Fix-It Fics

Challenging the Status Quo through Fan Fiction

Edited by
Kaitlin Tonti
Albright College

Series in Critical Media Studies

Copyright © 2024 by the authors.

All rights reserved. No part of this publication may be reproduced, stored in a retrieval system, or transmitted in any form or by any means, electronic, mechanical, photocopying, recording, or otherwise, without the prior permission of Vernon Art and Science Inc.

www.vernonpress.com

In the Americas:
Vernon Press
1000 N West Street, Suite 1200
Wilmington, Delaware, 19801
United States

In the rest of the world:
Vernon Press
C/Sancti Espiritu 17,
Malaga, 29006
Spain

Series in Critical Media Studies

Library of Congress Control Number: 2023950110

ISBN: 979-8-8819-0064-9

Also available: 978-1-64889-814-3 [Hardback]; 979-8-8819-0002-1 [PDF, E-Book]

Product and company names mentioned in this work are the trademarks of their respective owners. While every care has been taken in preparing this work, neither the authors nor Vernon Art and Science Inc. may be held responsible for any loss or damage caused or alleged to be caused directly or indirectly by the information contained in it.

Every effort has been made to trace all copyright holders, but if any have been inadvertently overlooked the publisher will be pleased to include any necessary credits in any subsequent reprint or edition.

Cover design by Vernon Press with elements from Freepik.

Table of Contents

	Acknowledgments	v
	Introduction: Fixing the Status Quo	vii
	Kaitlin Tonti	
	Albright College	
	Part One: Putting in the *Fix*	1
Chapter 1	**Fan Fiction Fixes for Queer Erasure in Mainstream Media**	3
	Percevile Forester	
	San Diego State University	
Chapter 2	**Beyond the Knot: Reparative Fiction and the Omegaverse**	19
	Paige Hartenburg	
	New York University	
Chapter 3	**Fannish Yiddish and Communal Becoming in the Rogue Archive**	35
	Ethan Calof	
	Vanderbilt University	
Chapter 4	**The Macro Fix-It: Practicing Activism through Fan Fiction**	53
	Darsey Meredith and Sharon Sutherland	
	Independent Scholars	
	Part Two: Fixing the Canon, Fixing the Author	71
Chapter 5	**Fan Fiction Fights Back: *Harry Potter* and the Effort to Build a Better Wizarding World**	73
	Laura Tolbert	
	Independent Scholar	

Chapter 6	'I have my version and you have yours': Fan Fiction and *Supernatural* Fans' Road to Damascus	91
	Anna Caterino *University of Milan*	
Chapter 7	"'This is all I ever wanted for you, Will. For both of us.' 'It's beautiful.'": *Hannibal* Post-Canon Fics and Queer Futurity	107
	Jamie MacGregor *Independent Scholar*	
Chapter 8	Fixing 'The Fixer': Fan Fictional Representations of *Wentworth*'s Joan Ferguson in Lesbian Relationships	121
	Kristy Smith *York University*	
	Part Three: Fixing Other Genres	137
Chapter 9	The Fix-It Novel: How Commercial Authors Instrumentalize Fan Fiction's Subversive Potential	139
	Amanda Boyce *Universität Trier*	
Chapter 10	Real-Life Magic: *Harry Potter* and the Fan Film Canon	157
	Jordan Hansen *Indiana University of Pennsylvania*	
Chapter 11	"It ruins the gritty realism of a man who fights crime dressed as a bat": Satire, Parody, and Multimodal Intertextuality in *Holy Musical B@man!*	171
	Meghan N. Cronin *Indiana University of Pennsylvania*	
	Index	187

Acknowledgments

I want to thank several people who were instrumental in making this book a reality. First, my husband, Jesse, for always providing encouragement as I barreled through the work and frustrations. I thank my parents, Lori and Andy, my close friends, and my colleagues for championing me in every project I endeavor. Thanks to the original participants of the panel who inspired this book, Laura Tolbert, and Ethan Calof. I express my gratitude to Vernon Press for showing interest in this project, especially to my editor Blanca Caro Duran, who was always there to answer my questions.

This book would also not exist without its primary inspiration, a fix-it fic by Elmie K-E titled "Little Achievements." Thank you for all your excellent writing, Elmie.

Thank you to Mel Lowery and Alexander Siddig, who made the performance of "Little Achievements" and the Sid City Social Club a reality.

Most importantly, thank you to fan fiction writers everywhere. You make the world a better place, one word at a time.

Introduction: Fixing the Status Quo

Kaitlin Tonti
Albright College

In an episode of Mindy Kaling's hit teen drama, *Never Have I Ever*, Kamala Nadiwadal, played by Richa Moorjani, is faced with an important decision complicated by culture and family. She must decide between marrying the man her family has chosen for her to stay with, or Steve, the man she had fallen in love with while away at school. In a scene where Kamala reunites with Steve to declare her love, she rambles, "I want to be with you even if you were from the wrong side of town and your dad was in jail for embezzling money." When he responds that he does not understand, she says, "I'm sorry, I just watched sixteen hours of *Riverdale*. Plus, some fan fiction where Jughead kisses Harry Potter."[1] *Never Have I Ever* will unlikely survive as a popular classic in the passing of time; however, this scene points to the permanent role that fan fiction has achieved in popular culture. It no longer resonates as a smaller appendage of fandom studies but has revealed its value as its own cultural currency.

Many now consider fan fiction as a literary art form; however, scholars continue to debate its purpose, practice, and relevance. Kamala's character is not meant to have participated in any fandoms or understood the significance of fan fiction, let alone know where to access it in the first place. This scene is read as a joke, an illusion of Kamala stepping into the teenage world that occupies her cousin Devi, the main character, as a way to navigate her own romantic failings. Nevertheless, Kamala's turn to fan fiction was her first action after being introduced to the *Riverdale* world. In other words, Kamala is immediately introduced to another outlet where the *Riverdale* narrative takes on new paths and overlaps with other fandoms. The implication is that fan fiction is just as powerful for a new viewer as the original content that drew in the consumer.

The beginnings and function of fan fiction are highly debated arenas of thought. Some suggest that fan fiction began with Arthur Conan Doyle's *Sherlock Holmes* series,[2] while others insist that fan fiction, as a larger component of fan

---

[1] *Never Have I Ever*, season 1, episode 3, "…gotten drunk with the popular kids," Kaling, Mindy, et al., writer, directed by Linda Mendoza, featuring Maitreyi Ramakrishnan and Richa Moorjani, aired April 27, 2020, Netflix.
[2] Arthur Conan Doyle, *The Complete Sherlock Holmes* (Garden City, N.Y.: Doubleday & Co), 1930.

studies, started with *Star Trek*[3] and the beginning of zine culture in the 1960s. If it is defined simply as "a form of collective storytelling," then some might argue that *The Odyssey*[4] and *The Iliad*[5] also function as forms of fan fiction.[6] Henry Jenkins' seminal text uses De Certeau's term "poachers" to demonstrate how writers use fan fiction to claim a spot in cultural production. He also suggests that "fans operate from a position of cultural marginalization and social weakness."[7] However, this is no longer the fan fiction writer of the twenty-first century. Fan fiction has developed as a literary form, and with the advent of open-access services such as *Archive of Our own* (*AO3*) and *Tumblr*, fan fiction writers have emerged from the limitations of subscribing to mailed zines, which has made their work as public as the original content. Furthermore, fan fiction is now a genre that has developed its own subgenres.

The Fix-It Fic

The central focus of this collection is the fix-it fic, a subgenre of fan fiction that Urban Dictionary defines as "fan fiction" where "characters who were originally dead in the actual books, shows, or movies are now alive and well… catastrophes are prevented by the author of the fan fiction and (almost) everyone gets the happy ending they deserved."[8] However, this definition of the fix-it fic is narrow and limiting in that recovering dead characters is the least of what the genre can accomplish. Lesley Goodman suggests that some popular interpretations of the fix-it fic attempt to define it as a vengeful outlet for angry fans to fix what the original creator or creators did wrong. However, she rejects this argument as still too simple, suggesting instead that "fan interpretation privileges the coherence of the fictional universe while downplaying the authority of the text, insisting that the author is not dead, but a failure and a disappointment."[9] Extending the definition of fix-it fics, this collection will explore the genre as a means of advocacy and activism. Fix-it fics allow writers to advocate for overlooked and underappreciated cultures and groups, and when in

---

[3] *Star Trek*, written by Gene Roddenberry, performed by William Shanter and Leonard Nimoy, (1966-1969).
[4] Homer, *The Odyssey*, ed. Robert Fitzgerald (Garden City, NY: Doubleday), 1961.
[5] Homer, *The Illiad*, ed. Robert Fitzgerald (Garden City, N.Y: Doubleday), 1974.
[6] Kristina Busse, "Introduction," *The Fan Fiction Studies Reader*, ed. Kristina Busse and Karen Hellekson (Iowa City: Iowa UP, 2014), 4.
[7] Henry Jenkins, "Textual Poachers," *The Fan Fiction Studies Reader*, ed. Kristina Busse and Karen Hellekson (Iowa City: Iowa UP, 2014), 28.
[8] "Fix-It Fics," *Urban Dictionary*, January 14, 2017, https://www.urbandictionary.com/define.php?term=fix%20it%20fics.
[9] Lesley Goodman, "Disappointing Fans: Fandom, Fictional Theory, and the Death of the Author," *The Journal of Popular Culture* 0, no. 0 (2015): 1-15. https://doi.org/10.1111/jpcu.12223

conversation with each other, it becomes a form of activism. As both advocacy and activism, fix-it fics serve as both a personal evolution for the individual writers and as an extension of awareness into the larger public that challenges heteronormative, abled, and white privileged perspectives. In other words, the fix-it fic author writes with the intention of changing the status quo.

Kristina Busse and Karen Hellekson's seminal work on fan fiction offers insight into how fan fiction scholarship is divided into several categories, including fan fiction as "an interpretation of the source text" and "fan fiction as individual engagement and identificatory practice."[10] Together, these functions point to how fan fiction is the intersection at which the individual practices and performs identity. The fix-it fic extends this idea to fix the stories that fail to recognize forms of bias. Fan fiction as a form of advocacy and activism demonstrates how the fan's interpretation and connection do not conclude at boundaries of the original content. Instead, these boundaries extend to challenge real-world social structures that ignore, invalidate, and promote hatred.

Fans find solace in fix-it fics because they can recreate the worlds they love as safe, comfortable places. Bronwen Thomas writes that fan fiction is a transformative force because it "offers a voice for marginalized groups…" in "seemingly safe or familiar storyworlds."[11] However, the fix-it fic as a form of advocacy and activism is to move beyond the text as a written source of comfort. Sometimes, writers find new aspects of their identity by creating fix-it fics. In a personal interview with Elmie K-E (known as almassi on *AO3*), a popular author in the *Star Trek: Deep Space Nine*, *Rabbit Lightning*, and *Good Omens* fandoms, they described fan fiction as an advocacy for the self, a means of exploration and understanding. They stated:

> But there's one constant throughline in a great deal of my work: gender exploration. I only recently noted it as personally significant and determined what my angle was. Specifically, I am drawn to writing masculine cisgender men engaging with and enjoying the feminine, more often than not as a sexual act. Trying makeup, wearing lingerie, imagining themselves as a woman. Occasionally I've written transgender characters, but the sexual aspect is absent under those circumstances. Although I am an AFAB nonbinary person who prefers a feminine presentation, the urge to write men seeking femininity turned out to be

---

[10] Busse, "Introduction," 8-9.
[11] Bronwen Thomas, "What is Fan Fiction and Why are People Saying Such Nice Things about it??," *Storyworlds: A Journal of Narrative Studies* 3, (2011), 1-24.

an unconscious reflection of myself, returning again and again in my writing. I cannot yet fully explain it, but I have recently been challenging myself to write more on this subject, and hopefully, I'll find the words so I can understand myself better.[12]

Elmie K-E's experience suggests that by exploring the creative realms they have come to admire, they have also ignited a desire to know themselves more intimately and thoroughly. In many cases, the greater recognition of the self through fan fiction, specifically fix-it fics, results in more opportunities for advocacy that extend to online community activism. Dean Leetal describes fan fiction as an "activism of care," defined as "activism that takes the social structure into account including the activists positioning and implements elements of care ethics."[13] Ze suggests that traditional activism results in some groups still being left out – especially those with physical disabilities. However, fan fiction writers take activism online, and with its public accessibility through forums such as *AO3*, they showcase worlds where underrepresented groups' existences are normalized and accepted. Through activism, for instance, slash fiction is not all that controversial but encouraged and consumed regularly. In other words, fan fiction as activism no longer only breaks the boundaries between fan and creator. It also makes the fan an advocate who uses their writing to showcase the possibilities of a world where acceptance, care, and empathy are universally and regularly practiced.

During the Covid-19 pandemic, Elmie K-E challenged the boundaries of fix-it fic activism when their story, "Little Achievements," was performed by the actors who originated the roles of both their characters.[14] Between April 2020 and October 2022, Alexander Siddig, the actor who played Dr. Julian Bashir on *Star Trek: Deep Space Nine* (*DS9*),[15] encouraged fans to join a Zoom session where they would have the opportunity to chat with Siddig, or Sid, as his fans call him. The meetings were scheduled twice a week (Tuesday and Friday) to accommodate the large international population that attended the Sid City Social Club meetings. Conversations ranged on various personal topics with every individual who spent fifteen minutes talking with Siddig. Eventually, the question of fan fiction arose, and so did conversations regarding the assumed

---

[12] Elmie K-E, "Interview," March 2023.
[13] Dean Leetal, "Those Crazy Fangirls on the Internet: Activism of Care, Disability, and Fan fiction," *Canadian Journal of Disability Studies* 8, no. 2, (2019), 46-73.
[14] Elmie K-E, "Little Achievements," *Archive of Our Own,* August 8, 2023, https://archiveofourown.org/works/26073979/chapters/63417001.
[15] *Star Trek: Deep Space Nine,* written by Rick Berman, performed by Avery Brooks and Nana Visitor (1993-1999), Paramount Pictures, TV Show.

romantic relationship between Siddig's character, Bashir, and actor Andrew (Andy) Robinson's character, Elim Garak.

Fan fiction featuring the relationship between Garak and Bashir, often referenced as "Garashir," is not a new phenomenon. Much like the assumed romantic relationship between Captain James Kirk and Spock of the original *Star Trek* series, Garak and Bashir's characters have attracted fan fiction authors for years. Of the over 5,000 works featuring the tag Julian Bashir/Elim Garak, most showcase fix-it fic features. [16] In several stories, the fix-it occurs at the point in the series finale, "What You Leave Behind," when at the end of the Dominion War, Garak and Bashir bid each other farewell with the promise of likely never seeing each other again.[17] Others place the fix-it during season two's "The Wire," when Bashir helps Garak overcome a near fatal addiction, and, in a moment of non-sexual intimacy, forgives Garak for "whatever it is you did."[18] In 2020, Siddig agreed to act with Robinson in producing "Little Achievements," also directed by Elmie K-E. On their *AO3* page, Elmie summarizes the play as "A *DS9* story about the everyday things we should be proud of."[19] However, what excited the first audience of over 192 people was when, in a moment of frustration, Garak asked Bashir, "What must I give to have a decent, uninterrupted conversation with my husband?"[20] This line confirmed many decades of fan suspicion: Bashir and Garak's relationship was of mutual, romantic attraction.

In my interview with Elmie, they state of the experience:

> Sid was afraid there would be backlash against me and what we made the characters say, but as far as I know, it hasn't come. I've seen celebratory memes, I've seen gifsets. I've seen articles and *YouTube* analysis videos. It's all been good stuff. I don't know what deeper effect "Little Achievements" had, at large, but when people recognize my name now, they recognize me for that.[21]

---

[16] Julian Bashir/Elim Garak on *Archive of Our Own*, https://archiveofourown.org/tags/Julian%20Bashir*s*Elim%20Garak/works

[17] *Star Trek: Deep Space Nine*, 176, "What You Leave Behind," directed by Allan Kroeker, May 31, 1999, Paramount Pictures.

[18] *Star Trek: Deep Space Nine*, 42, "The Wire," directed by Kim Friedman, May 8, 1994, Paramount Pictures.

[19] Elmie K-E, "Little Achievements."

[20] Elmie K-E, "Little Achievements."

[21] Elmie K-E, "Interview."

Elmie's humble analysis of their work underscores the significance of "Little Achievements" in how, through the performance, Siddig and Robinson affirmed their characters' relationship, thus replacing the original writers' portrayal of their characters in favor of the fans' interpretation. In an interview with Siddig, he states of "Little Achievements":

> I think the magic that Elmie conjures is rooted in their rare ability to edify implicitly while being overtly entertaining. A crowd of people on Zoom (all of us yearning for some respite from the dreariness of the pandemic) found "Little Achievements" to be a delight. It's a work that is, at once, gently reassuring, brimming with pathos and laugh-out-loud funny. It's nice to be reminded that raw humanity comes in so many surprising guises. On the day we read it for our group, we were lucky enough to have the inimitable Andy Robinson with us. I was lucky enough to be married to him for a short time! There were some beautiful things that arrived with that virus. How lucky we were...[22]

Siddig and Robinson's acceptance of their characters' roles as husbands in a post *Deep Space Nine* era produces the type of outreach that showcases fan fiction as a form of activism. Bashir and Garak's relationship, once confined to the fandom, is now widely known among all *Star Trek* fans, and only time will tell if it becomes more widely accepted. The performance is still cherished today, three years later. As Mel Lowery, writer, organizer of the Sid City Social Club, and producer of "Little Achievements," said:

> We knew the story would resonate with our audience. We also knew a significant portion of that audience would be delighted to have Sid and Andy perform their characters as an old married couple. More than two years later, we still receive comments from viewers just discovering the video who are entertained, comforted, and thrilled by "Little Achievements." Not bad for a no-budget, Zoom-based production.[23]

Elmie K-E's experience writing fan fiction is indicative of the journey for many fan fiction writers that evolves from the personal and results in public activism. For Elmie K-E, fan fiction began, and remains, a place of support in the face of debilitating health issues. However, they add that fan fiction is not just a venue for individuals to explore their personal existence, but also one that asks the public to join them in that adventure. As they state, "I do believe fanfic was the

---

[22] Siddig, "Interview."
[23] Lowery, "Interview."

Introduction   xiii

outreach program, soapbox, and public library gathering that allowed change to percolate, reaching new people who would care."[24] "Little Achievements" is just one example of how fan fiction can be a tool for challenging the status quo. Busse and Hellekson, Jenkins, and Thomas concur that fan fiction allows authors to break the confines of the original content and create safe spaces where their version of events exists online. The purpose of *Fix-It Fics: Challenging the Status Quo through Fan Fiction* is to expand the conversation about what fan fiction can accomplish, specifically the fix-it fic. Focused chiefly on queer cultural victories and struggles, the authors in this collection demonstrate how the hermeneutics of the fix-it fic reach beyond the boundaries of the individual fan fiction writer, thus creating a global space to highlight where cultural biases exist. In a world drastically changed by the Covid-19 Pandemic, this edited collection offers a variety of insights into different modes of the fix-it fic and how it moves beyond the individual exploration of identity to exist as a communal, online activist effort.

About the Book

The book is divided into three sections. The first is "Part One: Putting in the *Fix*," which delves into the precision of what the fix-it fic can accomplish. This section begins with Percevile Forester's "Fan Fiction Fixes for Queer Erasure in Mainstream Media," which broadly discusses the fix-it fic as a liminal space between the fan and anti-fan, where both excitement and ambivalence are motivating factors in writing. Using the theory of affective response, Forester examines the cultural frustration and exhaustion that occurs when fix-it fics come up against the mainstream media in a battle for control. Ethan Calof's "Fannish Yiddish and Communal Becoming in the Rouge Archive" examines how fix-it fic authors use Jewish culture and the Yiddish language to establish cross-cultural connections in the world that the fix-it author is revising. Paige Hartenburg's "Beyond the Knot: Reparative Fiction and the Omegaverse" explores the Omegaverse in *Voltron Legendary Defender* fix-it fics and demonstrates how the Omegaverse is a subgenre that re-imagines gendered hierarchy as a response to queerbaiting. Sharon Sutherland and Darsey Meredith's "The Macro Fix: Practicing Activism through Fan Fiction" analyzes fix-it fics that use the law and legal jargon to examine characters' points of view who have undergone injustice based on their sexual orientation.

"Part Two: Fixing the Canon, Fixing the Author" highlights how fix-it fics challenge the original creator's visions, thus fashioning a better environment for the characters. These chapters show how fix-it fics authors are activists in

---

[24] Elmie K-E, "Interview."

how they fight for acceptance by creating characters that challenge the original creator's lack of cultural awareness, specifically their anti-Queer stances. Laura Tolbert's "Fan Fiction Fights Back: The Effort to Build a Better Wizarding World" argues that *Harry Potter* fix-it fics erase Rowling's epilogue to counter her public, transphobic comments that dim the excitement that *Harry Potter* fans once found in the wizarding world. Anna Canterino provides an introspective on *Supernatural*'s lack of penance for several instances of queerbaiting in "'I have my version and you have yours': Fan Fiction and *Supernatural* Fan's Road to Damascus." The article also highlights the show's unstable relationship with fan fiction, consistently mocking the form throughout the series. Rounding out this section, Jamie MacGregor's chapter, 'This is all I ever wanted for you, Will. For both of us': *Hannibal* Post-Canon Fics and Queer Futurity" and Kristy Smith's chapter "Fixing 'The Fixer': Fan Fiction Representations of *Wentworth*'s Joan Ferguson in Lesbian Relationships" demonstrate the way fix-it fic authors offer characters who, the victims of queerbaiting by their original creators, a space for peacefully exploring life with their chosen partners.

"Part Three: Fixing Other Genres" considers how fix-it fics have leaked into other forms of multimedia. In "The Fix-It Novel: How Commercial Authors Instrumentalize Fan Fiction's Subversive Potential," Amanda Boyce analyzes the commercial authors who have used fan fiction to create stories that focus on characters hoping to change their favorite character's outcomes and thus their own, personal predicaments. Jordan Hansen's chapter, "Real-Life Magic: *Harry Potter* and the Fan Film Canon," analyzes the fix-it fic through the lens of fan films on *YouTube*, while Meghan N. Cronin analyzes the various incarnations of *Batman* and how theatrical satire critiques superheroes in "Satire, Parody, and Multi-Modal Intertextuality in *Holy Musical B@man*."

Ultimately, this book hopes to demonstrate fix-it fics essential and indispensable role in our cultural milieu. The fact that it has flourished and grown in its production, appearance, and purpose over the last several decades is a testimony to its lasting power and the momentous influence it has in the lives of those who read and write it. My own experience reading fan fiction brought me through the Covid-19 pandemic, offering a world that was accessible without fear of illness and one that offered a creative outlet in a moment that seemed so uncertain. I hope that for you, the person holding this book in their hands (or reading it online), a world of opportunity for reading, writing, advocating, and activism will come alive through fan fiction. The fix-it fic is no longer a taboo subject; it is an endless opportunity for imagination, feeling, and community empathy.

Bibliography

Busse, Kristina. "Introduction." In *The Fan Fiction Studies Reader*, edited by Kristina Busse and Karen Hellekson. Iowa: Iowa UP, 1-15.

Doyle, Arthur Conan. *The Complete Sherlock Holmes*. Garden City, N.Y.: Doubleday & Co., 1930.

Elmie K-E. "Interview." By Kaitlin Tonti, February 9, 2023.

———. "Little Achievements." *Archive of Our own*, August 23, 2020. https://archiveofourown.org/works/26073979/chapters/63417001.

"Fix-It Fics." *Urban Dictionary*. January 14, 2017. https://www.urbandictionary.com/define.php?term=fix%20it%20fics.

Goodman, Lesley. "Disappointing Fans: Fandom, Fictional Theory, and the Death of the Author." *The Journal of Popular Culture* 0, no. 0 (2015): 1-15. https://doi.org/10.1111/jpcu.12223.

Homer. *The Iliad*, edited by Robert Fitzgerald. Garden City, N.Y.: Doubleday, 1974.

———. *The Odyssey*, edited by Robert Fitzgerald. Garden City, N.Y.: Doubleday, 1961.

Jenkins, Henry. "Textual Poachers." In *The Fan Fiction Studies Reader*, edited by Kristina Busse and Karen Hellekson. Iowa: Iowa UP, 26-44.

Leetal, Dean. "Those Crazy Fangirls on the Internet: Activism of Care, Disability, and Fan fiction," *Canadian Journal of Disability Studies* 8, no. 2, (2019): 46-73. https://doi.org/10.15353/cjds.v8i2.491.

Lowery, Mel. "Interview." By Kaitlin Tonti, September 26, 2023.

Never Have I Ever. Season 1, episode 3, "…gotten drunk with the popular kids." Kaling, Mindy, et al., writer, directed by Linda Mendoza, featuring Maitreyi Ramakrishnan and Richa Moorjani. Aired April 27, 2020. Netflix.

Siddig, Alexander. "Interview." By Kaitlin Tonti, September 26, 2023.

Star Trek. Written by Gene Roddenberry. Performed by William Shatner and Leonard Nimoy. 1966-1969, Paramount Pictures. TV Show.

Star Trek: Deep Space Nine. Season 7, episode 175-176. "What You Leave Behind." Behr, Ira Steven, et al., writer. Directed by Allan Kroeker. Featuring Avery Brooks. Aired May 31, 1999. Paramount Pictures.

Star Trek: Deep Space Nine. Written by Rick Berman. Performed by Avery Brooks and Nana Visitor. 1993-1999. Paramount Pictures. TV Show.

Thomas, Bronwen. "What is Fan fiction and Why are People Saying Such Nice Things about it??," *Storyworlds: A Journal of Narrative Studies* 3 (2011): 1-24. http://doi.org/10.5250/storyworlds.3.2011.0001.

Wolfe, Robert Hewitt, writer. *Star Trek: Deep Space Nine*, season 2, episode 42, "The Wire." Directed by Kim Friedman. Featuring Andrew Robinson and Alexander Siddig. Aired May 9, 1994. Paramount Pictures.

Part One:
Putting in the *Fix*

Chapter 1

Fan Fiction Fixes for Queer Erasure in Mainstream Media

Percevile Forester
San Diego State University

Abstract: In this chapter, Forester addresses the popularity of slash fiction as a form of the fix-it fic. They suggest the fix-it fic challenges queer erasure and the instinct to show queerness in only tragic terms. They use negative affect theory to demonstrate how fans are not using it fix-it fics to express their dislike of the original content, but to highlight the larger cultural production that erases queer existences.

Keywords: queer erasure, slash fiction, Negative Affect Theory, LGTBQ+ communities, EWE (ending, what ending), *AO3*, tags, fanishness, fix-it fics.

***

For decades, fan studies scholars have directed their attention toward slash fan fiction, fascinated by its presence, interrogating its purpose, and scrutinizing the demographics that read and write it. Initially, much of this scholarship fixated on the heterosexual women engaging with slash fan fiction, interested primarily in unraveling the complex relationship between gender and erotics.[1] More recently, research has begun to reflect the engagement of queer demographics with slash fan fiction as well as its use as a stopgap to address a lack of quality queer representation in popular culture.[2] This chapter will focus on discussing queer (or slash) fan fiction as a response to queer erasure in mass media and an attempt to rectify its effects. However, it by no means is intended to figure this as the sole reason that queer fan fiction is written. Instead, it will

---

[1] For an overview of this early work, see: Henry Jenkins, "'Welcome to Bisexuality, Captain Kirk': Slash and the Fanwriting Community," in *Textual Poachers: Television Fans and Participatory Culture* (London: Taylor & Francis Group, 2012), 238.

[2] Diana Floegel, "'Write the story you want to read': world-queering through slash fanfiction creation," *The Journal of Documentation* 76, no. 4 (2020): 785.

focus on one of many reasons why slash fan fiction is produced: the desire to address and fix the societal tendency to erase and tragify queerness.

The word fix in fix-it fic suggests a contentious relationship with canon, an exasperation or frustration with a source text, or a recognition that something is broken. This phrasing implies a negative affect, which might seem contradictory when thinking of the fan and the anti-fan as binary identities, one entirely positive, the other entirely negative.[3] However, as Louisa Stein asserts, "negative or even anti-fannish feelings can exist alongside positive fannish feelings within the same community or within the same fan."[4] I suggest that Stein's idea of a fan who harbors both anti-fannish and fannish feelings describes much more accurately how fans typically interact with the texts of which they are fans. However, as Cornel Sandvoss notes, the word "fan" is a term that has come to encompass an incredibly broad range of people and groups, and different fan cultures interact differently with the objects of their fannish feelings.[5] For many fans who produce and consume transformative fan content, the liminal space between fan and anti-fan is a familiar one; their fannishness is often ambivalent. In fact, for many, their ambivalence is the very thing that drives their productivity.

Negative affective responses, especially when viewed through the lens of fix-it fics, are typically thought of as a direct response to dissatisfying aspects of specific texts. However, attention must be paid to the cultural contexts in which fandom is performed. Often, when fans respond negatively to a text, they also respond to a wider cultural problem that it represents, not exclusively to the text itself. While speaking broadly on anti-fandom, Jonathan Gray asserts that "we need a theory of *cultural exhaustion* to explain the frustration, anger, alienation, and hence anti-fandom that arise when an individual or community is constantly being misrepresented, not represented, insulted, and/or left out by media."[6] As Gray explains it, this exhaustion arises when an otherwise good piece of media reflects systemic oppressions and transforms a fan into an anti-fan. I would argue that textual poaching and participatory fandom are often similarly motivated; some fans may experience a more invigorating form of cultural *frustration* rather than cultural exhaustion and be fueled to productivity by their malcontent. To this effect, some fans consider their slash fan fiction

---

[3] This "atomic" model of fandom and anti-fandom was originally proposed by Jonathan Gray, but he himself has since recognized it to be flawed.
[4] Louisa Stein, "Dissatisfaction and *Glee*: On Emotional Range in Fandom and Feels Culture," in *Anti-Fandom*, ed. Melissa Click (New York: New York University Press, 2019), 98.
[5] Cornel Sandvoss, *Fans: The Mirror of Consumption* (Oxford: Polity, 2005), 7.
[6] Jonathan Gray, "How do I dislike thee? Let me count the ways," in *Anti-Fandom*, ed. Melissa Click (New York: New York University Press, 2019), 32.

production a political act,[7] a notion that suggests that there is something larger at stake to be fixed than the source text alone. This chapter will discuss specific categories of fan fiction, as well as (with the permission of their authors) pieces of slash fan fiction whose paratexts indicate that they seek to respond to and fix the impact of phenomena such as hetero- and cisnormativity, queercoding, and the "bury your gays" trope.

A Brief History of Queer Representation

Before discussing fan fiction, some historical context on representations of queerness in media may prove useful. In 1934, the Hayes Code was introduced in the United States, restricting depictions of queerness (among other things) in media. The code remained in place until the 1980s but didn't completely erase depictions of queerness. Instead, it relegated queerness to the subtext, only perceived by those attuned to its presence. Even when queerness was depicted in media explicitly, it was often cast in a negative light, with stories most often either represented as predatory or ultimately ending in tragedy.[8] In opposition to the dominant narratives, while the Hayes Code was in effect, queer communities began to create and circulate music, books, plays, and films of their own. However, post code, queerness was depicted much more openly in the mainstream. Some people have welcomed the increase in visibility, but others have mourned the loss of agency in the production of queer stories. The fact of the matter is that today, most mainstream media is still produced by heterosexual creators for heterosexual audiences and does not contain any depictions of queerness whatsoever. Even when queerness is included in mass media, it is produced for massive audiences, and many of the biases and regulations that shaped depictions of queerness in the Hayes Code era still linger today. The Hayes Code and the culture that shaped it played a prominent role in the obfuscation of queerness that many fans now notice in the objects of their fandom—an obfuscation that many find objectionable and seek to rectify in their fanfiction.

Heterosexuality? What Heterosexuality?

When searching for evidence of the undercurrent of spite that sometimes drives fan fiction production, one often needs to look no further than the paratext. The existence of the fix-it fic as a category of fan fiction and a tag on *Archive of Our own* (*AO3*) already proves this undercurrent. However, there is another tag of note that is pertinent to mention: EWE, or "Epilogue? What

---

[7] Crowgirl, qtd in Flogel, "'Write the Story You Want to Read,'" 785–805.
[8] Vito Russo, *The Celluloid Closet: Homosexuality in the Movies* (New York: Harper & Row, 1987).

Epilogue?" The tag is used by authors in the *Harry Potter* fandom and often serves both to indicate that works of fan fiction are not epilogue compliant and to criticize the content of the epilogue to the series. The tag is a tongue-in-cheek reference to the epilogue, written as though in anticipation that the fic author may receive questions about why their work has ignored its existence; in response, it implies that the author's disregard—or even disdain—for the epilogue is so strong that it effectively does not exist at all in their mind. Despite the transformative nature of communities that create and consume fan fiction, many fans are aware of how the dominant culture reads works and make efforts to distinguish between the text as they believe the author intended it to be read and the text as they read it. Their interpretations and analyses are intentionally and knowingly transformative, often indicating the extent to which the work is transformed in the tags. Generally, in fan culture, there is a line drawn between "canon" events, which take place in the text of the original work, and "AU," which are not canon-compliant and, therefore, take place in an "Alternate Universe" from the one that the author created. So, typically, a work that ignores something like an epilogue would be considered an AU. However, many fans do not consider EWE fix-it fics as AU,[9] denying the epilogue's inclusion as part of the text's canon. While some fans likely use the tag without harboring disdain for the epilogue, the way the tag is phrased—both in terms of what it includes and excludes—implies a certain level of malcontent. Over 14,500 works on *AO3* are currently using some variation of this tag, which means this anti-epilogue sentiment is relatively popular in the *Harry Potter* fandom.

The final chapter of *Harry Potter and the Deathly Hallows* contains the 1,627-word (approximately eight pages) long epilogue to the series. In this space, Rowling concludes the series by detailing a moment nineteen years after the events of the penultimate chapter. With the main conflicts resolved, she ties a bow to the personal lives of the three main protagonists, Harry, Ron, and Hermione, and the secondary antagonist, Draco, by depicting them all in heterosexual relations as they see their children off to school. The chapter ends with the sentence, "All is well."[10] This epilogue is part of a long-standing tradition in media in which characters are hurriedly pushed into heterosexual pairings. Furthermore, because of the emphasis placed on Harry's contentment, the implicit message is that the key to happiness is settling down with one's

---

[9] "Epilogue? What Epilogue?," *fanlore*, last modified January 10, 2022, https://fanlore.org/wiki/Epilogue%3F_What_Epilogue%3F.
[10] J. K. Rowling, *Harry Potter and the Deathly Hallows* (London: Bloomsbury, 2014).

heterosexual partner and having children,[11] a sentiment that is often echoed throughout our heteronormative society. The EWE tag is not exclusively used by authors of queer fan fiction nor as an implicit critique of heteronormativity in popular media. Many of the fics under this tag contain a heterosexual pairing. However, over half of the EWE writings are exclusively queer, indicating that much fan fiction creates more satisfying endings to the series for queer readers, thus, in a sense, fixing the heteronormativity that the epilogue promotes.

Beyond just the epilogue, though, many fans—and especially queer fans—have recently begun to view J. K. Rowling with distrust, considering a series of tweets she made recently that contained rhetoric invalidating trans identities.[12] Rowling has thus been a prime example in many debates regarding mindful consumption and the notion of separating the art from the artist. Many fans of Rowling's works teeter in the liminal space between fan and anti-fan, struggling to decide whether they believe it is ethical to continue engaging with texts that she produces. One such fan authored an exceptionally long *Harry Potter* fan fiction, which included several queer pairings and transgender characters. They ended their work with an extensive note condemning Rowling's actions and expressing the conflict they experienced while engaging with Rowling's work. They describe writing the fan fiction as cathartic and state:

> As JKR has gotten more hateful and dangerous in her crusade against trans people, I have found it difficult to want to associate any part of myself with her creations. This fic in a lot of ways was me trying to fix the things that always bothered me about canon . . . I think I've said my goodbyes to this fandom. It got me through a lot in my life, and I will always appreciate it for that, but I personally cannot keep engaging with the works and words of someone who doesn't believe I or my loved ones deserve human rights.[13]

The work addresses several elements beyond just the hetero and cis normativity that exists in canon. However, the author's use of the word "catharsis" and self-

---

[11] Audrey Fox, "Why the Harry Potter Film Epilogues Never Stood a Chance," *denofgeek*, July 15, 2021, https://www.denofgeek.com/movies/why-the-harry-potter-film-franchises-epilogue-never-stood-a-chance/.

[12] Abby Gardner, "A Complete Breakdown of the J.K Rowling Transgender-Comments Controversy," *glamour*, February 7, 2023, https://www.glamour.com/story/a-complete-breakdown-of-the-jk-rowling-transgender-comments-controversy.

[13] SomewheresSword, "Lily's Boy," *Archive of Our Own*, January 14, 2022, https://archiveofourown.org/works/30856244/chapters/90792109.

identification with transness implies that the work, at least in part, serves to provide an indirect fix for the impact that J. K. Rowling's transphobia has had on queer fans. This work is a great demonstration of how queer fans' sense of what they are fixing with their queer works sometimes goes beyond the text itself, instead extending to issues that the text serves to *represent*. The author's inclusion of several queer pairings fixes the heteronormativity that the narrative signifies, and, more significantly, the author's inclusion of several trans characters serves to fix the transphobia that J. K. Rowling, and by extension, her work, represents. The work does not highlight or fix any transphobic elements of the *Harry Potter* series. Instead, by nature of its attachment to J. K. Rowling, the inclusion of positive and accepting representations of trans characters in fan fiction serves, in and of itself, as a political statement against transphobia. Further, it intends to reassure the reader that, even if they regret the time and love they put into a series that has come to represent transphobia, they still entered a worthwhile community.

Even in fandoms where fans have a generally neutral or positive relationship with their text's creators, fanworks can be used to channel a negative affective relationship with the heteronormative cultural context. In the *Stranger Things* fandom, many of the show's characters are read as queer by fans—to the extent that Robin Buckley, Steve Harrington, Nancy Wheeler, and Eddie Munson are often referred to as "the fruity four."[14] However, Robin Buckley is currently considered the only canonically queer character in the show, as she is the only character who has come out on screen.[15] Furthermore, while Steve and Nancy are popularly read as queer, most fans recognize that there is scant textual evidence to support these readings in wider interpretive communities. Despite this fact, queer readings of Steve are widely accepted among slash fans, as is evidenced by the fact that the current two most written ships in the *Stranger Things* fandom on *AO3* both involve Steve in a queer relationship. Currently, 39% of all the fan fiction written on *AO3* for *Stranger Things* contains one or both of these pairings.[16] Fans generally seem content to read queerness into Steve's character only within their community. Nevertheless, there is no effort by the original creators to present Steve as queer in canon. Nor do fans tend to claim that he is purposefully coded as queer or even that he might be read as queer by anyone outside of this insular community. These fan fictions, by the

---

[14] "fruity" being an often pejorative, but in this case affectionate, term for queer people.
[15] *Stranger Things*, season 3, episode 7, "Chapter Seven: The Bite," directed by The Duffer Brothers, aired July 4, 2019, on Netflix, https://www.netflix.com/watch/80222778.
[16] This percentage was calculated on March 13, 2023, using the numbers on tag prevalence that *AO3* displays via the "sort and filter" function. The value was rounded down.

very nature of their existence (and the volume of their existence), respond to a phenomenon within media discourses that Monique Franklin identifies as a tendency for discussions of queerness to be "waylaid by an attempt to decipher authorial intent"—namely, the intent of the author of the original work.[17] These readings are knowingly subversive, unconcerned with whether characters are coded as queer by the original author. Many fans read Steve's characterization as one that is intended to be excessively heterosexual, an over-performance of masculinity. These readings are increasingly unconcerned with providing proof of queerness to dissenters. As *TikTok* user @jack_dearly puts it when listing characters who "are written so heterosexuality that it just circles back around to being bi": "I won't be taking criticism."[18] When queer fans refuse to take criticism on queer readings, they are reacting to a culture that gaslights them into submission, insisting that anything less than explicit queerness must be heterosexuality. Slash fan fiction about excessively heterosexual characters, like Steve, fix these conditions by refusing to shoulder the burden of identifying "canonical" textual evidence to justify queer readings. They return the obstinate energy of heteronormativity, mimicking and inverting the pervasive refusal to accept criticism of heterosexual readings in our society.

Scribbling in the Margins in Rainbow Pen

Fandom is not a monolith, and some fans still put a significant amount of stock in how texts are "meant" to be read. Interpretations of how texts are meant to be read and why vary from fan to fan. This can lead to debates over whether more prominent hints of queerness in a text are a result of queercoding or queerbaiting. Queercoding is the relegation of queerness to subtextual codes, minor details that signify a character's queerness. Queerbaiting, on the other hand, is a term that was created to protest the continual relegation of queerness to subtext, despite higher levels of tolerance for explicit queerness in media. Particularly, the term is meant to indicate that queer viewers are being baited into consuming the media by the prospect of queerness, despite a lack of intention ever to make that queerness overt, thereby verifying its queer readings in the eyes of the dominant culture. Because no creator is likely to outright admit to queerbaiting, whether certain examples qualify as queerbaiting is often heavily debated within fan communities, even amongst

---

[17] Monique Franklin, "Queerbaiting, Queer Readings, and Heteronormative Viewing Practices," in *Queerbaiting and Fandom: Teasing Fans through Homoerotic Possibilities*, ed. Joseph Brennan (Iowa: University of Iowa Press, 2019), 47.

[18] jack_dearly, "Fictional Bisexuals," *TikTok*, February 27, 2023, https://www.tiktok.com/t/ZTR7arhaJ/.

queer fans. However, this heightening debate indicates that many fans are generally getting quite tired of having their queer readings invalidated. As Roland Barthes notes, our society heavily prioritizes the notion of author intent when interpreting a text, to the point that authors have been given God-like authority over interpretations of their works.[19] The concept of queerbaiting shows that many queer fans still operate under this societal valuation of authorial intent, but also that many queer fans have begun to demand explicit textual representation. Constantly searching in the margins, seeing things where no one else does, is an alienating experience. Regardless of whether fans consider something queerbaiting, many are generally ready for more overt representations of queerness in our society, and that is often the target of queer fan's fixes. Elisabeth Schneider argues that when fans feel that they are being intentionally baited, "'Stealing' and recontextualizing those cultural products is an act of self-defiance—of self-empowerment, of activism."[20] I argue that self-empowerment and activism come not only as a defiant response to queerbaiting, but also as an overarching attempt to break free from the subtext and into the text, to urge others to notice the same coded details. Many of these stories tend to approach their subject matter as a fix-it that fixes the lingering effect of Haye's Code era subtleties more than anything else. Fix-it fics are loud and unapologetic, announcing their queerness boldly and openly, refusing to be relegated to the subtext, where culture can dismiss them at large.

The communities that produce slash fan fiction are aware that their interpretations are subject to greater interrogation than heterosexual readings of a character; they know that most people are not as attuned to signs of queerness as they are. Therefore, they pass along their proof of queerness reverently, lovingly, among those who do understand, in still-frames and videos of blink-and-you-'ll-miss-it details that feel ever-so-prominent when one is attuned to the right contextual clues. With these clues, they build their understanding of canon, common interpretations of characters as queer that are shared amongst members of a queer interpretive community, which allows for freedom from dominant heteronormative readings.

Some direct responses to queercoding are found in some *Stranger Things* fanworks about Eddie Munson, one of the aforementioned "fruity four," and another character, Will Byers. These characters are considered by many fans to be queercoded, and some who are part of this group are frustrated with the fact

---

[19] Roland Barthes, "The Death of the Author," in *Authorship: From Plato to the Postmodern: A Reader*, ed. Seán Burke (Edinburgh: Edinburgh University Press, 1995), 125-30.
[20] Elisabeth Schneider, "Reclaiming Queerbaiting: A Call to Action," in *Queerbaiting and Fandom: Teasing Fans through Homoerotic Possibilities*, ed. Joseph Brennan (Iowa: University of Iowa Press, 2019), 55.

that these characters' queerness is relegated to subtext. However, few fans interpret their coding as baiting. For many, their fix-it fics are not a direct response to the sense that they are being baited but rather to the pervasive feeling of invisibility that queer-coded characters represent.

One of the reasons that most fans do not consider Will's coding to be baiting is that many fans believe that Will Byers will eventually be confirmed to be gay. Several moments throughout the narrative exist in which his queerness is already toeing the line from subtextual to textual. One such moment occurs in season four and is the subject of *AO3* user bookinit's fix-it fic, "half a heart (without you)." In the original scene, Will is in a car with his friend Mike Wheeler, his brother Jonathan Byers, and Jonathan's friend Argyle. Throughout the season, there have been issues in Mike's relationship with his girlfriend, El, who lives with Will and is his close friend. In the car, Mike worries over his relationship with El. In the hopes of raising Mike's spirits, Will gives him a painting, the importance of which had been alluded to in previous scenes, most notably one at the beginning of the season in which Will is shown working on a painting as El narrates the scene, theorizing that the painting might be meant for someone that Will has romantic feelings for.[21] Another scene shows Will attempting to give the painting to Mike and failing, implying that its importance left him too nervous to feel comfortable giving it to Mike. Will finally gives Mike the painting, claiming that El commissioned it and describing how the painting is meant to represent her feelings for Mike. With the past two scenes in mind, the discerning audience member can infer that Will's description refers to his own feelings, not El's. Mike accepts the painting, and Will gives him a wobbly smile before turning and pretending to look out the window to hide the fact that he is crying.[22] In bookinit's fan fiction, rather than silently accepting the painting, Mike asks Jonathan to stop the car, then has a frank discussion with Will, admitting that he knows that Will is queer, but assuring him that he accepts him regardless. What makes this fan fiction notable is what the author says in the endnotes. Here, bookinit admits that, based on her personal experiences, the original scene was a realistic portrayal of queer realities but that she found it upsetting regardless for multiple reasons. Her most direct reasoning is that Mike seemed oblivious to Will's suffering and did not provide any comfort. However, she also provides a more abstract reason for finding the scene upsetting, stating that the subtextual nature of the scene allows people to deny Will's queerness, "when to someone who has been in that situation, it is

---

[21] *Stranger Things*, season 4, episode 1, "Chapter One: The Hellfire Club," directed by The Duffer Brothers, Aired May 27, 2022, on Netflix, https://www.netflix.com/watch/80229866.

[22] *Stranger Things*, season 4, episode 8, "Chapter Eight: Papa," directed by The Duffer Brothers, Aired July 1, 2022, on Netflix, https://www.netflix.com/watch/80229873.

painfully obvious what Will is going through. People are still able to deny it and ignore his sexuality because he hasn't outright stated anything."[23] Here, she makes it clear that the fan fiction's creation was driven, in part, by the desire to make the subtextual textual, not just due to her personal investment, but out of a larger sense that there is an injustice in writing queer stories in a way that allows that queerness to be denied or ignored. Her ambivalence reflects cultural frustration stemming from a persistent cultural denial of queer existence that this moment in the text represents.[24]

While many fans believe that Will's sexuality will be confirmed more explicitly in *Stranger Things*' canon at some point and, therefore, consider their frustration with his coding to be temporary, very few fans believe the same about Eddie Munson. Regardless, fans with knowledge of queer histories were more attuned to details about Eddie Munson's character that indicated his potential queerness than others. One detail is the handkerchief in Eddie's back pocket. In the 1970s and 1980s (the time in which *Stranger Things* is set), queer men would use hankies in their back pockets as a code to signify sexual preferences.[25] Fans quickly connected their gathered evidence and latched on to this detail so thoroughly that it now has a sortable tag on *AO3*: "Eddie Munson's Black Handkerchief," which, when used, signifies that a fanfiction will explicitly acknowledge the hanky and its significance. One such work, "Someone's Bound to Get It," by ShortAngryTwinks, takes place in between canon events, imagining a scene in which Eddie Munson's handkerchief is drawn to attention by another character, Billy Hargrove, and its coded meaning is confirmed. In public at first, the two dance around the subject, speaking in a combination of coded language and pointed gestures as they cobble together an idea of their respective preferences and negotiate a sexual encounter. However, when in private, they speak more candidly. As evidenced by this scene:

> Billy takes one look around his room and immediately zeros in on his handcuffs, eyebrows raising. "You really are into that S&M stuff."

---

[23] bookinit, "half a heart (without you)," *Archive of Our Own*, July 2, 2022, https://archiveofourown.org/works/40031733.

[24] Later in the note, bookinit explains that she anticipates that Will's queerness will be addressed further, just not in a satisfactory way: another reason behind her frustration. This didn't fit well into this chapter organizationally, but I did want to note that the cultural frustrations that drove her work extend beyond the relegation of queerness to subtext.

[25] J. Raúl Cornier, "Hanky Panky: An Abridged History of the Hanky Code," *historyproject*, April 23, 2019, https://historyproject.org/news/2019-04/hanky-panky-abridged-history-hanky-code0#:~:text=The%20hanky%20code%20was%20a,the%20purposes%20of%20sexual%20signaling.

"Yeah," Eddie says, "why else do you think I was wearing that black hankie?"[26]

Here, there can be no doubt about the meaning behind Eddie's handkerchief, no denial of the gathered evidence. This echoes a statement made by the author in the opening notes of the text, which asserts that the author feels that Eddie is intentionally coded as queer and that "I just wanted him to get some recognition for the fact that he's flagging . . . and thus, this fic was born."[27] Despite the fact that the author doesn't seem angry with the source text, he makes it clear in the notes that this fan fiction was born of dissatisfaction with the relegation of queerness to the subtext.

However, what is interesting about works like "Someone's Bound to Get It" is that some of them are not only responding to the relegation of characters' queerness to the subtext but also to the relegation of queer histories to the subtext. Some authors use the attention of their readers as an opportunity to educate and advocate, typically by incorporating elements of queer history into the text and making use of the end or beginning notes of the fan fiction to explain those elements. In "Someone's Bound to Get It," this occurs in the beginning notes when the author provides a lengthy paragraph of explanations and definitions surrounding handkerchief codes. Another fan fiction, "sub-culture," by palmviolet, explains references to queer culture and history in the 1980s that extend beyond the hanky code. This detail, in combination with the fact that one of the tags on the work reads, "queer history is so important, and this fic celebrates that," indicates that the author is very invested in the queer context in which the text is set.[28] In an interview with palmviolet, I asked about the motivation behind her work. She responded: "Part of the interest for me became this ability to play in a very specific cultural sandbox (the queer scene in 80s small town America against the background of the AIDS crisis) that *Stranger Things* isn't really engaging with, simply adjacent to, enough that it granted me access."[29] Palmviolet's insights reflect the significance that the 1980s holds for many people who are invested in queer history, as well as *Stranger Things*' removal from those histories, despite the presence of

---

[26] ShortAngryTwinks, "Someone's Bound to Get It," *Archive of Our Own*, July 1, 2022, https://archiveofourown.org/works/40005228.
[27] ShortAngryTwinks, "Someone's Bound to Get It."
[28] Palmviolet, "sub-culture," *Archive of Our Own*, May 30, 2022, https://archiveofourown.org/works/39308787?view_full_work=true.
[29] Palmviolet, in discussion with the author, 2023.

potentially purposeful subtextual references to them. While *Stranger Things* is set in the 1980s, much of the setting is purely aesthetic. It tends not to engage deeply with the historical contexts, aside from when it engages with the products that were consumed in the 1980s[30] as it pertains to nerd identities.[31] Despite this fact, the 1980s was a pivotal moment for the queer community in the United States. At this time, queer people were gaining visibility and acceptance, just beginning to be able to be more open with their queerness and taking part in incredibly effective direct action protests through groups in ACT UP. However, it was also a highly contentious period, so ACT UP was formed. Thousands of queer people died under a negligent administration as the AIDS epidemic tore through the community and hateful rhetoric circulated, firmly linking AIDS to queerness and positioning it as a low priority for the FDA and politicians who did not care at all for queer lives.[32] These histories are something that many people in the queer community are at least partially aware of, but there is a tension as we worry that we might lose sight of these histories, especially given that so many lives were lost, to the point where most people who identify as queer in the United States were not yet alive for the worst of the epidemic, if they had even been born at all.[33] The community is also keenly aware of the fact that most of us will learn about these histories from inside the queer community, as, according to GLSEN's 2021 national survey, the vast majority of students in the sixth through twelfth grades in America did not receive positive education on queer history in school.[34] Thus, the burden of education falls largely on the queer community itself. Evidently, the peritext of fan fiction is one of the spaces in which this occurs, as *Stranger Things* fan writers demonstrate when they capitalize on the 1980s setting and use it as an

---

[30] Kayla McCarthy, "Remember Things: Consumerism, Nostalgia, and Geek Culture in *Stranger Things*," *Journal of Popular Culture* 52, no. 3 (2019): 663-677.
[31] Percevile Forester, "Who're You Calling a Nerd?: How Identity, Marketability, and Nostalgia Impact Depictions of the 1980s in *Stranger Things*," *The International Journal of Creative Media Research* 10, (2023), accessed August 17, 2023, https://www.creativemediaresearch.org/post/who-re-you-calling-a-nerd-how-identity-marketability-and-nostalgia-impact-depictions-of.
[32] The dismissal of the AIDS epidemic also had ties to other forms of bigotry, but its roots in heterosexism were especially prominent.
[33] Nicolas Boyon, "LGBT+ Pride 2021 Global Survey points to a generation gap around gender identity and sexual attraction," *IPSOS*, June 9, 2021, https://www.ipsos.com/en-us/news-polls/ipsos-lgbt-pride-2021-global-survey.
[34] "The 2021 National School Climate Survey," *GLSEN*, 2021, https://www.glsen.org/sites/default/files/2022-10/NSCS-2021-Full-Report.pdf: 57.

opportunity to share their knowledge with a readership that they can safely assume is already interested in queerness as a topic. Though not all authors of *Stranger Things* fan fiction are invested in the historical contexts, and not all have an accurate idea of those contexts, for those who are and do, their projects offer an opportunity to fix the fact that most of the queer community does not have clear lines of access to accounts of its histories.

Unearthing Their Gays

Fix-it fics also respond to "bury your gays," a term that refers to the fact that a disproportionate number of queer stories have historically ended in death. This trope persists to this day, to the point that many queer viewers have come to expect queer stories to end in tragedy.[35] In keeping with the ethics of fan spaces, I feel obligated to warn that this section contains major spoilers, in the sense that I will be discussing characters who die in the canon of *Stranger Things*. *Stranger Things* serves as an interesting case study for the 'bury your gays' trope because, while Eddie Munson's status as queer is widely accepted among queer fans, his queerness was never confirmed, and thus, many fans were more exasperated than incensed. Furthermore, Eddie's character was introduced at the beginning of season four of *Stranger Things* and survived until the final episode of the season. However, because the season was released in two volumes, there was a month between Eddie's introduction and his death in which fans could produce content about him. Many fans anticipated his death, creating an odd new subgenre of fix-it: the pre-emptive fix.

In my correspondence with palmviolet, given that she began writing before Eddie died, I asked if she considered "sub-culture" a fix-it fic. In response, she explains: "I was already pretty convinced Eddie would die . . . so you could see sub-culture as a pre-emptive fix-it fic." During our discussion, palmviolet also drew my attention to the significance that this unique temporal relationship to canon has. As she puts it, "instead of assigning value to canon and then writing in opposition to it (and therefore privileging its importance as something that gives the fanwork meaning), Steddie[36] fix-its instead reject canon without even engaging with it, which diminishes the value of that canon itself."[37] While much of fandom has respect for canon that is on par with the dominant culture's regard

---

[35] Erin B. Waggoner, "Bury Your Gays and Social Media Fan Response: Television, LGBTQ Representation, and Communitarian Ethics," *Journal of Homosexuality* 65, no. 13 (December 15, 2018), 1886.
[36] The term refers to the pairing of Steve Harrington with Eddie Munson, the ship explored in "sub-culture."
[37] Palmviolet, in discussion with the author, 2023.

for an Author-God, carefully separating their own transformations from what is ordained by the author of the original work, that respect can be exhausted by continual disappointment in the products of mass culture. Palmviolet anticipated that the character she, and many other fans, had read as queer would be buried without confirmation of that queerness. Sensing disappointment on the horizon, she and many other authors pre-emptively created an alternative to canon, something other fans could respond to in lieu of volume 2.

Conclusion

According to Henry Jenkins, "fans are responding to products that are mass produced and distributed for commercial profit, and they intervene in those practices to generate forms of culture that more fully address their own fantasies, desires, and interests."[38] While this statement is true, many fans' responses to these products are not simply a response to the products themselves, but also to a wider cultural context, one that exhausts, excludes, and frustrates the marginalized. The texts produced by mass media are the bridge between marginalized fan communities and the dominant culture, a site where many of the slights on queer existence are read by fans. However, reading queerness into characters in these texts allows fan communities to form, and when they respond to individual texts, they are able not only to generate new forms of culture but also to work to rectify some of the slights that are consistently enacted by mass media and the dominant culture that produces it. This chapter detailed how fans use fan fiction to rectify some of the impacts of hetero- and cisnormativity, queercoding, and the "bury your gays" trope in mass media objects of fandom. Future research might find other ways in which fan fiction is an appropriately blatant response to popular culture media, which obscures and erases marginal identities in the interest of profitability.

Bibliography

Barthes, Roland. "'The Death of the Author.'" In *Authorship: From Plato to the Postmodern: A Reader*, edited by Seán Burke, 125-30. Edinburgh: Edinburgh University Press, 1995.

Bookinit. "half a heart (without you)." *Archive of Our own*. July 2, 2022. https://archiveofourown.org/works/40031733.

Boyon, Nicolas. "LGBT+ Pride 2021 Global Survey points to a generation gap around gender identity and sexual attraction." June 9, 2021. https://www.ipsos.com/en-us/news-polls/ipsos-lgbt-pride-2021-global-survey.

Cornier, J. Raúl. "Hanky Panky: An Abridged History of the Hanky Code." *historyproject*. April 23, 2019. https://historyproject.org/news/2019-04/han

---

[38] Henry Jenkins, "Fandom, Negotiation, and Participatory Culture," in *A Companion to Media Fandom and Fan Studies*, ed. Paul Booth, (2018), https://doi.org/10.1002/9781119237211.ch1.

ky-panky-abridged-history-hanky-code-0#:~:text=The%20hanky%20code%20was%20a,the%20purposes%20of%20sexual%20signaling.

Epilogue? What Epilogue?." *fanlore*. Last edited January 10, 2022. https://fanlore.org/wiki/Epilogue%3F_What_Epilogue%3F.

Floegel, Diana. "'Write the Story You Want to Read': World-Queering through Slash Fanfiction Creation." *Journal of Documentation* 76, no. 4 (2020): 785–805.

Fox, Audrey. "Why the Harry Potter Film Epilogues Never Stood a Chance." *Den of Geek*. July 15, 2021. https://www.denofgeek.com/movies/why-the-harry-potter-film-franchises-epilogue-never-stood-a-chance/.

Franklin, Monique. "Queerbaiting, Queer Readings, and Heteronormative Viewing Practices." In *Queerbaiting and Fandom: Teasing Fans through Homoerotic Possibilities*, edited by Joseph Brennan, 41-52. Iowa: University of Iowa Press, 2019.

Forester, Perceville. "Who're You Calling a Nerd?: How Identity, Marketability, and Nostalgia Impact Depictions of the 1980's in *Stranger Things*." *The International Journal of Creative Media Research* 10, (2023). https://www.creativemediaresearch.org/post/who-re-you-calling-a-nerd-how-identity-marketability-and-nostalgia-impact-depictions-of.

Gardner, Abby. "A Complete Breakdown of the J. K. Rowling Transgender-Comments Controversy." *Glamour*. February 7, 2023. https://www.glamour.com/story/a-complete-breakdown-of-the-jk-rowling-transgender-comments-controversy.

Gray, Jonathan. "How do I dislike thee? Let me count the ways." In *Anti-Fandom*, edited by Melissa Click, 25-41. New York: New York University Press, 2019.

jack_dearly. "Fictional Bisexuals." *TikTok*. February 27, 2023. https://www.tiktok.com/t/ZTR7arhaJ/.

Jenkins, Henry. "Fandom, Negotiation, and Participatory Culture." In *A Companion to Media Fandom and Fan Studies*, edited by Paul Booth, 2018. https://doi.org/10.1002/9781119237211.ch1.

———. "Welcome to Bisexuality, Captain Kirk': Slash and the Fanwriting Community." In *Textual Poachers: Television Fans and Participatory Culture*. London: Taylor & Francis Group, 2012.

McCarthy, Kayla. "Remember Things: Consumerism, Nostalgia, and Geek Culture in *Stranger Things*." *Journal of Popular Culture* 52, no. 3 (2019): 663-677.

Palmviolet. "sub-culture." *Archive of Our own*. May 30, 2022. https://archiveofourown.org/works/39308787?view_full_work=true.

Rowling, J. K. *Harry Potter and the Deathly Hallows*. London: Bloomsbury, 2014.

Russo, Vito. *The Celluloid Closet: Homosexuality in the Movies*. New York: Harper & Row, 1987.

Sandvoss, Cornel. *Fans: The Mirror of Consumption*. Oxford: Polity, 2005.

Schneider, Elisabeth. "Reclaiming Queerbaiting: A Call to Action." In *Queerbaiting and Fandom: Teasing Fans through Homoerotic Possibilities*, edited by Joseph Brennan, 54–56. University of Iowa Press, 2019.

ShortAngryTwinks. "Someone's Bound to Get It." *Archive of Our own*. July 1, 2022. https://archiveofourown.org/works/40005228.

SomewheresSword. "Lily's Boy." *Archive of Our own*. January 14, 2022. https://archiveofourown.org/works/30856244/chapters/90792109

Stein, Louisa. "Dissatisfaction and *Glee*: On Emotional Range in Fandom and Feels Culture." *Anti-Fandom*, edited by Melissa Click, 81-101. New York: New York University Press, 2019.

Stranger Things. Season 3, episode 7, "Chapter Seven: The Bite." Directed by The Duffer Brothers. Aired July 4, 2019, on Netflix. https://www.netflix.com/watch/80222778.

———. Season 4, episode 1, "Chapter One: The Hellfire Club." Directed by The Duffer Brothers. Aired May 27, 2022, on Netflix. https://www.netflix.com/watch/80229866.

———. Season 4, episode 8, "Chapter Eight: Papa." Directed by The Duffer Brothers. Aired July 1, 2022, on Netflix. https://www.netflix.com/watch/80229873.

"The 2021 National School Climate Survey." *GLSEN*. 2021. https://www.glsen.org/sites/default/files/2022-10/NSCS-2021-Full-Report.pdf: 57.

Waggoner, Erin B. "Bury Your Gays and Social Media Fan Response: Television, LGBTQ Representation, and Communitarian Ethics." *Journal of Homosexuality* 65, no. 13 (2018): 1877–91.

Chapter 2

Beyond the Knot: Reparative Fiction and the Omegaverse

Paige Hartenburg
New York University

Abstract: In this article, Hartenburg considers the inner complexities of the Omegaverse as a trope of fix-it fic that uses patriarchal structures to ultimately challenge them. She examines how alpha-beta-omega uses utopic biological components to reconsider power dynamics in patriarchal hierarchy while correcting narratives that use queerbaiting but ultimately promote only a heteronormative lens.

Keywords: omegaverse, A/B/O, heat, bonding, queerbaiting, biology, reproduction, pregnancy, patriarchal, *Voltron: Legendary Defender*, tags, fix-it fics, *AO3*.

***

Death came knocking in early August 2018. Scythe in hand and warrant signed, the accused were made aware of their sentence and were offered a deal: stop queerbaiting, or else. The charges, delivered in the form of several violent threats to the creative team behind the animated Netflix series *Voltron Legendary Defender* (2016-18), left many bystanders baffled by the extent to which some fans went to defend their interpretation of the fictional characters. Show creators Joaquim Dos Santos and Lauren Montgomery, both self-described fans of the original *Voltron* series (1984-85), were surprised by the fandom's response to the show's potential romantic plotlines. While the original animated mecha-space series was not known for centering character romance, fans of the Netflix adaptation, many new to the franchise, quickly developed an intense shipping culture between the popular characters.[1]

---

[1] Shipping culture (shipping): fan content/behavior that pairs two characters together, usually romantically and/or sexually. In fan fiction, this is largely known as "slash fics." Shipping culture, at its core, is an exploration of different power dynamics, intimacies, and relationships that may or may not have been excluded from the central canon.

Queering the gender and sexuality of the main protagonists, the fan interpretations of *Voltron: Legendary Defender* (*VLD*) were much more diverse than the show itself, reimagining the narrative to reflect the new audience, many of whom also identified as LGBTQ+. In 2018, as the show entered its seventh season, it was announced that a main cast member would come out as gay. Fans were ecstatic about this potential, waiting to see which of their headcanons would be legitimized. When it was revealed that the team leader, Shiro, would receive a boyfriend, though he would later die at the end of the episode, many fans were hurt, angry, and demanded an explanation. In "An Open Letter to the *VLD* Fandom," Joaquim Dos Santos commented on fans' polarized reactions, saying, "We knew people would be affected by the loss of Adam (Shiro's partner); we just could not have predicted how profound that loss would be," before denouncing the "aggressive behavior," and "lashing out," on the side of fandom.[2] The voice actor for green paladin Pidge, Bex Taylor-Klaus, also took to social media to voice their exhaustion towards the situation, "Please. Just be Kind … I'm tired of threats. I'm tired of having to consider canceling con appearances due to safety concerns. I'm just… tired."[3]

However, tensions in the fandom would only continue to rise with the release of the show's eighth and final season, a mere four months following the Shiro scandal. As the series concluded, fans were devastated to learn that none of the character conclusions aligned with fandom expectations, as calls for queerbaiting and racial profiling left many fans demanding that show personnel address the supposed failures of the finale. In a now-revised post on *Instagram*, voice actor Tyler Labine (voice of yellow paladin Hunk) criticized fans' responses to the show: "What will all fall by the wayside in due time is all the unwarranted hate and vitriol that the dark side of this fandom has let seep into this precious world. THAT is all just noise, and I refuse to listen."[4] From the perspective of the show creators, the *VLD* fandom had morphed into a hateful mob; all comments or critiques were seen as obsessive and crazed fan behavior. This belief seeped into other fan communities, many viewing *VLD* as a toxic fandom entrenched in shipping culture. As the fandom attempted to recover from the devastating season finale and rejection from show creators, many were left wondering: how did the fandom get to this point? How can fans move forward as a community with so much hurt, mistrust, and trauma?

---

[2] Joaquim Dos Santos (@JDS_247), "An Open Letter to the VLD Fandom," *Twitter*, August 13, 2018, 9:44.
[3] Bex Taylor-Klaus (@IBexWeBex), "Dear #Voltron fans," *Twitter*, August 10, 2018, 8:11.
[4] Tyler Labine (@tlabine), "To my fellow #Paladins," *Instagram*, December 15, 2018.

You Are What You Read

The goal of this chapter is to explore how queer fandom responds to and integrates trauma into its narratives, tracing how the popular yet notorious genre of the Omegaverse emerges as a response to queerbaiting and the identity culture of contemporary fandom. Answering this question requires establishing the cultural tone of fandom spaces during the height of *VLD*'s popularity. In 2016, queer fandom was in a state of recovery. From 2002 to 2012, popular community hubs *LiveJournal* and *FanFiction.net* repeatedly deleted mass amounts of fan content and accounts under the guise of removing child pornography. In practice, however, the deleted material largely centered on depictions of queer relationships, which right-wing activist groups claimed promoted "controversial situations" to teens and children.[5] Regardless of their actual content, the loss of queer media was heavily felt in fandom spaces, where fan works serve as critical infrastructure in organizing fandom. Fan content materialized different interpretations of a text in a shareable way, providing spaces for like-minded fans to discuss and engage with headcanons and theories in comment sections, discussion boards, and forums. This element of fandom was incredibly impactful on LGBTQ+ readers, who could easily organize and access queer content and community through the platforms' hyper-specific search tools. The porn purges, as a result, were harmful beyond removing targeted content, directly attacking how queer spaces operated in fandom. Fans reported feeling traumatized by the sudden erasure, which "also result(ed) in significant social losses" as friendships and communities vanished from key fandom hubs.[6] However, while the porn bans were directed mainly at queer content, the responses and protests from fans were more general, focusing on fan authority and free speech. Despite some petitions to remove the ban receiving upwards of 20,000 signatures, this effort did little to change the new policies. Displaced from the literary marketplace and embittered by the porn purges, fandom saw a departure from *FanFiction.net* and *LiveJournal* into different online spaces.

Fandom changed in two significant ways following the porn bans. First, in response to the erasure of NSFW fandom content, *Archive of Our own (AO3)* was created in 2009 to protect and curate fan works. Managed by the newly established *Journal of Transformative Works and Culture*, the creation of *AO3* supposedly marked a reclaiming of fandom spaces from corporate and political influences. However, while this project was successful in preserving fan works, Diana Floegel highlights how the shift to *AO3* separated fan works from the

---

[5] Declan McCullagh, "Mass Deletion Sparks LiveJournal Revolt," *CNET*, May 31, 2007.
[6] Diana Floegel, "Porn Bans, Purges, and Rebirths: The Biopolitics of Platform Death in Queer Fandoms," *Internet Histories: Digital Technology, Culture, and Society* 6, (2022): 90-112.

community, stating, "*AO3* is primarily an archive; it does not bill itself as a social media platform," lacking popular pages like community forums that were essential sites for previous fandom discourse.[7] Something was needed to supplement the lack of a community hub on *AO3*, and the blogging platform *Tumblr* rose to the occasion. This new space resulted in the second significant change in fandom as the community integrated into *Tumblr*'s identity-centric ecosystem. As Angela Nagel described in her book *Kill All Normies*, *Tumblr*'s gender-fluid culture aligned with fandom's role in representing fan identities and experiences, exploring issues of trauma resulting from "mental ill-health, physical disability, race, cultural identity, and intersectionality."[8] Fandom synergy with *Tumblr* introduced a new set of terminology to fan spaces, which centered on pathologizing identity and individual experience to access community spaces. *Tumblr*'s use of academic and psychological terms merged with fandom's preoccupation with establishing authority over a text: real fans versus imposters, valid headcanons versus indulgent projections. As Lily Winterwood described, *Tumblr*'s academic language provided a sense of legitimacy to fan readings:

> (On *LiveJournal*) Fan debates that spiral out of control used to be called wank… Nowadays, these similar arguments on *Tumblr* and *Twitter* are called discourse, a term co-opted from academia which lends gravitas and credence to the arguments being expounded in the post. Similarly, squick in old fandom simply implied a visceral dislike of a given topic, but the new fandom term trigger makes someone's aversive feelings towards that topic more intensely personal and potentially traumatic.[9]

As the lexicon of fan behavior was transformed by academic and psychological terms, fandom became a language for diagnosing identities, traumas, and experiences. While not exclusively the result of *Tumblr*, fandom's allegorical nature was heightened by the platform's emphasis on identity. Mainstream marketing teams, including the team behind *VLD*, developed viral strategies for attracting this audience by assigning viewers to in-universe characters through pseudo-personality tests; whether one prefers chocolate or vanilla ice cream was treated as psychological signifiers to map viewers onto specific characters. This relationship was more extreme in fandom itself, as the characters one related to became linguistic shorthand to describe mental illness, relationships

---

[7] Floegel, "Porn Bans," 100.
[8] Angela Nagle, *Kill All Normies: The Online Culture Wars from Tumblr and 4chan to the Alt-right and Trump* (Hants, UK: Zero Books, 2017).
[9] Lily Winterwood, "Discourse Is the New Wank: A Reflection on Linguistic Change in Fandom," *Transformative Works and Culture*, 27 (2015).

with others, hopes, dreams, and identities. *VLD* fans identifying with Lance could translate to depression with an inferiority complex, while identifying with Keith could translate to anger and abandonment issues. However, at the core of this hybrid sensibility, between personal enjoyment as a viewer and diagnosis, was media discussion, "shipping wars and other fandom wank are now being treated with the same lexicon and seriousness as academic discourse ... given the same amount of weight as psychological triggers."[10] Once based on individual preferences, fandom practices became a culture of validation. Any preference outside one's personal relationship to the central narrative could be interpreted as an attack against one's person and autonomy. Fan fiction's ability to provide material readings of certain characters and dynamics addressed many fans' hyper-personalized analogous relationships with their favorite media. In other words, fandom became immersed in a language of identity, fan fiction acting as an arena for verbalizing this connection and providing community infrastructure for reimagining canonical narratives through a lens of intersectionality.

This era, spanning roughly from 2008 to 2018, is when some of the most notable, infamous examples of fandom became popular. The erotic content became a point of interest for those looking in on fandom from the outside. Creators behind popular characters and narratives were often asked to comment on the "fandom question," mainly represented as a discussion of LGBTQ+ readings of the characters. Fans could watch actors and original creators, official figureheads within fandom spaces, discuss their feelings on popular ships and other headcanons while engaging with the same materials. However, as some fans wanted to believe, this acknowledgment did not impact who was given recognized authority over a narrative and its characters. As Michael McDermott described, "the dynamic between fan and producer can be understood as a 'contest' over meaning, with a key goal being 'ownership over and claim of a single authentic textual meaning and story.'"[11] Concerns over authorial preservation, deeply ingrained in fandom and creative cultures alike, led to conflicting beliefs over how mainstream media should interact with online audiences. While the culture prioritized personal authorial integrity, fandom was often an extension of identity. Fandom no longer only described a series of behaviors or actions but was used as a diagnostic language for understanding one's identity. As a result, the dynamic between fandom and creator was not just a context for narrative authority; it was also a fight over fans' ability to self-identify as a legitimate form of reading a text. Shipping became a

---

[10] Winterwood, "Discourse Is the New Wank," 18.
[11] Michael McDermott, "The Contest of Queerbaiting: Negotiating Authenticity in Fan–Creator Interactions," *Journal of Fandom Studies* 6, no. 2 (2018): 133.

critical form of mobilization within these spaces, allowing users to act out their identities through the language and medium of fandom. This practice gave additional potency to queerbaiting, which became the go-to term to describe any instance in which a canonical text did not recognize the legitimacy of a queer reading of the characters and narrative. Queerbaiting, described by Joseph Brennan as "an allegiance to issues of queer visibility without actually delivering on such an allegiance in any tangible way," became a kind of trauma, further responding to the culture of suffering that had become central to *Tumblr's* identity politics.[12] The queer potential of the reimagined character, belonging almost entirely to the fandom's creativity, rarely lived up to the actuality of the narrative. As a result, fan communities mourn lost futures, narratives, and characterizations in terms of the characters and as representations of real identities, relationships, and people. To explore how this multifaceted shift in fandom appeared within its creative works, I turn to a genre infamously known for its depiction of queerness, toxic relationships, and fetishistic sex. It's time to enter the Omegaverse.

Welcome to the Omegaverse

The Omegaverse, also known as Alpha Beta Omega dynamics (A/B/O), is a genre not only defined by its complicated power dynamics but also its complex and overarching world-building used to address fandom issues with a source narrative.[13] Pulling from canonical narrative elements or alternative universes, A/B/O is a fanfiction/erotica genre exploring an alternative reality in which humanity is born with biologically defined second genders. While these roles often align with performative norms surrounding real-life gender, the Omegaverse explicitly defines its identities through biology centered on pregnancy and reproduction. Alphas reflect traditional masculinity intended to reproduce with Omegas, the female-coded characters.[14] While A/B/O dynamics

---

[12] Joseph Brennan, *Queerbaiting and Fandom* (University of Iowa Press, 2019), 1.

[13] It is important to note the term A/B/O is spelled similarly to a slur towards Aboriginal Australians. In line with other scholarship on the Omegaverse and to reflect the language of the community, I have chosen to keep the term, with each use slashed to avoid similar spellings.

[14] It is essential to note that the Omegaverse overwhelmingly focuses on masculine queer relationships, while female characters and relationships are limited or completely excluded from the genre. For comparison, *AO3* houses 12,455 fan fiction tagged femslash A/B/O dynamics, making up roughly 8% of fan fiction available in the category. Heterosexual pairings make up roughly 14% or 22, 285 fan fiction. The role of gender within the Omegaverse is also complicated by the genre's prevalence in depicting trans-masculine characters, as explored by J.T. Weisser in their essay, "Transmasculinities and Pregnant Monstrosity: *Hannibal* Omegaverse Fan-Fiction," published by *Cultivate* in 2019.

have a notorious reputation for graphic and fetishistic sex, it continues to be one of the most popular genres on websites like *AO3*, *FanFiction.net*, and *Wattpad*. According to Luz Marina Delgado Diaz, traces of the Omegaverse can be seen as early as 2009, but the genre did not explode in popularity until 2017, in line with anxieties over another porn purge, this time from *Tumblr* (although the official ban would not be put in place till late 2018).[15] As of writing this essay, *AO3* alone has 29,888 published works related to Omegaverse and 157,454 texts published under the Alpha Beta Omega dynamics tag. Despite the genre's vast popularity in online spaces, little scholarship focuses on the Omegaverse, how its emergence responds to more significant trends in fandom, and why this controversial genre has gained so much popularity in recent years. Within this limited research, scholars of the genre tend to focus on the depiction of consent and gender roles. Milena Popova analyzes A/B/O through their ability to explore complex negotiations of consent within the genre's imagined social hierarchy:

> By positing a world with a radically different configuration of genders and sexualities to ours, readers and writers playing in this shared universe can examine gender roles as either driven by the strange biology of the Omegaverse, or socially constructed (or both) ... The biological or social construction of different genders and sexualities can be seen as leading to sometimes radically different, and sometimes strikingly similar, dominant sexual scripts in the societies depicted in Omegaverse fiction.[16]

While Popova's arguments are crucial in understanding the themes and functions of this genre, she only gestures to A/B/O's role within fandom communities and larger narratives of trauma and identity. By contextualizing the tropes and themes of Omegaverse within larger narratives of fandom identity, I will demystify the genre for those internal and external to fandom. Through exploring the Omegaverse beyond its negotiation of sex and analyzing the genre's depiction of society, family structures, and biology, I will define how the Omegaverse incorporates the trauma of queerbaiting, centering queerness as the ultimate and final conclusion for its characters. By co-opting medical and academic language, which responds to trends common throughout *Tumblr*-age fandom, the Omegaverse can legitimize pairings beyond individual interpretation to the level of biological and universal structures.

---

[15] Luz Marina Delgado Diaz, Patricia Alexandra Ubillus Brena, Giancarlo Cappello, "Omegaverse o la forja de un universo fanfiction," *Contratexto* (2022).

[16] Milena Popova, "'Dogfuck Rapeworld': Omegaverse Fanfiction as a Critical Tool in Analyzing the Impact of Social Power Structures on Intimate Relationships and Sexual Consent," *Porn Studies* 5, no. 2 (2018).

These pairings are then used to address areas of a source canon that do not align with fandom expectations and attachments, placing these connections at the center of the narrative universe and transforming the work into the creative property of fandom.

To further traverse Omegaverse fanfiction, I will explore four key tropes — the heat and bonding, body modifications, societal implications, and the pack — that I have found across A/B/O narratives. All quotes used in my analysis were pulled from fanfictions uploaded to *AO3*, under the Alpha/Beta/Omega dynamics tag and center Keith and Lance (known in the fandom as Klance) as the primary pairing.[17] Through my study of these tropes, I will outline how the Omegaverse integrates trauma, both in terms of queerbaiting and other forms of LGBTQ+ trauma, into the narrative structure of fan fiction, addressing the tension between fans, the original narrative, and its creators.

Trope One: The Heat and Bonding

The heat may be the most documented of all the elements associated with the Omegaverse. Describing a period of increased fertility for Omegas, in its most basic form, symptoms of heat include fever, bodily aches, arousal, and declined mental functioning. Behaviors like nesting, bonding marks, and mating also occur during this time.[18] Heats are usually cyclical and serve as the penultimate moment in many A/B/O narratives. While not as common, Alphas also experience their own form of heat called a rut, which includes similar symptoms to their Omega counterparts with more emphasis on aggression and anger. Omega heats can trigger an Alpha's rut and vice versa. Popova described the heat as the underlying force that defines the "power imbalance between Alphas and Omegas," aligning with dominant Western scripts about gender and sexuality, which place vaginal-coded bodies as submissive to phallus-coded individuals.[19] However, while Alphas tend to be placed in traditionally masculine roles, which carries significance when interpreting power dynamics, within the structure of a heat, Omegas are given the most space and representational power on a narrative

---

[17] I will limit my discussion of these narratives to their depiction of the Omegaverse, focusing on statements that invoke the genre to justify character behavior, world-building, and narrative structure. As a result of the vastness of the material, I will need to make some generalizations that will overlook different variations of the Omegaverse. For example, I will not explore fanfiction centering non-Omega/Alpha pairings or the figures like the Beta, Delta, or Gamma.

[18] Nesting: An Omegan impulse to build safe spaces for heat, pregnancy, labor, and comfort. Nests are usually described as plush and soft, comprised of forged items from members of their pack. Bonding Marks/Mating: during a heat or rut, Alphas and Omegas can bond/mate. Bonding marks often solidify a relationship and signal mate status to the rest of the pack.

[19] Popova, "Dogfuck Rapeworld," 19.

level. Although Alphas are the socially dominant group, Omega authority is the most powerful in places like nests, where heat is biologically intended to occur (although this does not happen in every narrative). For example, in "Spicy Little Kitten" by may10baby, when Lance (Alpha) demanded entry into Keith's (Omega) nest, he was playfully told he would need to "earn it," despite the pair already having sex (without mating).[20] "They Call Me The Taylor," by zeerogue, includes a similar scene where Lance (Alpha) was told not to intrude on Keith's (Omega) nest and agreed due to respecting Keith's position as an Omega.[21] The nest is one of the few places of consent within the Omegaverse, albeit somewhat on a surface level. It is a gate meant to be opened rather than a fortress of protection. Though it seems like this dynamic would place more control with the Alpha, bonding centers on Omegan pleasure as a form of power, serving as the central focus and perspective of many A/B/Os as well as the leading, but not dominant, body within the sexual scripts. While the Omega, like the nest, is meant to be conquered by the Alpha, A/B/O narratives largely focus on the Omega: their consent is often the most verbalized within the narrative, their arousal is repeatedly used as the inciting event, and their pleasure often solidifies bonding (this is not always the case, but those narratives often include other tags like non-consensual (noncon) or rape). "Mating Bond" by whitehorsetiger describes receiving a bonding mark from the perspective of the Omega (Keith), highlighting the "burning pleasure" that overtook his senses while Lance's (Alpha) perspective is distinctly absent.[22] "Jealousy Thy Name is Keith," by TilDeathDoWeLove25, similarly positions Omega's pleasure and bonding, "Keith (Alpha) finally marked him (Lance, Omega), the noise soon turning into yet another of pleasure."[23] While mating marks invoke connections to possessive patriarchal values by focusing on the feminine-coded Omega and centering their pleasure, mating does not function as an oppressive institution. This is a significant shift in how power and consent function within the Omegaverse. Here, power is created through an exchange of pleasure. It is not just penetrative but a symbiotic relationship between body, soul, and identity. The heat and bonding weave queerness into the social fabric of the Omegaverse, legitimizing the pairing beyond attraction at the social and universal levels. Kristina Busse described this tendency as an element of larger fan behavior. She writes, "Fandom generally seems to prefer happy over

---

[20] May10baby, "Spicy Little Kitten," *Archive of Our Own*, February 27, 2018, https://archiveofourown.org/works/11998587.
[21] Zeerogue, "They Call Me The Taylor," *Archive of Our Own*, April 2, 2021, https://archiveofourown.org/works/28325850.
[22] Whitehorsetiger, "Mating Bond," *Archive of Our Own*, April 10, 2019, https://archiveofourown.org/works/18422781.
[23] TilDeathDoWeLove25, "Jealousy Thy Name Is Keith," *Archive of Our Own*, April 7, 2018, https://archiveofourown.org/works/14246628.

unhappy and soul mates over one-night stands."[24] In the popular fanfiction "Enslaved," by Mer_kitty, the heat is described as "the most sacred and beautiful act," all-consuming in its impact on the Alpha and Omega.[25] Author Caeseria writes similarly about the Omegaverse, highlighting the heat as "intense, both of them (Keith and Lance) connected not only by the bond itself but also by emotion to each other. They were...barely able to be apart for the first few days."[26] Within both narratives, the heat, while relying on the archaic language of patriarchal possession, emblematic of this genre's equivalent of marriage, holds an essential role in the functioning of society. This positions Klance as an element of larger universal, biological, and social traditions. In this way, the heat, divinely approved and required, moves beyond conversations of consent and into the realm of communal recognition. The pairing is validated within patriarchal and omnipresent structures, which creates outcomes that are fixed and immutable, transforming the initial queerbaiting into a secure and definitive relationship.

Trope Two: The Body

A/B/Os are most infamous for their impact on the characters' bodies. Fandom authors have incorporated a myriad of pseudo-biological language to explain the physical manifestations of secondary genders. Scent glands at the base of the neck release personalized odors to attract potential mates and serve as the spot of a mating bite. Unique vocal cords allow Alphas and Omegas to "chirp" and "growl" to express emotional distress as well as provide additional power to command members of the pack (a power usually, but not exclusively, reserved for Alphas). Alpha's phallus can swell at the base to "knot" during intercourse, and Omegas produce a wet substance called "slick" when aroused.[27] Most notoriously, Omegas, regardless of their primary genders, can support pregnancy and give birth. Some narratives like "Enslaved" by Mer_Kitty and "The darkness in his eyes" by NSkellington, extend the presence of secondary genders by providing autonomous consciousness to the primal voices external to the characters themselves, using physical qualifiers like pacing and preening to describe the imagined physicality of the secondary

---

[24] Anne Jamison and Kristina Busse, "Pon Farr, Mpreg, and the rise of the Omegaverse," *FIC: Why Fanfiction is Taking Over the World*, ed. Anne Jamieson (Dallas TX: Smart Pop, 2013).
[25] Mer_Kitty, "Enslaved," *Archive of Our Own*, October 25, 2022, https://archiveofourown.org/works/13357761.
[26] Caeseria, "Be Alive With Me Tonight," *Archive of Our Own*, February 25, 2022, https://archiveofourown.org/works/20074594/chapters/47544118.
[27] Knotting: during sexual climax, the base of the Alpha phallus will expand, allowing the Alpha to "lock" themselves into the Omega, keeping their semen inside their partner.

genders.[28] While biological changes vary across A/B/O narratives, it is common for the characters, specifically the Omegas, to feel dysphoric about their bodies. "It's not a problem until it's a problem...," by Lynn1998, opens their narrative on this theme, "Lance was certain he wasn't meant to be an omega. His first heat made him feel like a hole with legs."[29] A similar pattern is found at the beginning of "Your Sex I Can Smell" by HedonistInk and Heikijin, which describes Lance's first heat as humiliating due to his male identity.[30] "What Else Could a Virgin Omega Do" by realfakedoors and The_Broken_Dreamer adds an additional component to this element, writing how Lance (an Omega) "felt like he lost a bit more of his sanity each time" (he experienced a heat). He wondered if other Omegas had this much trouble or if he was just an oddity," highlighting how the physical sensation of secondary genders challenges his sense of self and consciousness, furthered by the queer-coded questioning of Lance as an "oddity."[31] The dysphoria felt by the Omega in these narratives, mirroring real-life experiences of queer dysphoria, is rooted in an individualized interpretation of the symptoms. These are not problems necessarily faced by all Omegas, but rather the unpaired Omega (in these cases, Lance). As the narrative continues, the heat occurs, and Lance and Keith romantically unite; this is depicted as the "cure" for the Omega's dysphoria as what was once dysphoric becomes natural, an essential piece to connecting the two characters. What was once painful is replaced with a truer understanding of self, revealed through sex, and solidified by the biological function of the A/B/O dynamic. Fixing the narrative to address fandom interpretations, the Omegaverse is a revelation in addition to a correction, addressing fandom anxieties about identity and validation while also directly overriding source authority. In doing so, the Omegaverse not only fixes the source canon but provides an answer to queer dysphoria, depicting a solution rooted in community rather than isolation.

Trope Three: Society

One of the most interesting elements of the Omegaverse is its significance beyond individual character interactions, serving a pivotal role in determining how the narrative universe operates. While A/B/O societies can share haunting

---

[28] NSkellington, "The darkness in his eyes," *Archive of Our Own*, February 5, 2021, https://archiveofourown.org/works/29003238/chapters/71180409.

[29] Lynn1998, "It's not a problem until it's a problem...," *Archive of Our Own*, August 25, 2020, https://archiveofourown.org/works/16611974/chapters/38936732.

[30] HedonistInk and Heikijin, "Your Sex I Can Smell," *Archive of Our Own*, January 27, 2017, https://archiveofourown.org/works/8738485/chapters/20034571.

[31] realfakedoors and The_Broken_Dreamer, "What Else Could a Virgin Omega Do?," *Archive of Our Own*, Octtober 21, 2019, https://archiveofourown.org/works/8101726/chapters/18566056.

similarities to real-life social practices and power structures by centering queerness and, more specifically, centering the eventual coupling of Klance, these structures take on a particular role within the narrative both as oppressive and as the element of the story that will incite their coupling. Within the limited scholarship surrounding A/B/O, one of the most common overarching arguments is that the genre balances a precarious relationship between challenging normative standards of gender and sexuality while restricting representation to patriarchal standards. This relationship is true within the world-building of many Omegaverse narratives, as the female-coded Omegas are often treated as weak, inferior, or Alpha property. However, this analysis does not discuss the role of the Omegaverse in exploring queer trauma while ensuring the pairing of specific characters. In "Breathe me in, Breathe me out" by Queerklancing, in a scene where Lance (who is secretly an Omega) and Keith (Alpha) are locked in a closet after Lance's heat is triggered by space slavers, the author writes that, "Omegas are not exactly the first choice when it comes to fighter pilots," explaining why Lance chose to hide his secondary gender.[32] Here, the oppression faced by Omegas, while critiqued by the narrative, is also crucial for inciting Keith and Lance's eventual bonding. Without oppression, the heat and subsequent relationship would not happen, denying the function of the fan fiction that promises the eventual coupling of two specific characters. Other popular Omegaverse narratives like "Enslaved" by Mer_Kitty[33] and "Be Alive With Me Tonight" by Caeseria[34] envision Keith and Lance undercover as bonded Alpha and Omega in gendered societies feature similar oppressive elements, simultaneously voicing character disgust over the "barbaric … patriarchal society" while maintaining these elements as natural, necessary elements of the character's relationship; "At what point did they decide that any of the genders shouldn't bond, that bonding was shameful, that it was a showcase of genders running wild, giving into baser instincts that humanity no longer needed?"[35] Patriarchal power serves a very particular role within the Omegaverse. It is a challenge (and, to a certain extent, a trauma) experienced by both characters that can only exist before the pair's coupling. By mating and bonding, the trauma, bodily dysphoria, and oppression faced by these characters, especially the Omega, are incorporated into the core of the relationship and subsequently healed by the mere confirmation that the

---

[32] Queerklancing, "Breathe me in, Breathe me out," *Archive of Our Own*, April 9, 2017, https://archiveofourown.org/works/10581339.
[33] Mer_Kitty, "Enslaved."
[34] Caeseria, "Be Alive With Me Tonight."
[35] Mer_Kitty, "Enslaved."

relationship is secured both socially and biologically. This acceptance also heals the Alpha, whose internal conflicts over control, power, and consent are resolved by the finality of bonding that secures the couple's relationship. Like much of fan culture, trauma is placed at the heart of the Omegaverse, allowing fans to process and resolve tensions born from social structures that seek to regulate and remove sections of society deemed as non-normative. While A/B/O dynamics do not necessarily destabilize these structures, the genre celebrates personal success and acceptance, correcting specific issues caused by the subjugated relationship between fans and original creators.

Trope Four: The Pack

Beyond the implications of the Omegaverse on sexuality, the body, and society, its most essential result, outside of the potential for pregnancy, is the pack. Pack dynamics replicate many found family narratives, centering on a group of people brought together not by blood but by affection and familial care. As Kali Wallace wrote, "Found family stor(ies are) an exploration of how the path a character actively chooses for their future" heals a traumatic past, highlighting the genre's role both in depicting narratives of trauma and imaginative futures.[36] Found family narratives are particularly impactful in LGBTQ+ communities. As a marginalized community, queerness is distinct from other identities in that it is not inherited from family lineage or nationality. Queerness is something grown into as a part of one's self-actualization. Found family narratives fit within this process, both culturally as an element of coming into one's identity and as a real-life survival response to queer oppression and violence. A/B/O furthers this structure, providing a biological element to legitimize the new family. Each member has a clear role, and the identities within the Omegaverse and subsequent family structures incorporate trauma of mating, dysphoric bodies, and social expectations as validating forces for the family structure. While these dynamics mirror the oppressive elements of cisheteronormativity through queering the represented bodies, A/B/Os reflect queer futurity within the language and expectations that have become associated with the genre. For example, in "Want" by JustSomeGirl92, the narrative begins with an established Alpha/Omega couple (Shiro and Matt) discussing the joys of being a mated couple and deciding to purchase Lance (a "mail-order" Omega) for Keith (Alpha and Shiro's brother):

> If the younger man (Keith) was lonely and there was so much anger in him, he had to fight himself constantly to keep control (of his secondary gender). Shiro had confessed to Matt that he saw how desperately Keith

---

[36] Kali Wallace, "Exploring the Dark Side of Found Family," *Tor.com*, 2021.

needed someone to anchor him, to help him feel calm and maybe even happy. Keith deserved someone to love him the way Matt did Shiro, someone to care about him and be his stability.[37]

Within this narrative structure, the pack provides more than community; it regulates one's biology and identity. Additionally, through the inclusion of biology, the Omegaverse can fix and define character relationships on a structural level, legitimizing pairings within the fandom universe. This structure feeds into larger conversations on identity and community in fandom spaces. As fandom reorganized itself following the porn bans and shift to *Tumblr*, Omegaverse narratives provided space to negotiate the new sense of community felt by fandom members. Combined with the identity politics of *Tumblr*, which permeated many of the common tropes of A/B/O dynamics, the Omegaverse served to both imagine and legitimize fandom readings of a text, correct discrepancies between fandom interpretation and source narrative dependent on fans' relationship with their favorite characters.

Death and Rebirth

Through exploring the Omegaverse, the connection between LGBTQ+ trauma, corrective narratives, and fandom is evident. Responding to a long history of queerbaiting and erasure, the Omegaverse writes queerness through the impact it leaves on the body, with its violence and heteronormic tendencies responding to larger structures that attempt to confine narrative authority to a single group. Through the Omegaverse, A/B/Os center queerness as biologically and universally definitive for these characters, leaving little room to push the boundaries of representation within the rigid structures of the narrative. The Omegaverse is a complicated genre made more intricate by its surrounding culture. Responding to specific traumas of queerbaiting and projection, the Omegaverse repairs a broken universe and a broken fan, each healed by the futurity and certainty an A/B/O can provide. While A/B/Os are criticized for their depiction of cisheteropatriarchial values, it is essential to reflect on the genre's role as an extension of fan identity, trauma, and culture rather than an isolated creative trend. The Omegaverse, in all its intricacies, both problematic in its highly patriarchal troupes and emblematic of considerable community trauma, is a genre representative of the dissolving relationship between queer fandom spaces and mainstream creatives. In an attempt to fix a faulty conclusion or validate community expectations, the unique and, at times, drastically different

---

[37] JustSomeGirl92, "Want," *Archive of Our Own*, November 9, 2017, https://archiveofourown.org/works/12656517/chapters/28845105.

world of the Omegaverse highlights how fandom addresses the scars of its past, reviving a narrative in a new life following the death of its source material.

Bibliography

Brennan, Joseph. *Queerbaiting and Fandom*. The University of Iowa Press, 2019.

Caeseria. "Be Alive With Me Tonight." *Archive of Our own*. February 25, 2022, https://archiveofourown.org/works/20074594/chapters/47544118.

Delgado Diaz, Luz Marina, Ubillus Brena, Patricia Alexandra, and Giancarlo Cappello. "Omegaverse o la forja de un universo fanfiction." *Contratexto* (2022): 129-151.

Dos Santos, Joaquim (@JDS_247). "An open letter to the *VLD* fandom." *Twitter*. August 13, 2018, 9:44.

Floegel, Diana. "Porn Bans, Purges, and Rebirths: The Biopolitics of Platform Death in Queer Fandoms." *Internet Histories: Digital Technology, Culture, and Society* (2022): 90-112.

HedonistInk and Heikijin. "Your Sex I Can Smell." *Archive of Our own*. January 27, 2017, https://archiveofourown.org/works/8738485/chapters/20034571.

Jamison, Anne, and Kristina Busse. "Pon Farr, Mpreg, and the Rise of the Omegaverse." In *FIC: Why Fanfiction Is Taking over the World*, 288–94. Dallas, TX: 2013.

JustSomeGirl92. "Want." *Archive of Our own*. Nov 9, 2017, https://archiveofourown.org/works/12656517/chapters/28845105.

Labine, Tyler (@tlabine). "To my fellow #Paladins." *Instagram*. December 15, 2018.

Lynn1998. "It's not a problem until it's a problem…" *Archive of Our own*. August 25, 2020, https://archiveofourown.org/works/16611974/chapters/38936732.

May10baby. "Spicy Little Kitten." *Archive of Our own*. February 27, 2018, https://archiveofourown.org/works/11998587.

McCullagh, Declan. "Mass Deletion Sparks LiveJournal Revolt." *CNET*, May 31, 2007.

McDermott, Micheal. "The Contest of Queerbaiting: Negotiating Authenticity in Fan–Creator Interactions." *Journal of Fandom Studies* 6, no. 2 (2018).

Mer_Kitty. "Enslaved." *Archive of Our own*. Octtober 25, 2022, https://archiveofourown.org/works/13357761.

Nagle, Angela. *Kill All Normies: The Online Culture Wars from Tumblr and 4chan to the Alt-right and Trump*. Hants, UK: Zero Books, 2017.

NSkellington. "The darkness in his eyes." *Archive of Our own*. Feb 5, 2021, https://archiveofourown.org/works/29003238/chapters/71180409.

Popova, Milena. "'Dogfuck Rapeworld': Omegaverse Fanfiction as a Critical Tool in Analyzing the Impact of Social Power Structures on Intimate Relationships and Sexual Consent." *Porn Studies* 5, no. 2 (2018): 175-191.

Queerklancing. "Breathe me in, Breathe me out." *Archive of Our own*. Apr 9, 2017, https://archiveofourown.org/works/10581339.

realfakedoors and The_Broken_Dreamer. "What Else Could a Virgin Omega Do?" *Archive of Our own*. October 21, 2019, https://archiveofourown.org/works/8101726/chapters/18566056.

Taylor-Klaus, Bex (@IBexWeBex). "Dear #Voltron fans." *Twitter.* August 10, 2018, 8:11.

TilDeathDoWeLove25. "Jealousy Thy Name Is Keith." *Archive of Our own.* April 7, 2018, https://archiveofourown.org/works/14246628.

Wallace, Kali. "Exploring the Dark Side of Found Family." *Tor.com,* 2021.

Weisser, J.T. "Transmasculinities and Pregnant Monstrosity: *Hannibal* Omegaverse Fan-Fiction." *Cultivate: The Feminist Journal of the Centre for Women's Studies* (2019).

Whitehorsetiger. "Mating Bond." *Archive of Our own.* April 10, 2019, https://archiveofourown.org/works/18422781.

Winterwood, Lily. "Discourse Is the New Wank: A Reflection on Linguistic Change in Fandom." *Transformative Works and Culture* 27 (2015).

Zeerogue. "They Call Me The Taylor." *Archive of Our own.* April 2, 2021, https://archiveofourown.org/works/28325850.

Chapter 3

Fannish Yiddish and Communal Becoming in the Rogue Archive

Ethan Calof

Vanderbilt University

Abstract: In this article, Calof looks at fix-it fic authors who apply Jewish culture, language, and tradition to canonically non-canonically Jewish pop culture, specifically characters, to imagine Jewish futures and spaces. They consider the fix-it fic as an archival site where individuals can explore their heritage as part of a marginalized community. Calof seeks to establish the fix-it fic and *Archive of Our own* (*AO3*) as a reparative archive that evokes the possibility of a minority futurity.

Keywords: Jewish, rogue, archive, Yiddish, culture, tradition, minority futurity, community building, tags, *AO3*, fix-it fics.

***

On September 8, 2022, fanfiction author bloodscout published the one-chapter long, one-shot fanfiction, "make me aware of being alive."[1] The story was a "slash" fic featuring male/male erotic romance in ways not explicitly canonical, based on the fourth season of the popular Netflix series *Stranger Things*. In this fic, bloodscout chose Eddie Munson, a fan-favorite character who is tragically killed in the season finale, as their romantic lead alongside fellow fan favorite Steve Harrington. Nevertheless, beloved metalhead Eddie is given a characteristic in "make me aware of being alive" that he is not given in the original series. bloodscout makes him Jewish. As part of their exploration of Eddie's romance and Jewishness, bloodscout drops bits and pieces of Yiddish in their prose to emphasize his faith and budding connection with Steve. While the two are cooking together, Eddie slaps Steve's behind flirtatiously and says, "Now, gey aroys, get your tuchas out of my kitchen, or I'll never finish in time."[2] In another,

---

[1] bloodscout, "make me aware of being alive," *Archive of Our Own*, September 8, 2022, https://archiveofourown.org/works/41569509.

[2] "Gey aroys" means "get out" in Yiddish, while "tuchas" means behind. Both are transliterated.

Eddie apologizes silently to his mother for using a Christmas-themed challah cover with "antshuldigt," or "sorry" in Yiddish. All these transliterated Yiddish terms are defined in a glossary by bloodscout at the end of their story, along with an explanation for why they are using Yiddish in a non-Yiddish story, on a non-Yiddish website, about a non-Jewish character, and tagging it as #Yiddish in the fanfic's metadata. Their metadata and paratext solicit a dual audience of Yiddishkeit amateurs and Yiddishkeit experts. In their author's notes, they write both "We deserve NJB[3] Eddie!!!" and "Quick note that I am not Jewish (yet!! I get dunked nxt yr)[4] and most definitely don't have jewish family, so I rly rly hope I haven't gotten anything wrong."[5] They are simultaneously identifying as an in-group member and soliciting those with deeper ties to Yiddish. Through *Archive of Our own (AO3)*, bloodscout has a venue for experimentation and growth. Yiddish is their tool, and is part of a broader tradition of cultural performance through fanfiction archives that is broader than just Yiddishists. They are using the language of a Yiddish past and merging it with the dialogues and canonical texts of contemporary pop culture, writing for audiences both Jewish and non-Jewish, and, in the process, providing a model for fellow Yiddish enthusiasts to play both imagining and creating a Yiddish future. They are searching for and reifying a new branch of "Yiddishland," which Jeffrey Shandler defines "as a virtual locus construed in terms of the use of the Yiddish language"[6] in a non-Yiddish, non-Jewish, non-institutional, experimental world. Their fic is a fix-it fic on a dual level: creating a space for Yiddishness and Jewishness in the original gentile world of *Stranger Things* and creating a space for queer, non-linear, communal growth in various conceptions of Yiddishland. To borrow from Abigail de Kosnik, these authors are rogue archivists in search of fellow rogues.

De Kosnik refers to fanfiction archives, among many other communal-based archival processes, as "rogue" or counter-hegemonic archives. According to De Kosnik:

> What I call *rogue archives* are defined by: constant (24/7) availability; zero barriers to entry for all who can connect to the Internet; content that can be streamed or downloaded in full, with no required payment, and no regard for copyright restrictions (some rogue archivists digitize only

---

[3] NJB is an abbreviation for Nice Jewish Boy.
[4] In this case, "get dunked" refers to the mikvah, a ritual bath in Judaism for those converting to the faith.
[5] bloodscout, "make me aware."
[6] Jeffrey Shandler, *Adventures in Yiddishland* (Berkeley: University of California Press, 2005), 33.

what is already in the public domain); and content that has never been, and would likely never be, contained in a traditional memory institution.[7]

The internet narrows power gaps that have characterized traditional archives, introducing "some measure of democratization" in De Kosnik's framing,[8] and a fanfiction archive like *AO3* is inherently democratized by virtue of its unbarred access and thriving discourse community. An individual fanfic exists at once as repertoire (by performing an artistic reinterpretation of an already existent property), archive (due to its tagging, its searchability, its many layers of categorization and metadata), text, paratext (many authors supplementing their stories with authorial notes that explain their intentions and choices), and social forum (through its comment section, providing a place for direct feedback and ensuing author-reader dialogue). Fanfiction's uniqueness comes from how foregrounded all these existences are and how much the form and genre of fanfiction incentivize direct community building rather than making it a secondary part of the process. It foregrounds all levels of canonical fixes: fixes in representation, fixes in story continuity, and fixes on all other identity bases.

Suppose one uses fan fiction to explore one's heritage or a marginalized community. In that case, it accelerates the ability to seek and find solidarity from other community members, with the only barrier to entry being an internet connection. Fan fiction archives do not purport to contain the same degree of ossified past-ness that a stable state archive often perpetuates, with the instant posting and archiving lending a degree of immanence and accessibility that a more traditional archive does not. However, they share the same principles of revision, interpretation, and ultimately restorative imagination of an alternate community using the language of the dominant discourse. In fanfiction such as bloodscout's "make me aware of being alive," the author is imagining themselves and their Jewishness in a broader non-Jewish cultural dialogue, with Yiddish as a tool for deepening these connections. These imaginations are corrective and space-building at once. They create their own form of "becoming," a Gil Z. Hochberg term for art that plays with historical archives to imagine a more just society. Her theories of archival imagination and "becoming" come from her analysis of Palestinian artists using archiving to craft revolutionary or critical art. In examples such as director Kamal Aljafari using recycled Israeli media to convey contemporary Palestinian life and loss in Jaffa, archives no longer hold to Aleida Assmann's formation of archives as "past as past" and instead are used to build a future-

---

[7] Abigail De Kosnik, *Rogue Archives: Digital Cultural Memory and Media Fandom* (Cambridge: The MIT Press, 2019), 2.
[8] De Kosnik, *Rogue Archives*, 16.

oriented framework.⁹ Hochberg's formulation of "becoming Palestine" removes any spatiotemporal cloistering of the *nakba* as a trauma that happened "back then" and ensures that its long-running effects are recognized as present as well, in order to generate a sense of futurity by imagining a new archival site. Thus, silences and violences of the past are rendered visible and overcome.¹⁰ The "becoming" in "becoming Palestine" signifies the creation of new collectives, contingencies, and revisions of the historical record, with the ultimate aim of imagining a radical societal transformation along the axes of anti-colonial justice.

While Yiddish fanfiction authors are writing around a social situation that doesn't match the scale of tragedy in the *nakba*, they are creating a dual niche that had not previously existed. These authors carve a space for Yiddish and Jewish heritage within fannish works and a contemporary approach to Yiddish that evades its metalinguistic, unearned reputation as a language fixed in the past and more dormant in the present. Like Aljafari using the tools of Palestine's colonizers to create liberatory Palestinian art, Yiddish fanfiction authors use the tools of gentile media to create deeply Jewish content. Fandom spaces create different sorts of minoritized solidarities or possibilities than other existent internet spaces for Jewish heritage languages, such as *Ladinokomunita*, a decades-old message board exclusively for speakers of Ladino or Judeo-Spanish. It is a visible, public, and open practice largely populated by queer young women with a vested interest in various popular culture properties. It is largely pseudonymous, providing a measure of safety to participants who fear ostracization, yet vast degrees of community and discourse are formed around these pseudonyms. It is not a "closed" group, with many Yiddish-inflected fics featuring extensive author notes and vocabulary lists for non-experts. Yet, it is ultimately oriented towards a concrete representation of Yiddishkeit (or Jewishness) meant to be appreciated by fellow stakeholders in the Jewish community and culture. Because it is a rogue archive created simultaneously with its archiving, it creates a space for Yiddish experimenters inherently more democratized than other publishing methods or location-based Yiddish organizations such as YIVO in New York. It is both performance and lesson, with Yiddishists of various skill levels experimenting with the language and soliciting advice on how to propel their knowledge forward, creating a barrier-free Yiddishland. These texts simultaneously gather and render visible new Yiddish collectivities outside of location-based institutions. It is strategically archiving the material of an external property of the dominant property (such

---

⁹ Gil Z. Hochberg, *Becoming Palestine: Toward an Archival Imagination of the Future* (Durham: Duke University Press, 2021), 70-71.
¹⁰ Hochberg, *Becoming Palestine*, 31.

as *Stranger Things* for bloodscout) by selecting and adapting in such a way as to provoke a sense of imminent, open, roguish minoritarian futurity. The fiction fixes both the gentile canon and the faltering archive.

Just like offline communities, digital fan communities are subject to the same forces of white supremacy and systemic racism that affect the world at large and threaten many marginalized artistic ventures. Legacy Russell captures the tension between hypervisibility and invisibility that internet users from Black and queer communities are forced to navigate with her formulation of the "glitch." While internet technology increases the odds that one will be able to find community across time and space, it also increases one's visibility as a target for violence and harassment, collapsing the same bounds of space and time. She writes, "The paradox of using platforms that grossly co-opt, sensationalize, and capitalize on POC, female-identifying, and queer bodies (and our pain) as a means of advancing urgent political or cultural dialogue about our struggle (in addition to our joys and our journeys) is one that remains impossible to ignore."[11] In fandom spaces specifically, Rukmini Pande identifies the role of whiteness as an "unexamined structuring force,"[12] affecting not only which fans are treated as mainstream but also which romantic ships are normalized for exceedingly popular media properties such as *Star Wars*.[13] While Yiddish fic ultimately has a much smaller audience than hashtag-based communities or popular media ship wars, it is still constituted broadly by the forces of digital whiteness that undergird all fannish communities, as adherence to a broader community's norms ensures that it will be noticed, deemed as fannishly legible, and collect members to form a digital community.

In this paper, I analyze Yiddish fanfiction with various degrees of linguistic integration. Some of the chosen fix-it fics are written entirely in the Yiddish language, while others, such as "make me aware of being alive again," are written predominantly in English with a few Yiddish terms transliterated. In these fanfictions, Yiddish serves as a medium of storytelling and as an object of fandom in and of itself, giving itself the potential to fix both the fandom on which it writes and the Yiddish canon more broadly. Yiddish fanfic authors engage with the language similarly to how they and others approach the fandoms within which they write: they adapt it to new situations, reading queerly and creating a corpus of glitched literature at the intersection of the imagined space of Yiddishland and secular mass culture. It is an extension of Shandler's conceptions of the Yiddish postvernacular, taking a heritage

---

[11] Legacy Russell, *Glitch Feminism: A Manifesto* (Brooklyn: Verso, 2020), 24.
[12] Rukmini Pande, *Squee from the Margins: Fandom and Race* (Iowa City: University of Iowa Press, 2018), 12.
[13] Pande, *Squee*, 10-11.

language as a heritage object and contouring it onto unconventional contemporary art forms, including queer reading practices. It is also beholden to Rebecca Margolis' critique and extension of Shandler's postvernacular, where she introduces the concept of the transvernacular, where "Yiddish appears as a fluently spoken language produced by, and for, non-fluent Yiddish speakers."[14] And ultimately, it serves as a model for archival imagination, transposing the work of two canons (Yiddish cultural heritage and widely known popular culture) into an entirely new generative space where they become objects of fandom. Its uploading creates a roguish, unfettered community, unbound by any level of linguistic or financial mastery or institutional dogma, fixing the absence of secular Yiddish communities stemming from decades of Ashkenazi Jewish North American assimilation. It is making Yiddishland "live" amidst the multiple temporalities of the Internet, creating a model for a potential Yiddish future based on a Yiddish past. Margolis writes that the Covid-19 pandemic has led to the creation of a vibrant digital Yiddish infrastructure,[15] and there is also a lengthy tradition of Yiddish art being used to comment on non-Jewish social issues and media in America, such as 1931's *Mississippi* by Y. Gotlib about the Scottsboro Boys.[16] Yiddishland on *AO3* merges these two legacies, remixing them into a new archive that presents a model for communities beyond just contemporary Yiddish. It is oriented specifically toward experts and amateurs, soliciting dialogue, kinship, and, ultimately, shared growth.

Yiddish-Exclusive Fanfiction: A Case Study

At the time of this chapter's writing in February 2023, there were five fanfictions on *AO3* written predominantly in Yiddish, which are labeled ייִדיש in Hebrew letters, under language. A further 76 are tagged as #Yiddish, an indicator that Yiddish language or content is significant within the body of the story. Sticking exclusively to works tagged as Yiddish establishes a self-selecting discourse community in the archive that directly sees participation in digital Yiddishland as relevant to readers. While it is important to identify the broadness of Yiddish in fandom, it is far more important to show the self-identification of these

---

[14] Rebecca Margolis, "New Yiddish Film and the Transvernacular," *In Geveb: A Journal of Yiddish Studies*, December (2016), 2. https://ingeveb.org/articles/new-yiddish-film-and-the-transvernacular.

[15] Rebecca Margolis, "Forays into a Digital Yiddishland: Secular Yiddish in the Early Stages of the Coronavirus Pandemic," *Contemporary Jewry* 41, no. 1 (2021): 71–98. https://doi.org/10.1007/s12397-021-09379-x.

[16] For more on the historical intersections of Yiddish art and North American culture, please see Amelia Glaser's *Songs in Dark Times: Yiddish Poetry of Struggle from Scottsboro to Palestine* (Cambridge: Harvard UP, 2020).

works *as Yiddish* than to impose an external categorization on them. The self-identification and tagging in fanfiction are not solely paratextual but textually integral. It establishes how a reader reacts to a text, delineating which themes are relevant. Tagged Yiddish generates a sense of kinship and community that discordant or incidental displays of Yiddish may not contain. If there is an act of cultural recognition in the archive, it starts with self-recognition, lending it legibility *as* Yiddish fanfiction.

Of the five fanfics from three authors tagged as in the Yiddish language on *AO3*, three are by the same author, and all cover different fandoms across different eras, mediums, and genres. Timemidae's work is a translation of their English fanfic on *The Man From U.N.C.L.E.* (1964-1968),[17] [18] theodcyning writes on dybbuk lore and Jewish mysticism,[19] [20] and Griboslav_Muhomorovich's remixed Isaac Bashevis Singer's "Yentl the Yeshiva Boy" (1962)[21] and Joseph Mlotek's *Yidishe Kinder* series (1959 and 1975),[22] with the third a femslash fic[23] based on the Ever Given's 2021 obstruction of the Suez Canal.[24] What all five texts have in common is that they are linked explicitly to totems of Ashkenazi history, whether or not they are addressing an explicitly Ashkenazi text. Singer's and Mlotek's texts were written originally in Yiddish, while dybbuks have been a key element of Yiddish folklore since S. Ansky's 1920 play *The Dybbuk*. In their oeuvre, Griboslav_Muhomorovich allows us to see the many valences of fannish Yiddishland. They dedicate their poem "די שיף און דער קאנאל"[25] to long-deceased Yiddish poet Zishe Landau, inspired by Landau's poem "Who leads the ships which go across the seas." Their works are also all a single chapter long and all shorter than a thousand words, with the longest piece, "Yentl with

---

[17] Timemidae, "דערציונג," *Archive of Our Own*, January 30, 2022, https://archiveofourown.org/works/36769666.

[18] A brief plot summary of "Dertziyung": spy Illya Kuryakin is cast as Jewish in the fic, which details how he accumulated the skills of his spycraft from his turbulent, pogrom-influenced childhood.

[19] theodcyning, "די אונגעהײַערע צוױשנספֿער פֿונעם װאָרט," *Archive of Our Own*, January 22, 2022, https://archiveofourown.org/works/36584920.

[20] A summary of theodcyning's fic: the narrator lives in the Pale of Settlement before the Russian Revolution and deals with their father's death and his reanimation as a dybbuk.

[21] Griboslav_Muhomorovich, "Yentl with Zombies, or Der Tsurik-Kumer," *Archive of Our Own*, November 21, 2021, https://archiveofourown.org/works/35259529/chapters/87870172.

[22] Griboslav_Muhomorovich, "רבֿקלה און גיטעלע," *Archive of Our Own*, March 7, 2021, https://archiveofourown.org/works/29904543/chapters/73598562.

[23] Unlike slash fic, which centers on male/male erotic romance, femslash fic centers on female/female queer romance.

[24] Griboslav_Muhomorovich, "די שיף און דער קאנאל," *Archive of Our Own*, March 27, 2021, https://archiveofourown.org/works/30303696.

[25] Transliterated as "Di Shif un Der Kanal," translated as "The Ship and the Canal."

Zombies, or Der Tsurik-Kumer," topping out at 754 words. For context, the longest completed work tagged as Yiddish (i.e., as including Yiddish content rather than Yiddish exclusive) is "Harry Potter and the Muggleborn Prolet," at a total of 178,338 words, written by ComradeTortoise.[26] The vast gap presents Yiddish-exclusive fanfiction as an experiment, one focused on internal language growth and smaller scale community, with no clear intent or desire to serve as an external education on Jewishness or Jewish language. It is a specific archive devoted to specific comprehension. Yiddish is not merely symbolic but communicative in these cases. While, Yiddish tagged fic such as "make me aware of being alive" uses Yiddish as a medium for Jewishness, Yiddish-exclusive authors are focused on Yiddish as Yiddish, a much more explicit gesture to a "becoming" Yiddishland. Both are fixes to a Yiddish-deficient pop culture sphere, but the latter turns Yiddish from an ingredient to the entire recipe.

By digging more deeply into these works, the self- and communal-educational dimensions of these Yiddish exclusive fanfictions become more apparent, as well as the spectrum of linguistic skills these Yiddish performers must accommodate through their prose and paratext. Griboslav_Muhomorovich's command of Yiddish evolves across their three fanfictions, which were written over approximately nine months: "רבקלה און גיטעלע"[27] on March 7, 2021; "די שיף און דער קאנאל" on March 21; and "Yentl with Zombies, or Der Tsurik-Kumer" on November 21. "Rivkele Un Gitele" features incredibly simple sentences, no tenses beyond the present, few to no clauses, and a limited vocabulary that matches up closely with the dictionary in the first volume of Sheva Zucker's seminal and widely used Yiddish textbook, *Yiddish: An Introduction to the Language, Literature & Culture* (1994). Griboslav_Muhomorovich's first four sentences are as follows:

גיטעלע גייט אין שול. רבקלה גייט אין שול. גיטעלע און רבקלה גייען אין שול. אין שול, גיטעלע זאָדט "איך קען אַ יידיש ליד!" און זינגט אַ ליד. רבקהלע הערט דאס ליד און טראכט: "גיטעלע זינגט אזוי שיין!"[28] [29]

And translated into English:

---

[26] For even further context, this fanfiction has a higher word count than four of the seven *Harry Potter* novels.
[27] Transliterated as "Rivkele Un Gitele," translated as "Rivkele and Gitele," the diminutive forms of Rivka and Gitl.
[28] Griboslav, "Rivkele."
[29] Transliterated: Gitele geyt in shul. Rivkele geyt in shul. Gitele un Rivkele geyen in shul. In shul, Gitele zodt "Ich ken a yidish lid!" un zingt a lid. Rivkele hert dos lid un tracht: "Gitele zingt azoy sheyn!"

Gitele goes to school. Rivkele goes to school. Gitele and Rivkele go to school. In school, Gitele says, "I know a Yiddish song!" and sings a song. Rivkele hears the song and thinks: "Gitele sings so beautifully!"[30]

The limited vocabulary indicates a beginning learner rather than one experienced in Yiddish, with the text mostly adhering to a basic subject-verb-object structure. There is only one preposition and one conjunction, only one adjective or adverb, and many words are repeated. There are also a few spelling and vocabulary errors: "זאָדט" should read as "זאָגט" (zodt vs. zogt), and "רבבקלה" has an extra letter in one of its iterations in this excerpt. The preposition "אין" is used for "to" when the slightly more complex "צו" (tzu) would be more proper. Later sentences include minor errors such as missed verb conjugations, missing or added letters, and mistranslations, indicating that this text is written originally in Yiddish rather than penned in English and fed through a translation service. Griboslav_Muhomorovich indicates their awareness of these missteps in the comment section. In their replies to other users, they thank them for their corrections – the corrections and thanks are both issued in simple Yiddish. In contrast, the English language fanfiction by Griboslav_Muhomorovich from March 2021, "The Tay Bridge Disaster But It's About the Ever Given Blocking the Suez Canal," shows off complex vocabulary, as well as poetic phrasing and rhythm, such as the use of "o'er" and "'twas."[31]

What's most notable about this fic is not that the text, notes, and comments point to a beginning language learner who is using *AO3* to learn the Yiddish language and solicit feedback. It is the dedication Griboslav_Muhomorovich gives to creating fanfiction legible as femslash and a queer reading of Mlotek's non-romantic text, even with their limited vocabulary, that is notable. Yiddish practice and community are contouring to the cultural norms of the archive, creating Yiddishland inside the rogue archive, a glitch within a glitch. In other words, they are fixing Yiddish's pop culture near-invisibility by merging it with the benchmarks of fannish community-building. Rivkele and Gitele's romance proceeds clearly: Rivkele compliments Gitele's singing, they walk home together,

---

[30] Translation mine.
[31] Griboslav_Muhomorovich, "The Tay Bridge Disaster But It's About the Ever Given Blocking the Suez Canal," *Archive of Our Own*, March 26, 2021, https://archiveofourown.org/works/30274038; None of this is meant to be a condemnation or a critique of the quality of Griboslav's work in any way. Language learning is challenging. Yiddish has notably few online educational resources (for example, Yiddish Duolingo had yet to come online at the time of Griboslav's first fic, and it is an incredibly bold move to share public experimentation with a language that is new to you, no matter what the language is.

Rivkele encourages Gitele to follow her dreams of being a singer and offers to be her songwriter, and at the end of the story, they agree to be partners. Partners, in Yiddish, is an English transliteration and carries a specific double entendre for English readers that might not exist for solo Yiddish speakers: they are partners in song and partners in love. The symbolic resonance of the vocabulary is heightened by the paratextual material that Griboslav_Muhomorovich includes with their story: their tags include "F/F" (female/female, or femslash) and "LGBTQ+ Jewish Character(s)." The author notes foreground the flirtation, reading, "Gitele has been singing songs in class for years. Today, somebody takes notice." The characters, as two stock figures from a Yiddish children's book read queerly, position Yiddish as both the *medium* of fandom and the *object* of fandom. Griboslav_Muhomorovich's experimental fiction is directly, explicitly building a queer Yiddishland using artifacts of a Yiddish past in a space dedicated to alternative queer reimaginations.

The combination of Yiddish fannish imagination and queer reading undergirds Griboslav_Muhomorovich's restorative worldbuilding in their other works. We can see them progressing in both their language skills and ability to depict queer intimacy more fully in their target language. Their second work, "Di Shif un Der Kanal," features an expanded vocabulary incorporating adverbs, prepositions, subject and object pronouns, more complex clauses, and past tense verbs. Like "Rivkele un Gitele," "Di Shif" features a Yiddish double entendre legible primarily to English speakers rather than to native Yiddish speakers. During the Ever Given's fateful voyage, they write, "I'm coming my love," she says quietly,"[32] a reference to both the ship's arrival in the canal and English slang for orgasm. While the romance plot in "Rivkele" revolves around singing and a short walk home, the introduction of past tense to the story allows for a more comprehensive sense of eroticism featuring a longer-term romance, conflict over the future, modulation of tone to heighten the ship and canal's connection, and an ultimate consummation.

Dedicating the story to Zishe Landau adds another layer to their Yiddish fandom and another valence to its canon expansion and fixing/modernizing of Yiddish. The use of Yiddish speaks to a desire to engage with the language while making Landau an interlocutor, creating non-linear, queer kinship between the fanfic and a much deeper Yiddish cultural legacy. The invocation of Landau is as much a statement of intent as it is an homage, imagining a past that can illuminate the present (in this case, the Suez Canal blockage) and can be carried forth into the future (in this case, a continued expansion of Yiddishland and Yiddish culture under the umbrella of the fannish, roguish community). The

---

[32] In the original Yiddish: """איך קומט, ליבע," זי זאָגט שטיל"." In transliteration: """Ich kumt, libe," zi zogt shtil." Translation mine.

fact that this story was later translated into English by another user, dandelionbunny, only heightens this sense of kinship and sense of future-oriented preservative performance. As she writes in her translation's author notes, "As a Yiddish speaker, I love making sure our art is accessible to learners and curious folks alike, and this is... This is apparently no exception."[33] Griboslav_Muhomorovich's linguistic experimentation no longer belongs to them alone – it is "our art," resituating it as a performance of a heritage object, adding another layer of exposure in the rogue archive, and interpreting it as born-Yiddish and thus worthy of canonization in English.

Griboslav_Muhomorovich's third and final – for now – Yiddish fanfiction, "Yentl with Zombies," certifies their inherited stewardship of Yiddish fanfiction. Their author notes affirm their position as student and ambassador, acknowledging the words they had to find from a Yiddish-English dictionary and creating an online flashcard deck to help other language learners. Just like the allusion to Landau in "Di Shif," the fanfiction's use of zombies is grounded in Ashkenazi Jewish history. They mention how Yaniv, the original setting of "Yentl the Yeshiva Boy," is within the current Chernobyl Exclusion Zone; as a result, they explicitly blur the timelines of Yentl and Chernobyl to imagine a reality where science fiction tropes of the nuclear apocalypse have been suffused with Yiddishkeit and thus create a sense of contemporary Chernobyl "becoming" Yiddishland. The story still fits comfortably within the *AO3* tropes in femslash, and Alternate Universe (AU) tropes are common in all fandoms and solicit beta readers in its tags. The choice of Yentl as the specific orienting object of fandom, a story that intentionally plays with gendering as the titular character tries to pass as male to go to a yeshiva, links Griboslav_Muhomorovich with decades of commentary on the queer Yiddishist valences of the narrative.[34] The prose and grammar are advanced to a level where they would not be immediately distinguishable as a second language user were they not to state so upfront. The sentences are complex, the paragraphs are delineated and formed, they use a wide array of tenses, and their use of metaphor and symbolism is clear. In one section, Yentl says that her desire to learn the Torah "burned hotter than the fire," juxtaposing the two sources of inspiration for "Yentl with Zombies."[35] The ultimate act of Griboslav_Muhomorovich's self-

---

[33] dandelionbunny, "The Ship and the Canal," *Archive of Our Own*, October 20, 2022, https://archiveofourown.org/works/42510135.

[34] For a quick literature review of Yentl's position in queer Yiddish culture, I'd recommend Naomi Seidman's 2011 "Reading "Queer" Ashkenaz: This Time from East to West."

[35] The original Yiddish: " נאָך דעם אויפֿרייס האָט זי געוואָרן פֿאַרגלייבט אַז זי מוז לערנען זיך די תורה — זי איז פֿאַרברענט הייסער ווי דער אויפֿרייס, און אפֿשר צוליב דעם, אַז ער האָט פֿאַרשטאַנען אַז דער וועלט פֿון פֿאַר דעם וועט נישט אומקערן זיך. האָט ר. טודרוס אָנגעהויבן לערנען מיט איר די תורה ." Translated by me: "After the explosion she became convinced that she must learn the Torah – she burned hotter than the explosion, and maybe because of that, because he understood that the world from before would not return, Rav Tudrus began studying the Torah with her."

incorporation into the broader narrative of Yiddishland is the shift in their requests for feedback. Rather than asking solely for feedback on grammar and spelling, they write, "If I may claim so, I'd say that I have enough Yiddish now that you can also give me criticism on style and content, which I would also be greatly appreciative of!"[36] The fact that this story so far only has one chapter of its promised many does not diminish it as a mark of achievement. Griboslav_Muhomorovich's repertoire has progressed from instrumental yet queered Yiddish language practice to fluid Yiddish prose and reimagining canonical texts. The fact that the entire process is enshrined in a broader fanfiction archive is indicative of an unwillingness to ossify Yiddish in the past but to show it evolving, adapting, and creating a future that corrects metanarratives of Yiddish death both through its instantiation and its content. The Yiddishland archival "becoming" comes from the twin queering of Yiddish history and secular, non-Yiddish culture.

Fannish Yiddish versus the Yiddish Postvernacular and Transvernacular

One of Margolis' key departures from Shandler's concept of the Yiddish postvernacular comes down to their differing weight on the symbolic nature of contemporary Yiddish media, particularly projects aimed at non-native speakers and primarily English users. Shandler's postvernacular focuses less on conversational Yiddish and more on discrete examples of Yiddish where "the very fact that something is being said (or written or sung) in Yiddish is at least as meaningful as the meaning the words being uttered—if not more so."[37] In contrast, Margolis rejects what she calls the "underlying assumption that Yiddish will be encountered in pieces" inherent to his conception.[38] Her Yiddish transvernacular is predicated on works such as the *YouTube* series "YidLife Crisis,"[39] which attempts to recreate a world where secular Yiddish spaces in Anglophone countries are as vibrant and multifaceted in the twenty-first century as they were at the start of the twentieth. Because these anti-assimilatory works are often created for English speakers, lines of Yiddish communication in filmed media are rendered in English subtitles, thereby creating full measures of communication under a logic of Yiddish becoming rather than isolated or atomized Yiddish. She ends her piece reflecting on the potential for cyberspace as a possible venue for an expanded Yiddish

---

[36] Griboslav, "Yentl."
[37] Shandler, "Yiddishland," 22.
[38] Margolis, "New Yiddish Film," 15.
[39] Jamie Elman and Eli Batalion, "YidLife Crisis," *YouTube* video, modified August 17, 2023, https://www.youtube.com/watch?v=v3auB1Bf4YM.

transvernacular for both language learners and experts, riffing off Tsvi Sadan's 2011 study on the Yiddish "cyber-vernacular." She writes optimistically:

> Perhaps with more and more projects in the transvernacular that feature fluently-spoken Yiddish dialogue in diverse contexts and addressed to varied audiences, the discourse about Yiddish as "dead" or "dying" will finally give way to discussion about what Yiddish is today and can become in the future.[40]

Years later, in 2021, she explores how Covid-19 has created the conditions for an expanded, more fluid digital Yiddishland for learners of all levels. She highlights many new resources, including a weekly Zoom meeting called *Shmueskrayz*, the Yiddish word for conversation, where Yiddish speakers of all levels gathered for moderated conversation practice. This space was hosted by *Vaybertaytsh*, a feminist Yiddish podcast that sits comfortably with Griboslav's visions of Yiddish as a queered, counter-hegemonic language that is creating space for progressive imagined futures.[41] While neither *Vaybertaytsh* nor *Shmueskrayz* were active at the time of this essay,[42] both exemplified a similar ability to Yiddish fanfiction authors to maximize the potential of digital technology and the Internet to bind together Yiddish speakers from disparate geographic locations into a community, be accessible to all levels of learners, and foster a roguish and queer affirming attachment to the language and culture. The Covid-19 pandemic weakened in-person bonds while incentivizing digital adaptation for those who previously hesitated to form online communities. Margolis' digital Yiddishland capitalizes on this fresh availability. Internet-based communities correct any geographic fixity of Yiddish-speaking circles.

However, it would be a mistake to assume that the fanfictions, whether Yiddish-exclusive or Yiddish-inflected, are an extension of prior organizational pushes for digital Yiddishland. Neither are they an Internet-based elaboration of Margolis' 2015 transvernacularism. First, the work on *AO3* is not organizational in any fashion whatsoever. In the spirit of the purest rogue archives, there's no hierarchy of value, no scheduling, no concrete rules of engagement, and the only expectations for what Yiddishness might mean are self-assigned and self-solicited. Griboslav_Muhomorovich solicits feedback on their Yiddish grammar in "Rivkele un Gitele" not because of an institutional commitment to proper Yiddish or proper grammar but because of an individual desire to experiment, grow, and perform their language skills. That

---

[40] Margolis, "New Yiddish Film," 30.
[41] Margolis, "Forays," 86.
[42] *Vaybertaytsh*'s most recent episode was published in December 2021.

is not to say that these attributes are invisible in communities such as *Shmueskrayz*; rather, it is to say that instead of flocking to a dedicated Yiddish center to learn one's Yiddish, these authors are creating a Yiddishland enclave within a space that is not explicitly Jewish, through the conventions of the said non-Jewish space, by merging Yiddish and secular culture, correcting cultural erasure of Yiddish and gaps in contemporary Yiddish community. It is crucial to underline that *AO3* is neither a Jewish space, nor one dedicated to education, nor one about experimentation with language. It heralds itself as an archive without a sense of favor, with minimal censorship or moderation, and protecting a broader fandom community. The most concrete methods of Yiddishland expansion in *AO3* include tagging, bookmarking, and commenting. A fan fic is an extension of Yiddishland if it declares itself as such rather than being a part of Yiddishland due to its position as a communal axis. It is a community entirely at the whims of its users, yet one whose community exists through its enshrining, a semi-permanence that exists only so long as it is individually perpetuated – or, in other words, an archive only as strong as its ongoing repertoire enables it to become. It merges conventional visions of Yiddishland with an explicitly secular, archival scaffolding, a placement of Yiddish outside of Yiddish rather than Yiddish as its own whole.

The corrective merging of Yiddishland with non-Jewish secularity introduces the second key nuance between Margolis' communities, Shandler's postvernacular objects, and the works tagging themselves as Yiddish on *AO3*. While Shandler champions Yiddish as a primarily symbolic gesture, and Margolis emphasizes conversational Yiddish as the avenue for imagining a coherent imagined Yiddishland, fannish Yiddish closes any perceived gaps between the two in ways both great and small. Similar to *YidLife Crisis*, Griboslav_Muhomorovich's fanfictions create a dialogic, artistic, transvernacular Yiddishland, yet this is far from the extent of how fannish Yiddish is deployed. Searching through the tagged Yiddish, we see an array of different engagements of Yiddish that belie an optimism for a Yiddish future as-of-yet-reached, a fix to presentist malaise. In "make me aware of being alive," they use Yiddish as a way to explore their own Jewishness, remarking that they are in the middle of their process of converting to Judaism and including a Hebrew and Yiddish to English dictionary for any non-Jews encountering their fanfiction.[43] In another ongoing fanfic, *X-Men* slash fic "Growing Pains" from Aidaran and StarTravel, they link Erik Lensherr's use of Yiddish to his survival of the Holocaust and their desire to authentically represent Yiddish to their heritages. They write, "Since Aidaran has the same Ashkenazi roots (though she learned only a few words

---

[43] bloodscout, "make me aware."

from her family), it felt like a way of reconnecting with her heritage."[44] Griboslav_Muhomorovich's dialogic exists in the same space as bloodscout and Aidaran as both use their tickets of Yiddishland to create a sense of coherence no matter how large or small their language command. Fannish Yiddish connects a Yiddish past to a Yiddish future through however many contemporary Yiddish works each author has access to and can read queerly, whether just a symbol or budding skill, and contours itself for a wide range of potential Yiddishists through its tagging rather than a single, specific, homogenous audience.

Conclusions

Fannish Yiddish is polysemic due to the multifarious ways its authors identify as part of Yiddishland. Rather than scaling from beginner learners to advanced, Yiddish engagement in fandom runs the gamut from non-learners to fluent language speakers, with the same author occasionally occupying multiple places on that spectrum like Griboslav_Muhomorovich has throughout their prose. Rather than having a stable symbolic value, fannish Yiddish represents everything from authentic religiosity to secularity to a complete absence of Jewishness – after all, there's no religion that a sentient ship such as the Ever Given could possibly convert to. Above all, fannish Yiddish contains an overwhelming ethos of play and discovery, whether self-discovery or communal discovery, while simultaneously creating the Yiddishland it aims to discover by inserting itself as a fix to a fully secular rogue archive. The work Yiddish fan fiction does by merging contemporary, mass market, secular media discourses with a Yiddish timeline of past, present, and future, placing it at a unique nexus between fix-it fics and fiction that honor the original source material. The fixes being modeled are less plot-based and more paratextual in nature. Yiddish fic authors are not challenging any perceived plot failings of an object of fandom, such as a canonical ending that alienates fans or an underdeveloped character. Rather, they are queering and correcting the gaps between the twin spaces in which they reside: fanfiction archives and the Yiddish canon. Yiddishland is gaining queer genealogy that dismantles metanarratives of Yiddish death, erasure, or atomization. Rogue fanfiction archives are expanding with the fic to accommodate a new sense of play: language play, featuring language as both medium and subject.

The works used as settings for these experimental, educational fics are relevant so far as the author can link them to the broader Yiddish canon, no matter how natural these affiliations are within the original works. Griboslav_Muhomorovich connecting the Ever Given and Suez Canal to

---

[44] Aidaran, and SoMuchMoreThanYouKnow (StarTravel), "Growing Pains," *Archive of Our Own,* May 15, 2022, Chapter 2.

Yiddish history may not necessarily be the most intuitive. However, by playing with this link in the fannish form, they are performing an act of Yiddish fannish community building that exists primarily because of the unique repertoire and archival dimensions of fan fiction. They are building a community external to institutions or more publicly recognized spaces, one whose barrier to entry is an interest in the Yiddish language, a desire to grow it, and a willingness to queer the language and history just as fan fiction fundamentally queers its original works. This ultimately expands the possibilities of Yiddish existence beyond the established ideals of the postvernacular and transvernacular, morphing language performance into a tool of self-expression. By applying a fannish lens to Yiddish and a Yiddish lens to fan studies, this chapter and these fanfic authors can elaborate on the importance of experimental or ludic spaces in a metalinguistic analysis of a language and its various communities. The non-hierarchical, unfixed space of fandom and *AO3* allows for roguish participation that enables the multiplicity of vernacular Yiddish in a model that could apply to a wide array of other projects of Yiddish exploration or fannish community building. In addition, it complicates any inherent links between Jewishness and Yiddish usage, as the more fluent and complete Yiddish fan texts create a linguistic genealogy that subordinates any potential "Jewishness" in Yiddish to the fan fiction conventions revealed in a twin queered look at Yiddish. Ultimately, these fics and the communities forming around them are authoring their own processes of "becoming": becoming Yiddish, becoming a fan, and becoming a counter-institutional rogue.

Bibliography

Aidaran, and SoMuchMoreThanYouKnow (StarTravel). "Growing Pains." *Archive of Our own*, May 15, 2022. https://archiveofourown.org/works/38974206/chapters/97703922.

bloodscout. "make me aware of being alive." *Archive of Our own*, September 8, 2022. https://archiveofourown.org/works/41569509.

dandelionbunny. "The Ship and the Canal." *Archive of Our own*, October 20, 2022. https://archiveofourown.org/works/42510135.

De Kosnik, Abigail. *Rogue Archives*. Rogue Archives, 2019, https://doi.org/10.7551/mitpress/10248.001.0001.

Griboslav_Muhomorovich. "די שיף און דער קאנאל." *Archive of Our own*, March 27, 2021. https://archiveofourown.org/works/30303696.

Griboslav_Muhomorovich. "רבקלה און גיטעלע." *Archive of Our own*, March 7, 2021. https://archiveofourown.org/works/29904543/chapters/73598562.

Griboslav_Muhomorovich. "The Tay Bridge Disaster But It's About the Ever Given Blocking the Suez Canal." *Archive of Our own*, March 26, 2021. https://archiveofourown.org/works/30274038.

Griboslav_Muhomorovich. "Yentl with Zombies, or Der Tsurik-Kumer." *Archive of Our own*, November 21, 2021. https://archiveofourown.org/works/35259529/chapters/87870172.

Hochberg, Gil Z. *Becoming Palestine: Toward an Archival Imagination of the Future*. Durham: Duke University Press, 2021.

Margolis, Rebecca. "Forays into a Digital Yiddishland: Secular Yiddish in the Early Stages of the Coronavirus Pandemic." *Contemporary Jewry* 41, no. 1 (2021): 71–98. https://doi.org/10.1007/s12397-021-09379-x.

Margolis, Rebecca. "New Yiddish Film and the Transvernacular." *In Geveb: A Journal of Yiddish Studies*, December 2016. https://ingeveb.org/articles/new-yiddish-film-and-the-transvernacular.

Pande, Rukmini. *Squee from the Margins: Fandom and Race*. Iowa City: University of Iowa Press, 2018.

Russell, Legacy. *Glitch Feminism: A Manifesto*. Brooklyn: Verso, 2020.

Shandler, Jeffrey. *Adventures in Yiddishland*. Berkeley: University of California Press, 2005.

theodcyning. "די אונגעהייַערע צווישנספֿער פֿונעם װאָרט." *Archive of Our own*, January 22, 2022. https://archiveofourown.org/works/36584920.

Timemidae. "דערציונג." *Archive of Our own*, January 30, 2022. https://archiveofourown.org/works/36769666.

Chapter 4

The Macro Fix-It: Practicing Activism through Fan Fiction

Darsey Meredith and Sharon Sutherland
Independent Scholars

Abstract: In this article, Sutherland and Meredith consider the fix-it fics from a practical, legal standpoint in how it offers the opportunities to explore real-life scenarios and how one might respond. Specifically focusing on activism, fix-it fics authors create low-stake environments where they can practice advocacy and representation. Sutherland and Meredith use the omegaverse and legal personhood to illuminate how writers create offshoots of their favorite fictional worlds where they can practice activism, both individually and communal based, and litigation without risk or concern.

Keywords: macro-fix, activism, law, legality, advocacy, representation, omegaverse, legal personhood, ethics, community, fix-it fics, tags, *AO3*.

***

Introduction

As the breadth of discussion in this book shows, fan fiction offers a wide variety of opportunities to fix canon narratives, examine existing stories through the lens of marginalized communities, and turn beloved characters into avatars for readers who do not see themselves in the original fictional world. In this chapter, we focus on a further step in that exploration: we examine some of the many ways in which fan fiction not only explores real-life social challenges but also offers an opportunity to rehearse resistance and protest.

While much fan fiction uses familiar characters to explore and decry the individual impacts of social injustice or, alternatively, create and celebrate better societies for the marginalized, a smaller number of stories place characters at the center of a narrative of social change. Through protest and legal battles, beloved characters play out a fight for large-scale social change. This form of fix-it fic activism offers a unique opportunity for both experienced and new writers to test ideas against a fictional adversary and to practice activism in a safe, low- stakes environment. Just as importantly, fix-it fics offer unique opportunities for community feedback and engagement around ideas. There is both immediacy of response and ongoing dialogue between authors and readers. A fan fiction community can encourage and improve the author's ideas and inspire and embolden others to join more actively in attempting to fix real social injustices; in this way, it serves as a rallying space for activism. In this paper, we draw on examples of fix-it fics that engage directly with legal argument, political activism, and other efforts to create social change to demonstrate the considerable potential of fix-it fics as space for imagining, practicing, and inspiring broad social fixes.

Social Activism in the Omegaverse

In exploring social activist narratives within fan fiction, it is fitting to begin with a genre unique to fan fiction and specifically used in fix-it fics: the Omegaverse (often described as Alpha/Beta/Omega dynamics, or "A/B/O"). Mariann Gunderson defines the Omegaverse as "an alternate universe consisting of a cluster of tropes involving humans with animalistic traits, inspired by the popular imagination of wolf biology and behavior, the rewriting of sex, gender, and the human reproductive system, and dynamics of dominance and submission."[1] Within this universe, people are "gendered" as Alpha, Beta, or Omega. While several tropes common to A/B/O fan fictions are traced to earlier fandoms,[2] the origin of the Omegaverse is commonly identified as developing within the *Supernatural* fandom, then spreading rapidly across multiple fandoms.[3]

While most Omegaverse stories focus on romantic and sexual relationships between characters,[4] a significant subset utilizes the Omegaverse framework as a site for dystopic explorations of social structures based on gender. This subset of A/B/O fiction is often highly misogynistic, with Omegas (usually) possessing fewer rights than other genders. Omegas are commonly portrayed as controlled and even owned by Alphas. Sexual slavery is a frequent social framework. Similarly, even when societies provide more equal rights to all genders, common tropes examine dubious consent to sexual acts. Omegas may be unable to control their sexual desires while in heat; more often, however, these dystopic A/B/O societies excuse rape by Alphas when in a rut or when exposed

---

[1] Marianne Gunderson, "What Is an Omega? Rewriting Sex and Gender in Omegaverse Fanfiction" (MPhil diss., University of Oslo, 2017), 15.
[2] Kristina Busse, "Pon Farr, Mpreg, Bonds, and the Rise of the Omegaverse," in *Fic: Why Fanfiction Is Taking Over the World*, ed. Anne Jamison (2013), 316-22.
[3] norabombay, "Alphas, Betas, Omegas: A Primer," *Archive of Our Own*, last modified September 21, 2015, https://archiveofourown.org/works/403644.
[4] Gunderson, "What is an Omega?"

to an Omega in heat. The consequence is that many A/B/O fictions examine current rape culture through stories set in this alternate reality.

Dystopic fiction, in general, features "a non-existent society described in considerable detail and normally located in time and space that the author intended a contemporaneous reader to view as considerably worse than the society in which the reader lived."[5] At the same time, dystopic critiques must be recognizably anchored in existing social conditions in order to be effective.[6] Within the Omegaverse, authors may depict extreme victim blaming and shaming in ways that reflect real-world failures of our legal systems and demonstrate the worst impacts of legal regimes that enshrine and maintain sexist perspectives on sexual violence or other forms of coercive control. For authors, developing extreme visions of current cultural issues may clarify the risks of inaction. For readers, these dystopias may serve as a warning or a call to action. Given the unique engagement between fan fiction authors and readers, these dystopias may also lead to active community discussion, raising awareness, participation, and critique in safe and supported ways that are not typically available for most other media.

Of particular interest in exploring the potential for macro fix-it fics, authors use the Omegaverse tropes to examine how legal systems and protests might address societal failings in this universe and, by extension, may apply to gendered rape culture in our society. As an example, "A Hole in the World" is a *Supernatural* fix-it fic focused on the popular pairing of Dean Winchester and Castiel (or "Destiel"). Dean is an Omega who has returned to his hometown after years away to attend his father's deathbed. Castiel is the Alpha doctor who cares for Dean's comatose father following the drunk driving accident that eventually ends his life. As Dean is leaving the hospital following his father's death, he is attacked by a group of Alphas who previously gang-raped him shortly after his first heat at the age of thirteen. Dean tries to fight back, expecting to die in the attempt, but he is saved by Castiel, who happens to come into the parking lot in time to beat several of the assailants and scare off the others.

As a lengthy work at 302,280 words, "A Hole in the World" gives considerable attention to the developing relationship between Dean and Castiel.[7] A

---

[5] Lyman Tower Sargent, "The Three Faces of Utopianism Revisited," *Utopian Studies*, 5(1) (1994), 1-37. https://www.jstor.org/stable/20719246.
[6] Sharon Sutherland and Sarah Swan, "Margaret Atwood's *Oryx and Crake*: Canadian Post 9/11 Worries," *From Solidarity to Schisms: 9/11 and After in Fiction and Film from Outside the US*, ed. Cara Cilano (2009), 221.
[7] AnnalieseMichel, "A Hole in the World," *Archive of Our Own*, March 6, 2016, https://archiveofourown.org/works/849926.

significant focus of the story, however, is the preparation for and participation in several criminal and civil suits arising from the attempted rape. Initially, criminal charges are pressed against both Dean and Castiel for assault against the would-be rapists. At the same time, the assailants filed a civil suit for assault against Castiel and his employer, which at the time of the attack was the hospital. Further complicating the legal landscape, the assailants are also facing both criminal charges and a civil countersuit filed by Dean's brother and lawyer, Sam Winchester. While there is some care taken to distinguish civil and criminal actions, there is nonetheless some conflation in service of plot advancement, placing focus primarily on the trials against Dean and Castiel.

By focusing on these trials, the author can engage the very familiar courtroom drama framework to exaggerate the problems inherent in many trials focused on sexual assaults: victim blaming and reliance on unreliable gendered stereotypes when framed within the A/B/O world are both deeply disturbing and disturbingly familiar. The criminal prosecutor and civil plaintiffs' counsel seek to use Dean's past rape against him, both as supposed evidence of his consent and for its value as a threat to humiliate him on the stand in hopes of convincing him (or Castiel) to settle. Fortunately, with a fair judge presiding, Dean can reference the past rape as support for his claim of self-defense in this instance. Asked on the stand, "Were you in fear for your life? Did you believe you were in danger?" Dean replies, "I didn't 'believe' crap. I knew exactly what those assholes were capable of, because they'd done it before not even a week after my first heat. ... So, was I in fear for my life? Sure. Because I would have made those assholes kill me this time rather than go through that again."[8]

The impact of this statement and the relative success of Dean's defense (and the eventual conviction of his attackers) are the first signs of a shift in this society's beliefs about rape. At the time of the first attack, the clear evidence of violent assault on Dean's thirteen-year-old body did not stand up against the testimony of a gang of hometown boys; years later, Dean's testimony is believed and is sufficient, albeit with additional corroborating evidence from Castiel. However, this indication of a positive shift is not the end of the characters' legal battles for social change; it merely sets the stage for even more egregious abuse of the justice system. As the American public famously witnessed during the O. J. Simpson trials,[9] a civil trial differs from a criminal trial. Though they are based on the same set of facts, they may allow for very different evidence. In "A Hole in the World," the attackers' lawyers attempt to intimidate Dean and Castiel by

---

[8] AnnalieseMichel, "A Hole in the World."
[9] O. J. Simpson was found not guilty of the murder of Nicole Brown Simpson and Ronald Goldman in criminal court but was found legally responsible for their deaths in a wrongful death action in civil court.

making it clear that they will call evidence of the most horrific experience in Dean's life, a period of four months when he was held captive, drugged, and sex-trafficked. To escape any criminal consequences at the time, Dean's captor wrote a cheque to Dean's father for "services rendered," reflecting a societal understanding that an Omega is their parent's property. Ultimately, Dean makes the argument that settling the civil case would be tantamount to paying his abusers. With that motivation, the entirety of chapter 29 is devoted to Dean's testimony in Castiel's criminal trial[10]: the survivor's voice is heard in a way that too rarely occurs in the real world – clear, impactful, and believed.

The sliver of justice experienced through the criminal and civil trials, while gained through a process that is demonstrably unjust and retraumatizing for survivors, leads Dean's brother/lawyer/and now Alpha guardian (following their father's death) to suggest that Dean "sue the government" to challenge Omega guardianship laws. This human rights challenge (which quickly becomes a class action suit) is a central focus in the latter portion of the story as it makes its way up to the U.S. Supreme Court.[11]

Overall, "A Hole in the World" demonstrates how fan fiction can use familiar characters to bring immediate empathy and understanding to systemic issues in the legal system and in relation to cultural biases. Similarly, retaining highly recognizable elements of the U.S. court system within this alternate universe connects the imagined world and the real world more viscerally. Interestingly, the author added a note when posting chapter 53 indicating that between writing and posting that chapter, "civil rights protests, uprisings, riots, and on-campus sexual assaults being ignored or dismissed have been in the news nearly every day…"[12] While the author is concerned that the work focuses on the love story between Dean and Castiel, and so might be perceived to minimize current events, we would suggest that embedding real-world issues within the familiar tale serves a positive purpose: it brings the discussion to a wider audience while humanizing the legal concerns. Examining the injustices inherent in this Omegaverse and sharing them through beloved characters deepens readers' empathetic responses while still allowing them to engage critically with a world that resembles their own without being overwhelmed. Just as courtroom dramas give a recognizable face to legal issues, and science fiction can provide a slightly removed lens through which to view current events, exploration of such challenges within Omegaverse fix-it fics creates

---

[10] AnnalieseMichel, "A Hole in the World."
[11] The author draws on minor characters as additional members of the class to illustrate a broader range of gendered harms resulting from this society's rules.
[12] AnnalieseMichel, "A Hole in the World."

both a visceral understanding of the challenges of rape culture and space for the creation of considered legal and activist responses.

Exploring Legal Personhood through Fan Fiction

Legal personhood has been a common theme of science fiction since its inception[13] and continues to be an important theme in many modern science fiction, fantasy, and superhero franchises.[14] It is consequently unsurprising to see the same themes developed in fan fiction building on those franchises. However, interrogations of who is human under the law can also be a fundamental question in another unique fan fiction genre, creature fic, stories in which familiar human characters are reconceived as creatures and non-humans.

A particularly well-developed example of this use of fan fiction is "Halflings" by Unforth,[15] another Destiel AU fiction that casts Castiel as a half-octopus and Dean as his human owner. In the story's universe, half-human hybrids are common pets for humans despite demonstrably equivalent capacity with humans in reasoning, feeling, and all other common measures of legal personhood. Dean and Castiel develop strong feelings for each other despite their awareness of the problematic power dynamic inherent in Dean's ownership of Castiel. Throughout the story, Dean and Castiel become activists for halfling rights: they attend protests, are arrested for their participation, and work with a halfling rights lawyer to challenge the laws that deny halflings human rights. They begin their foray into activism by protesting the notably restrictive Kansas "Statute 40.15.4b, which denies halflings the right to accuse humans of crimes against their person."[16] They continue through years of litigation, media interviews to raise awareness, and attendance at protests. Eventually, Dean chooses to emancipate Castiel despite emancipation being illegal in their version of the United States. This action leads to the climactic scene: waiting for the Supreme Court to deliver its verdict on halfling personhood, based on a comparison of the Thirteenth and Fourteenth Amendments of the U.S. Constitution.

---

[13] While there is considerable scholarly debate about what the first work of science fiction was – and what *is* science fiction – Mary Shelley's *Frankenstein* (1818) is commonly central to that debate and raises the question of the definition of humanity as a primary theme.

[14] A few examples of the many franchises that focus on personhood as a fundamental theme are *X-Men, Dark Angel, Humans, Altered Carbon, Battlestar Galactica, Kyle X-Y,* and *Westworld.*

[15] Unforth, "Halflings," *Archive of Our Own,* last modified June 19, 2018, https://archiveofourown.org/works/5483762.

[16] Unforth, "Halflings."

After more than 100,000 words of character development and reader investment in the trial's outcome, the emotional impact of the decision (granting halflings human rights) and the vicarious excitement felt through the characters' responses reward the reader. Just as many scholars argue that reading fiction has the potential to evoke empathy when the story emotionally transports readers,[17] we suggest that stories of successful activism can encourage, through empathy, a commitment to righteous causes and inspire both reflection and, potentially, action in the reader. In a lengthy story like "Halflings," it is even more likely that readers who reach the climactic scenes are invested in the characters and emotionally transported by their success.

Explorations of legal personhood necessarily resonate with critical examinations of racist legal and social structures, historical and current. A second example of activist creature fix-it fics, "Have Your Steak (And Eat It Too)," here forth referenced as "Have Your Steak,"[18] is much more explicit than most, both in illuminating racism and critiquing the division of federal and state powers in the United States of America. This real-person fiction (RPF) is based on the EXO fandom and draws on the actual members of that South Korean-Chinese boy band. Drawing on Asian, primarily Korean, protagonists allow the fiction to develop a critical outsider perspective that raises questions about the alternate universe depicted and about the real-world U.S. issues reflected.

In the world of "Have Your Steak," humans have created human-animal "hybrids." In most societies around the world, hybrids have limited rights but are protected from the most egregious forms of slavery and abuse. In the United States, however, "person" is defined as "a member of the species *Homo sapiens*," and only persons have protected rights. Without constitutional protection, each state has legislated regarding hybrids: North Dakota determined that hybrids are "livestock," but because they are not regulated by the U.S. Department of Agriculture, a legislative loophole has left all hybrids unprotected by any oversight for their wellbeing. The fix-it fic begins with Kim Jongdae, a Korean lawyer, joining an international team of lawyers, social workers, and other professionals brought to North Dakota to support more than six hundred hybrids rescued from a "designer hybrid cattery" where they have been locked in cages for breeding for up to thirty years and sold as pets and sex slaves.

The international support team is comprised almost entirely of Asian professionals because the breeders prided themselves on "foundation stock"

---

[17] P. Matthijs Bal and Martijn Veltkamp, "How Does Fiction Reading Influence Empathy? An Experimental Investigation on the Role of Emotional Transportation," *PLOS ONE*, January 30, 2013, https://doi.org/https://doi.org/10.1371/journal.pone.0055341.

[18] XiuChen4Ever, "Have Your Steak (And Eat It Too)," *Archive of Our Own*, last modified March 14, 2020, https://archiveofourown.org/works/22122100/chapters/52801963.

from Asian countries. Essentially, this means that hybrids used for the breeding program were brought to the United States from Korea, China, and Japan and illegally deprived of the rights they had in their countries of origin. As Jongdae observes, the racism inherent in breeding Asian half-human hybrids for "that ideal cat-eyed aesthetic" cannot escape criticism as eugenics, regardless of legal definitions of hybrids as non-human.[19]

Like "Halflings," "Have Your Steak" follows a romantic couple, Jongdae and Minseok, a snowlynx hybrid, navigating a legal system that reflects the real-world U.S. system. The fact that Jongdae is a Korean lawyer brings a critical lens to all aspects of the system. Not only does the fix-it fic critique the imagined laws regarding hybrids, but it also critiques the federalist model of state rights that allows for a shocking disparity in the rights of hybrids from state to state. While framed as a question of hybrid rights, the applicability of this critique to current debates around abortion access and 2SLGBTQIA+ rights is clear. Jongdae and his fellow Asian lawyers seek to work within the U.S. system, a system that strikes them as unjust and irrational. Their perspectives raise questions about assumptions about fundamental social systems that might not be explicit in a fix-it fic with American lawyers working within a system familiar to them.

One element of activism that receives particular attention in "Have Your Steak" is the use of social media to build public support and shift attitudes to hybrids. Concurrently with legal issues, the international team of hybrid advocates and support workers creates a viral holiday video of hybrids answering the question, "What do you want for Christmas?" The youngest hybrids charm viewers with their simple wishes for any of toy since they have never had one before, while Minseok touches the hearts of many with his wish for his children, whom he has never met, "to be loved."[20] When it is clear that some humans will always believe the video is a trick and that hybrids cannot talk or think, Minseok and the daughter he meets accidentally go on live television to be interviewed about their experiences and their personhood. Much like the courtroom-based fix-it fics that practice legal arguments, "Have Your Steak" provides practice at shifting popular opinion through media initiatives.

AUs and Mary Sues: Activist Training Without Risk

Fix-it fics not only inspire activism in readers, but they are also a potential space for authors to practice activist work. This practice might take the form of rehearsing legal arguments through the development of a courtroom drama, as seen in "A Hole in the World," or writing speeches for characters engaged in

---

[19] XiuChen4Ever, "Have Your Steak (And Eat It Too)."
[20] XiuChen4Ever, "Have Your Steak (And Eat It Too)."

protests and media interviews, as occurs in "Halflings" and "Have Your Steak." Of course, this kind of rehearsal and opportunity to hone arguments could occur within any form of fictional writing. Where fan fiction arguably offers something different than other types of writing is in the creation of a "Mary Sue" (or "Gary Stu") character – a practice that most other forms of fiction resist and often denigrate. In fan fiction, a Mary Sue is an original character introduced into a fan-made work "who is important in the story, possesses unusual physical traits, and has an irrelevantly over-skilled or over-idealized nature."[21] Often, a Mary Sue character is an "idealized version of an author"[22] who overcomes some significant obstacle in the narrative, even succeeding where canon characters failed in the original narrative. The Mary Sue character also offers the potential to test activist actions without the limitations faced by canon characters who have prescribed personalities and skills. A Mary Sue can have the exact combination of identities, skills, and new ideas that best support the author's argument.

In an incomplete Marvel Cinematic Universe fan fiction, "The Collars," by Piertotumshore,[23] a police officer/mutant/vigilante original character is put in a difficult position when the fictional New York Police Department is considering adopting a new piece of technology: power dampening collars. The original Mary Sue character, Alex, argues against using these collars, citing health risks to enhanced individuals who might rely on their powers for survival or healing. They argue:

> "How would you feel if you had to wear a collar that stopped the only thing preventing you from dying? Imagine if you had to put one of these on someone you know... For those of you that know Spider-Man's identity, would you feel comfortable using one of these on him? I know I wouldn't."[24]

When these arguments are not enough to sway the entire department, Alex identifies as a mutant and demonstrates the effects of these collars on themself. This action convinces the rest of the police department. Finally, Alex teams up with Daredevil and Spider-Man to neutralize the collars' effects, suggesting that they continue to worry about what the police might do with this technology in

---

[21] "Mary Sue," TV Tropes, accessed April 2, 2023, https://tvtropes.org/pmwiki/pmwiki.php/Main/MarySue.
[22] Leila Tudury, "Mary Sue," Dictionary.com, January 19, 2021, https://www.dictionary.com/e/fictional-characters/mary-sue/.
[23] Piertotumshore, "The Collars," *Archive of Our Own*, last modified January 11, 2022, https://archiveofourown.org/works/36360331/chapters/90650548.
[24] Piertotumshore, "The Collars."

the future. The concern in "The Collars" exists within the framework of canon stories. Marvel has touched on anti-mutant technology in different stories and forms of media.[25] How is a mutant's power understood in relation to the use of force laws? Should laws be used to balance and restrict some forms of power? Moreover, how does one decide who is a danger to society and should have their powers restricted?

Building a narrative that raises these questions alongside an explicit consideration of police violence and police willingness to use anti-mutant technology draws parallels to real-life concerns around police activity in 2022 (when the fan fiction was posted).[26] While the author is unlikely to be in a position to question the real-world police face-to-face on their tactics, this fix-it fic gives them a chance to test a few arguments in a zero-stakes environment. Do the police respond with empathy to questions about the safety of the people with whom they interact? How much more empathy do they show for friends or minors?[27] When Alex shows their colleagues the power-dampening collars in use, they immediately show signs of pain and suffering. Does that demonstration aid in bringing more police officers to the side of less violence? Or might it instead encourage them to see the tools as effective ones? If they cannot be convinced of an empathetic approach to policing, what must the activists do to stay safe? Each of these questions raised within "The Collars" has applications to real-world policing and reflects similar questions facing protestors and activists in 2022, who might be facing police forces armed with their own version of the "collar" – pepper spray, rubber bullets, or other riot gear.

At the end of "The Collars," Piertotumshore includes a note to their audience, stating, "Let me know if you want me to add more to this," [28] thus inviting readers to engage with the work and with the unanswered questions about justice and policing. They are open to continuing the story and imagining further the potential effects of the power-dampening collars on Alex, Spider-Man, Daredevil, and the rest of Hell's Kitchen. Such conversations are at the heart of fan fiction communities, allowing authors and readers to cultivate dialogue, debate, and learning.

---

[25] Marvel has used variations on power-inhibiting collars to contain and control mutants in comics, movies, and television shows. The foci of the canon stories have not, however, been the act of resisting or petitioning against their use.

[26] Two years after George Floyd's death at the hands of police sparked national (and international) calls for police reform and defunding, Mapping Police Violence reported that police killed more people in 2022 than in any year in the previous decade (https://mappingpoliceviolence.us). Media reports of many of these killings ensured that police violence was at the forefront of civic discourse.

[27] Alex uses Spider-Man as an example here because he is known to be a minor at only sixteen years of age.

[28] Piertotumshore, "The Collars."

A *Les Misérables* Modern AU fix-it fic, "The Things I Say," by zade,[29] follows Grantaire searching for his soulmate while working with a modern activist group ("Les Amis") to stop the construction of a jail near their school, touches on similar questions to "The Collars." Once again, the idea of activism certainly exists within the original text, but the specifics are altered to test a different kind of action. In this case, rather than building a barricade and having a shootout with soldiers, Les Amis dumps sugar in the concrete mix being used on the jail's foundation. They name the issue quite clearly as one of systemic racism as the school they are a part of is predominantly non-white, and they understand the jail's construction as an intentional statement about what the police and government expect of those students. The act of dumping sugar is, therefore, an act of protest intended to strike the finances of those building the jail and to impede the construction. Despite a chase through the construction yard, Les Amis gets away with only a few minor injuries and no arrests.

Unlike the original story of *Les Misérables*, zade's story ends with the group celebrating a tangible action they could take and the clever ways they could keep from being discovered. The activists in the story are never caught, so there is no examination of the legal ramifications of their actions; the story's focus is the planning and execution of a protest action, and it supports a hopeful reading that they might well have gotten what they wanted in the end. According to the tags on zade's story, this fix-it fic is intended to be read with the understanding that the characters are people of color themselves, responding to personal experiences of disenfranchisement within racist schools and justice systems. The author also uses *AO3* tags to share that they are a person of color as well, so "do not @ me."[30] Their notes to readers indicate that while they intend the characters to be read as people of color, zade "left it vague so you can insert your own headcanons."[31] For readers from different backgrounds, this fix-it fic is an invited site for envisioning their own connection to the fight against racism.

As a form of rehearsal for activism, the story identifies what might go wrong in carrying out the protest, and it imagines solutions for each of those possibilities. The characters brainstorm possible actions and ask practical questions about planning and execution. The author may not suggest that readers follow directly in Grantaire's footsteps, but they have laid out a clear set of questions that readers should ask themselves when planning their acts of protest.

---

[29] zade, "The Things I Say," *Archive of Our Own*, last modified December 10, 2020, https://archiveofourown.org/works/27985131.
[30] zade, "The Things I Say."
[31] zade, "The Things I Say."

Morality Considerations and Public Perception

If fix-it fics are a site for practicing activist action, then they can also be a site for practicing activist thought. Questions about how to maintain moral high ground when fighting against oppression have an entirely different set of stakes if those being oppressed have superpowers. Taking superheroes and supervillains as subjects to examine those moral questions allows the authors and the readers to dig deeply into the possible results of the protest. It also acknowledges the position protesters hold if they work to maintain the public's trust and respect. A superhero, beloved by all, will be held to a certain standard of action that a supervillain might choose to ignore. Which of these two positions is more effective for protest? Or is there a middle ground between the morally righteous superhero and the burn-it-down-and-start-over supervillain? In "Détente,"[32] Charles Xavier (Professor X) and Erik Lehnsherr (Magneto) from the *X-Men: First Class* movie universe face the same conflict that the characters have faced in many *X-Men* works: how do they keep mutants safe in a predominantly human society? In this fix-it fic, Charles and Erik take on the same roles as they do within the *X-Men* movie universe, one a publicly-appreciated pro-mutant professor, the other the violent, radical leader of the Brotherhood of Mutants. However, we get another look at what may be happening behind the scenes. The author, stickmarionette, considers the strategy if Charles and Erik were worked together privately while publicly at odds. In this scenario, they maintain a disagreement on methods of activism but call on one another for backup during several politically important events.

In chapter 2 of "Détente," titled "Equilibrium," Charles and Erik are focused on destroying a mutant research facility run by the CIA. Charles gives information to Erik and the Brotherhood so that they can effectively pursue their attack on the facility. When the mission is complete, Charles shapes the public narrative of the attack to invoke sympathy from humans toward mutant kind, despite the level of violence the Brotherhood demonstrates when destroying the facility. Throughout the story, Charles is clear that he is willing to do what it takes to protect mutants, including, when necessary, using his telepathic powers to push a particular narrative into the minds of the human public. Erik is similarly willing to do whatever it takes to destroy the CIA's dangerous facility, including acts of violence and murder.

The story illustrates several moments where Charles and Erik communicate telepathically to set up plans for pro-mutant political action. Erik questions Charles' willingness to employ violent means of protest, communicating, "This

---

[32] stickmarionette, "Détente," *Archive of Our Own*, last modified November 25, 2011, https://archiveofourown.org/works/283320/chapters/451017.

will be an act of war, Charles. Don't come crying to me when you realise the cost."[33] Charles responds with his reasoning, "There's no war. We act in self-defense, and to expose an anti-American conspiracy. The people deserve to know what their government are doing with their tax money."[34] In this telepathic exchange, the mutants agree that they are willing to do whatever is necessary to protect themselves and their people, even acts of violence.

The audience is familiar with stories of mutant resistance, but the cooperation between Xavier's school and the Brotherhood introduces a new kind of activism to the X-Men universe. It challenges our understanding of morally justifiable action when pushing for societal change and our understanding of 'good guys' versus 'bad guys.' After all, if Professor X and Magneto were secretly working together, then the violent actions of the Brotherhood were condoned (and supported) by the heroic X-Men. The moral high ground is not held clearly by either party; the only difference in tactics is how they manage public perception. Charles uses his human and mutant skills to protect public perception of the larger group (mutant-kind), while Erik uses extreme force to push for immediate, radical change. This story posits that activism and social change require multi-tiered approaches, and those pushing for change, whether they hold the position of 'superhero' or 'supervillain,' must work together to be most effective. Perhaps it might also serve as a warning for activists to keep an eye on their own moral compass, as well as the public's perception of their acts.

The Macro-Macro Fix-It: Litigation in the Fix-It Fic

As we have noted, fix-it fics offer an opportunity to examine and practice legal arguments. This may take the form of human rights litigation, as seen in "A Hole in the World" and "Halflings," using the mechanism of lawsuits as a tool against social oppression. In some fan fiction, however, authors have taken the fix-it a step further and written fan fiction about real-world litigation. In "The One About Wolf Porn,"[35] *The Good Fight*'s Diane Lockhart represents a real-world author using the pseudonym Zoey Ellis in a fictionalized version of a lawsuit commonly known as the "Omegaverse litigation." In the real-world matter, *Quill Ink Books, Ltd. V. Soto a.k.a. Cain*,[36] Ellis's publisher pursued a claim on her behalf against another writer, Cain, and their publisher, Blushing Books, in response to takedown notices under the *Digital Millennium Copyright Act* (the

---

[33] stickmarionette, "Détente."
[34] stickmarionette, "Détente."
[35] SiderumInCaelo, "The One about Wolf Porn," *Archive of Our Own*, June 20, 2021, https://archiveofourown.org/works/32073559.
[36] *Quill Ink Books, Ltd. v. Rachelle Soto, a.k.a. Addison Cain* (E.D. Va. 2019). Case No. 1:19-cv-476.

DMCA) filed against Ellis's books based in the Omegaverse. Cain claimed that Ellis's books infringed the copyright in her own Omegaverse-based books, and Ellis sought damages for defamation and intentional interference with business interests.[37] Ultimately, Blushing Books settled the claims against the company, and Cain was successful in a Motion to Dismiss, so the matter never went to trial. It did, however, attract a large amount of fan attention and discussion about "who owns the Omegaverse?"[38] That question was never determined by the court. The Motion to Dismiss determined that there was no actionable defamation claim, no tortious interference with business interests, and no statutory conspiracy: Omegaverse copyrightability was irrelevant to those conclusions.

The fix-it fic version of this litigation begins with the same basic premise: a lawsuit filed by Ellis's publishers against Cain because of a takedown notice. However, it fixes things by having the matter go to trial, where the law regarding Omegaverse copyright is addressed more clearly. Attorney Diane is the protagonist here rather than any individuals directly involved in the real litigation. As such, the story follows the highly unrealistic timeline of most cases in *The Good Fight* (and most television courtroom dramas). Thus, Diane is handed a case file, and there is an almost immediate scene shift to court. The plaintiff and her expert witness, real-world fan fiction scholar Dr. Kristina Busse (who was retained as an expert for Ellis in the real lawsuit), give cogent and persuasive testimony. The defendant's arguments are not given equal attention, so it is no surprise when Diane wins a decisive victory. Diane tells her colleague following the trial, "We got a declaratory judgment that Ellis's books are lawfully published, and an injunction against the defendants bringing any more complaints of copyright infringement."[39] In other words, the fix-it fic decides differently than the actual court and promotes the legal conclusion that many fans wished to hear in the real-world case: if the court declared the books were lawfully published, then, by implication, the Omegaverse was not subject to copyright protection. In the story, the fictional Dr. Busse's definition of the Omegaverse as a "folksonomy" that shares some tropes[40] is understood to be endorsed by the court.

---

[37] Quill Ink Books, Ltd. originally alleged six tortious actions. Only three were permitted in the District Court.
[38] The case attracted sufficient attention that *The New York Times* published an article on the topic titled, "A Feud in Wolf-Kink Erotica Raises a Deep Legal Question: What do copyright and authorship mean in the crowdsourced realm known as the Omegaverse?" Alexandra Alter, May 23, 2020 (updated May 29, 2020), https://web.archive.org/web/20200611030407/https://www.nytimes.com/2020/05/23/business/omegaverse-erotica-copyright.html.
[39] SiderumInCaelo, "The One about Wolf Porn."
[40] SiderumInCaelo, "The One about Wolf Porn."

There are numerous additional fan fiction explorations of real-world case law[41] and even RPF fan fiction about real-world Justices that further demonstrate the potential for fan fiction as a space for critiquing case law. Perhaps unsurprisingly, among the forty-three stories tagged as "U.S. Supreme Court" in *Archive of Our own* (*AO3*), eleven recent stories discuss *Roe v. Wade*.[42] These include stories that cast real-world Justices into the Omegaverse, where male Justices are impregnated and unable to obtain abortions.[43] Other cases that have their own fan fiction include *Obergefell v. Hodges*[44] and *Buck v. Bell*,[45] while the late Supreme Court Justice Ruth Bader Ginsberg has her own tag in *AO3*.[46] Similarly, a search for events such as "U.S. Capitol Riot January 6, 2021" demonstrates the engagement of authors in the re-working, and consequent reflection on current events.[47] While the number of fan fictions that engage directly with current events and legal issues in this way is small, the potential for intentional growth of this practice is intriguing. What opportunities does fan fiction offer for law school assignments that humanize the litigants in case law in ways that build empathy and understanding of the impacts of legal decision-making? How might one rehearse persuasive reasoning through a story where the impacts of emotion and relationship can be examined alongside logical arguments? Certainly, the examples we have seen of fan

---

[41] This includes at least one other fan fiction that engages with the Omegaverse litigation – the *Star Wars* AU, "Tits v. Porny" by jeeno2, *Archive of Our Own*, April 6, 2020, https://archiveofourown.org/works/18115103/chapters/42825197, but its focus is on the relationship between junior lawyers rather than on the legal issues in the case.

[42] An additional eight stories are tagged "Roe v. Wade" but take place in other fandoms rather than as Supreme Court RPFs.

[43] For example, "Johnny Robert's Hypocwisy" by Chaosinfurgency, *Archive of Our Own*, September 26, 2022, https://archiveofourown.org/works/39892362, "God Bless America" by BunnySoap, *Archive of Our Own*, July 30, 2022, https://archiveofourown.org/works/39929001, and "Supreme Court Justice Samuel Alitoo (with two o's to avoid legal problems) gets matpat mpregged" by Vivid_IGuess, *Archive of Our Own*, June 25, 2022, https://archiveofourown.org/works/39869223, all deal with pregnancies of male Justices.

[44] *Obergefell v. Hodges* is explored directly in a 2019 *West Wing* fan fiction, "Obergefell v. Hodges" by Charowak, *Archive of Our Own*, May 16, 2019, https://archiveofourown.org/works/18852391/chapters/44743792 and other stories; however, legalization of same-sex marriage as a result of the case (tagged "US Legalization of Same-Sex Marriage") is an important element in many more stories.

[45] In "glaze defects" by thepolysyndetonaddictsupportgroup, *Archive of Our Own*, February 17, 2022, https://archiveofourown.org/works/37198735, Matt Murdock (the blind superhero Daredevil) contemplates the social meaning of *Buck v. Bell*'s decision on involuntary sterilization of people with disabilities.

[46] A search for Ruth Bader Ginsburg as a fictitious returns twenty-three works.

[47] An *AO3* search on April 4, 2023, produced thirty-six stories tagged for the Capitol Riot.

engagement with law and protest suggest that fan fiction has unexplored learning and development possibilities.

Conclusion

As much as fix-it fics offer a space to fix narrative wrongs for beloved characters, they also offer a space for fans to examine and rehearse fixes for social injustice in the real world. Fix-it fics like "A Hole in the World," "Halflings," and "Have Your Steak" offer an opportunity to build and rehearse persuasive legal arguments and play out potential media campaigns aimed at changing public opinion on topics impacting oppressed populations. Other fix-it fics, such as "The Things I Say" and "Détente," imagine engagement in other forms of public protest and system disruption. Tying these arguments and movements to beloved characters imports pre-existing empathy, creating greater understanding for persons impacted by injustice and, perhaps, inspiring passion for change.

As seen, some fan fiction tropes uniquely support explorations of social injustice. Much as courtroom dramas and dystopias offer familiar frameworks for stories examining injustice, the Omegaverse and creature fics provide alternative frameworks that may resonate more within fandom communities. This resonance is a critical component of the potential for fix-it fics to act as calls to action: fan fiction is inherently created within the community and invites community engagement and exchange. Situating stories of activism and protest in this space invites, at a minimum, discussion and imagining around the potential for change. While, to date, there has been little intentional use of fan fiction for these purposes, the potential for macro fix-it fiction to aid individual activists and inspire communities is evident in an increasing number of works written in direct response to current events. We anticipate that these macro fix-it fics will develop and grow in frequency as each fix-it fic launches new conversations and new actions.

Bibliography

AnnalieseMichel. "A Hole in the World." *Archive of Our own.* March 6, 2016, https://archiveofourown.org/works/849926.

Alter, Alexandra. "A Feud in Wolf-Kink Erotica Raises a Deep Legal Question: What do copyright and authorship mean in the crowdsourced realm known as the Omegaverse?" *The New York Times*, May 23, 2020 (updated May 29, 2020). https://web.archive.org/web/20200611030407/https://www.nytimes.com/2020/05/23/business/omegaverse-erotica-copyright.html

Bal, P. Matthijs and Martijn Veltkamp. "How Does Fiction Reading Influence Empathy? An Experimental Investigation on the Role of Emotional Transportation." *PLOS ONE*. January 30, 2013, https://doi.org/10.1515/jlt-2015-0005.

BunnySoap. "God Bless America." *Archive of Our own.* July 30, 2022. https://archiveofourown.org/works/39929001/chapters/99983895.

Busse, Kristina. "Pon Farr, Mpreg, Bonds, and the Rise of the Omegaverse," *Fic: Why Fanfiction is Taking over the World.* Ed. Anne Jamison. Smart Pop Books, 2013. 288-94.

Chaosinfurgency. "Johnny Robert's Hypocwisy." *Archive of Our own.* September 26, 2022. https://archiveofourown.org/works/39892362/chapters/99886287.

Charowak. "Obergefell v. Hodges." *Archive of Our own.* May 16, 2019." https://archiveofourown.org/works/18852391/chapters/44743792.

Gunderson, Marianne. "What Is an Omega? Rewriting Sex and Gender in Omegaverse Fanfiction." MPhil diss., University of Oslo, 2017.

jeeno2. "Tits v. Porny." *Archive of Our own.* Last modified March 18, 2017. https://archiveofourown.org/chapters/42825197.

norabombay. "Alphas, Betas, Omegas: A Primer." *Archive of Our own.* Last modified September 21, 2015. https://archiveofourown.org/works/403644?view_full_work=true.

Piertotumshore. "The Collars." *Archive of Our own.* Last modified January 11, 2022. https://archiveofourown.org/works/36360331/chapters/90650548.

Sargent, Lyman Tower. "The Three Faces of Utopianism Revisited," *Utopian Studies,* 5(1(1994), 1-37. https://www.jstor.org/stable/20719246.

SiderumInCaelo. "The One about Wolf Porn." *Archive of Our own.* June 20, 2021. https://archiveofourown.org/works/32073559.

stickmarionette. "Détente." *Archive of Our own.* Last modified November 25, 2011. https://archiveofourown.org/works/283320/chapters/451017.

Sutherland, Sharon and Sarah Swan. "Margaret Atwood's *Oryx and Crake*: Canadian Post 9/11 Worries," *From Solidarity to Schisms: 9/11 and After in Fiction and Film from Outside the US.* Ed. Cara Cilano. Rodopi, 2009. 219-234.

thepolysyndetonaddictsupportgroup. "glaze defects." *Archive of Our own.* February 17, 2022 https://archiveofourown.org/works/37198735.

Tudury, Leila. "Mary Sue." Dictionary.com. Dictionary.com, January 19, 2021. https://www.dictionary.com/e/fictional-characters/mary-sue/.

TV Tropes. "Mary Sue." Accessed April 2, 2023. https://tvtropes.org/pmwiki/pmwiki.php/Main/MarySue.

Unforth. "Halflings." *Archive of Our own.* Last modified June 19 2018. https://archiveofourown.org/works/5483762.

Vivid_IGuess. "Supreme Court Justice Samuel Alitoo (with two o's to avoid legal problems gets matpat mpregged." *Archive of Our own,* June 25, 2022. https://archiveofourown.org/works/39869223.

XiuChen4Ever. "Have Your Steak (And Eat It Too)." *Archive of Our own.* Last modified March 14, 2020. https://archiveofourown.org/works/22122100/chapters/52801963.

zade. "The Things I Say." *Archive of Our own.* Last modified December 10, 2020. https://archiveofourown.org/works/27985131.

Part Two:
Fixing the Canon, Fixing the Author

Chapter 5

Fan Fiction Fights Back: *Harry Potter* and the Effort to Build a Better Wizarding World

Laura Tolbert
Independent Scholar

Abstract: In this article, Tolbert examines the fix-it fic through the *Harry Potter* wizarding world and its relationship to current political and cultural upheavals. She believes that the reasons for the uptick in creating and consuming fix-it fics were in response to the 2016 election of former President Donald Trump, the 2020 Covid-19 Pandemic, and J.K. Rowling's transphobic comments made via *Twitter*. In response, *Harry Potter* fans fixed the original stories to address trauma and stressors, thus reclaiming and reappropriating the wizarding world to serve a much broader, diverse population of readers.

Keywords: politics, culture, transphobia, stressors, trauma, diversity, reclaiming, reappropriating, acceptance, Harry Potter, fix-it fics, tags, *AO3*.

***

In 2008, nearly a year after concluding her wildly popular *Harry Potter* series, author J. K. Rowling stood before Harvard graduates and delivered the commencement address, focusing on harnessing the power of imagination for both oneself and the good of the wider world. "Imagination," Rowling stated then, "is not only the uniquely human capacity to envision that which is not [...] it is the power that enables us to empathize with humans whose experiences we have never shared."[1] Yet, a little over a decade later, this magical "power" was nowhere to be found.

As of June 6, 2020, Rowling exists in a precarious position in the cultural consciousness in the wake of her viral quote-tweet reaction to an article

---

[1] J. K. Rowling, "The Fringe Benefits of Failure, and the Importance of Imagination." Convocation speech, Harvard University, 5 June 2008, Cambridge, MA, https://news.harvard.edu/gazette/story/2008/06/text-of-j-k-rowling-speech/.

discussing "people who menstruate." She tweeted, "I'm sure there used to be a word for those people. Someone help me out. Wumben? Wimpund? Woomud?"[2] In the face of immediate backlash, Rowling did not back down but rather doubled down, continually defending her position. In one instance, Rowling claimed to "know and love trans people" herself, only to write, "...erasing the concept of sex removes the ability of many to discuss their lives meaningfully. It isn't hate to speak the truth."[3] This statement is simply one of many transphobic comments Rowling has made since 2020, and with every disparaging comment, *Harry Potter* fans the world over distanced themselves more from the creator of their favorite book series.[4]

The irony to Rowling's exclusionary beliefs is that when she first wrote the *Harry Potter* series, she created something that extended beyond herself as its author, especially regarding cultural stakes and social engagement. The series continues to inspire fan-created art and media nearly twenty-five years later. However, as with most beloved artwork, the *Harry Potter* series has never been without controversy. Prior to Rowling's transphobic comments, reader pushback to the text gained traction immediately following the conclusion of the series, noting its lack of meaningful diversity. Rowling then began a campaign of retroactive continuity, or "ret-con," to build more diverse elements into the series where there previously were none. For many readers, however, these measures were too little, too late, and their advent was often seen as tokenism and other cultural insults. Despite these attempts at inclusion, the wizarding world, a world where anything is possible still remains less than inclusive. Rowling's transphobic commentary, therefore, compounds preexisting cultural tensions surrounding the texts. It is at the intersection of textual controversy and flash-point reactions that the internet becomes relevant.

The advent of the internet and the subsequent rise of social media has allowed fandom to steadily grow in popularity in recent decades. As of the 2020s, social media platforms such as *Tumblr* and *TikTok* abound with interactions among fans establishing headcanons and creating art inspired by their favorite films, books, television series, or video games. Fans have also found a home on *Archive of Our own* (*AO3*), arguably the most well-known site

---

[2] J. K. Rowling (@jkrowling), "People who menstruate," *Twitter*, June 6, 2020, https://twitter.com/jk_rowling/status/1269382518362509313.

[3] J. K. Rowling (@jkrowling), "If sex isn't real," *Twitter*, June 6, 2020, https://twitter.com/jk_rowling/status/1269389298664701952.

[4] For a more comprehensive overview of Rowling's numerous transphobic statements, see Duggan, "Transformative Readings: Harry Potter Fan Fiction, Trans/Queer Reader Response, and J. K. Rowling." *Children's Literature in Education* 53 (2022): 147-168. https://doi.org/10.1007/s10583-021-09446-9.

for fan fiction on the internet. There are millions of fan-created stories, some less than a thousand words while others rival hefty tomes such as *War and Peace*, that reimagine the author's favorite media. For these authors, the *Harry Potter* series is a bountiful source of inspiration. When searching the tag "Harry Potter" on *AO3*, hundreds of thousands of fan fictions appear, but post-2015, the number and the popularity of these stories grew exponentially, with many of the most popular *Potter* fics on the site garnering thousands, if not millions of hits.

The reason for this increase in both the creation and consumption of fan fiction is twofold. I argue that the initial wave of fan fiction creation was due to the tensions surrounding the 2016 presidential election and the resulting wave of heightened political discourse both in the United States and abroad. The widespread proliferation of the prejudiced rhetoric spread by the Trump campaign impacted many marginalized communities, and the waves of support it garnered deeply affected those who were targeted by both ideological and, in some cases, physical attacks. Thus, that rhetoric represented a source of trauma for members of these communities. It should be no surprise that during Trump's tenure, *Harry Potter* fans were often vocal critics of him online. "A consistent lesson throughout the books and movies," as Anthony Gierzynski and Kathryn Eddy remind us, "is acceptance of those who are different from ourselves," a behavior that the Trump administration seemed to oppose directly.[5] The organization of *Harry Potter* fans in open opposition to Trump and what he represents, then, feels like an extension of the seemingly progressive ideals that Rowling herself advocates in her novels.

However, building on backlash concerning diversity in the texts, fan attitudes toward Rowling were further agitated by Rowling's 2016 acceptance speech for the PEN/Allen Foundation Literary Service Award, an award "bestowed to an author whose work embodies its mission to oppose repression in any form, and to champion the best of humanity."[6] In her speech, Rowling refers to Trump himself, stating that despite finding "him offensive and bigoted," "he has [her] full support to come to [her] country and be offensive and bigoted there," defending his rhetoric under the mantle of free speech. This shift in rhetoric was a departure from her 2008 claim that apathetic responses to harmful actions are an act of complicity.[7] When Rowling's political rhetoric intensified

---

[5] Anthony Gierzynsky and Kathryn Eddy, *Harry Potter and the Millennials: Research Methods and the Politics of the Muggle Generation* (Baltimore: The Johns Hopkins University Press, 2013), 12.
[6] J. K. Rowling, "2016 PEN/Allen Foundation Literary Service Award Acceptance Speech," Speech, New York City, 20 May 2016, *PEN America*, https://pen.org/multimedia/2016-penallen-foundation-literary-service-award-j-k-rowling/.
[7] Rowling, "The Fringe Benefits of Failure."

over the next several years, many fans saw this behavior as a breaking point, the culmination of a pressure that had been building for years, beginning in the wake of continued critical readings of Rowling's books. With this development, many fans of the *Potter* series, particularly queer and Trans fans, were faced with the notion that the wizarding world was no longer the haven it once was and that their participation in the fandom was not welcomed by its creator. Many stood in solidarity with the LGBTQ+ community in their shared grief over the "Rowling revelation" and stepped back from the author. The *Harry Potter* fan fiction community has taken a stand in response to the compounded effects of Trump's presidency and Rowling's statements.

Against the backdrop of heightened political discourse, I suggest that the second wave of fan fiction creation developed in response to the onset of Covid-19 and the first major incident of Rowling's transphobic commentary. To combat the feelings of isolation brought about by the worldwide quarantine in response to Covid-19, people flocked to social media in search of community. What many found was the connection that fandom affords, including the act of writing and reading fan fiction. Fan fiction becomes a phenomenon through social media; recommended reading lists are made, "book" clubs are created, and illustrations are drawn.

The rise in popularity of *Harry Potter* fan fiction since 2020 seems to reflect the fandom's desire to escape into familiar stories for emotional refuge; however, to do so necessitates reclaiming the magical nature of the wizarding world to create a more safe, inclusive community for all its participants. The result of this effort is an increase in the number of *Harry Potter* fix-it fics that address the trauma within the series to confront the real-world trauma brought about by the social stressors mentioned above. Many *Harry Potter* fix-it fics draw attention to the social structures that allowed Voldemort's ideologies to take root initially, and by consciously embedding diversity into these fictional spaces, these authors criticize and undermine the institutions that impede social progress, mirroring the frustrations with real-world social stagnation. This essay argues that the reclamation of the imaginative magic that inspired Rowling's creation of the series years ago is predicated upon the fandom's desire to use the series as an outlet for not only processing social trauma, but the wounds caused by Rowling's offensive and bigoted commentary as well. By first examining the *Potter* fandom and then utilizing Judith Herman's theories concerning trauma recovery as it relates to *Harry Potter* fan fiction, this essay demonstrates how pushing back on the limits of their own fan culture. Thereby, the author's influence that created it uniquely situates *Potter* fans as a force for change and acceptance within fan culture and in the world at large.

Henry Jenkins describes fan culture as a "participatory" one that necessitates active engagement with the text at hand.[8] This collaboration extends beyond a simple discussion of the text into the realm of reimagination, where fans take the work into their own hands with the creation of fan fiction and fan art. This act of communal participation makes the threads that bind fan communities together so strong. Where a single fan may have felt alone in their desire to see Harry Potter and Draco Malfoy in a relationship together, fan communities prove that they are not alone in that desire but also that many people agree with them. The impact of online fan communities, then, does not just lie with the exposure to new ways of viewing the original text; it also is rooted in the diversification of its participants that now have access to them because of the internet.[9] The community then, in response to its more diverse demographics against an ever-shifting cultural backdrop, naturally evolves to become more inclusive, simultaneously protecting its participants as well as the text at hand.[10] This is simply the newest manifestation of fan activism. A more diverse community constitutes a more diverse wizarding world and a shift in how that community prioritizes issues within itself in order to advocate for change.[11]

Within the *Harry Potter* community, fans have traditionally demonstrated a deep concern for the ethical and moral issues that Rowling herself emphasizes in the texts. Jenkins describes the activism of the Harry Potter Alliance, a fan activist group that mobilizes in response to cultural issues using "elements of the content world (and their accumulated meanings) as metaphors for making sense of contemporary issues."[12] Similarly, Gierzynski and Eddy find that millennial *Potter* fans are "more accepting [of] those who are different, […] more politically tolerant, […] more supportive of equality, […] less authoritarian, […] more opposed to the use of violence and torture, […] less cynical, [… and] evince a higher level of political efficacy" than those who are not.[13] These examples prove that the values embedded in the *Potter* series have had a marked effect on the development of fans' social and political views as adults, which manifests clearly in fans' relationship with fan fiction as a whole.[14]

---

[8] Rebecca Borah, "Apprentice Wizards Welcome," in *The Ivory Tower and Harry Potter*, ed. Lana A. Whited (Columbia: University of Missouri Press, 2002), 344.
[9] Jennifer Duggan, "Who writes Harry Potter fan fiction? Passionate detachment, 'zooming out,' and fan fiction paratexts on AO3," *Transformative Works and Cultures* 34 (2020): 2.2. https://doi.org/10.3983/twc.2020.1863.
[10] Henry Jenkins, "Cultural acupuncture: Fan activism and the Harry Potter Alliance," *Transformative Works and Cultures* 10 (2012): 2.3. https://doi.org/10.3983/twc.2020.1863.
[11] Duggan, "Who Writes?" 2.3.
[12] Jenkins, "Cultural Acupuncture," 1.9.
[13] Gierzynsky and Eddy, *Harry Potter and the Millennials*, 6.
[14] Gierzynski and Eddy, *Harry Potter and the Millennials*, 2.

The relationship between *Harry Potter* and its fans is also rooted in the notion of literature, including fan fiction, as an imaginative escape from real-world stressors.[15] Given Jenkins' thesis that fan culture is inherently a participatory one, it serves that writing fan fiction also provides the same type if not a more heightened form, of escape than what reading provides. This conclusion has been proven by years of psychological research that has found that "writing about personal or emotional experiences has beneficial effects for physical health and subjective well-being."[16] In other words, the act of writing provides a self-contained space for reflecting and reckoning with the experiences of daily life. For individuals who have experienced emotional trauma, writing about the events surrounding the trauma specifically is a proven way to process the event and subsequent emotions associated with the healing process.

The theoretical framework proposed by Judith Herman further expands on how the trauma recovery process works and, therefore, why writing may be such an effective step in that process.[17] For Herman, there are three stages to the recovery process: "the establishment of safety," "remembrance and mourning" in an attempt to reconstruct the story, and "reconnection to ordinary life."[18] For Herman, these steps are necessary to trauma survivors not only for reconstructing their view of the world but also for their own sense of identity. Once survivors see the opportunity for community in the world, they can see themselves as a participant within that community. Herman's detailed overview of the trauma recovery process and the importance of support groups to that journey easily translates to the importance of fandom and the creation of fan fiction. This process, when applied to fan fiction, grounds a unique opportunity for those interested in writing as a mode of recovery in that doing so allows them to explore their recovery through the lens of characters and stories that are already familiar to them, thereby providing an extra layer of emotional security that is necessary for recovery work. In establishing the emotional safety provided by both the familiarity with the characters and the anonymity afforded by online screen names, authors can project and thereby process residual emotions concerning their trauma by applying it to a preestablished framework. Interacting with fictional characters who share identity experiences creates a new approach to the trauma recovery process,

---

[15] Alaa Alghamdi, "The Past is Present and Future: Recurring Violence and Remaining Human in J. K. Rowling's *Harry Potter* Series," *IAFOR Journal of Arts & Humanities* 5 (Spring 2018): 62. https://doi.org/10.22492/ijah.5.1.04.

[16] Brianna Dym et al., "Coming Out Okay: Community Narratives for LGBTQ Identity Recovery Work," *Proceedings of the ACM on Human-Computer Interaction* 3, no. 154 (2019): 3. https://doi-org.ezproxy.bsc.edu/10.1145/3359256.

[17] Judith Herman, *Trauma and Recovery –From Domestic Abuse to Political Terror* (New York: Basic Books, 1992).

[18] Herman, *Trauma*, 155.

even if the writing is not intended to be explicitly therapeutic in nature.[19] Lastly, by sharing these stories with other fans who are familiar with the stories being used as a framework, as well as the themes explored within, fan fiction authors become activists that advocate for both themselves and the fan community at large. This engagement, Herman notes, allows a reshaping to occur, where "the group has a capacity to bear and integrate traumatic experience that is greater than that of any individual member" and allows the individual in recovery to "draw upon the shared resources of the group" to enable a re-integration into ordinary life once more.[20]

The ability to use fan fiction as a tool for re-integration is why the ever-increasing diversity of the *Potter* fandom allows space for creative and progressive interpretations of both the characters and the text itself.[21] In *Harry Potter*, the very existence of magic suggests that the possibility for pluralities of race, sexuality, or gender would be nearly limitless. This potential is where the appeal of *Harry Potter* lies for so many fans. Though the pairings and possibilities seem infinite, for these purposes, this essay focuses on two of the most popular "ships" in the *Potter* fandom: Dramione and WolfStar. The popularity of fics focused on Dramione, the shorthand for the romantic pairing of Draco Malfoy and Hermione Granger, and WolfStar, the ship name for Remus Lupin and Sirius Black, are the creations of dissatisfied fans and the tidy development of the canonical story arcs for these characters. When considering Rowling's conservative approach to the text, it becomes evident that she prioritizes a heteronormative, nuclear approach to the resolution of the books to appeal to a "happily ever after" sensibility. Hermione is rewarded with a loyal husband and family after losing her own, and while neither Sirius nor Remus survives to the series' conclusion, Remus does have a family with Nymphadora Tonks and their child, Teddy. For many fans, however, the unrealized possibility of these two pairings carries much more nuanced implications about the characters and the story itself. Superficially, these stories may seem interested in the realization of curious pairings Rowling never realizes; at their core, though, these specific relationships present an opportunity for narratives about the multitudes of trauma that these characters endure and how the exploration of that trauma and the attempt to recover from it creates an avenue for processing and modeling recovery that recalls Herman's theoretical approaches.

Of the most popular fan fiction to circulate through the *Potter* community recently is "Breath Mints/Battle Scars." The story follows the "eighth-year" trope, in which Hogwarts students are required to return to school post-war to

---

[19] Dym et al., "Coming Out Okay," 7.
[20] Herman, *Trauma*, 216.
[21] Duggan, "Transforming," 151-152.

complete their studies cut short by the Second Wizarding War. Upon returning to the castle, Hermione Granger faces the residual trauma of her experiences and is affected daily by PTSD-induced anxiety attacks. Granger, ever "the cleverest witch [her] age," is acutely aware of how futile the venture seems to put teenagers who have already survived a war back to classes.[22] Upon seeing Harry on the train, Hermione notes he "looks strange in his Gryffindor tie. Looks…wrong. Misplaced in the clothes of a child that he is not," and that the castle "would probably be better, in some sick, morbid sort of way, if it didn't look so much like it used to." [23] Indeed, she is aware that her "strange, new cluster of emotions she does not quite understand yet" is a sort of "coping mechanism" in the face of so much unresolved trauma.[24]

The significance of Hermione's trauma in "Breath Mints/Battle Scars" to her complexity as a character cannot be overemphasized. Throughout the series, Hermione represents bravery and courage, a steady hand in the face of a storm. For many people, particularly young women, Hermione is a role model, the standard for being strong *and* smart. The focus on Hermione's intelligence in the series is mirrored in her psychological struggles in "Breath Mints/Battle Scars"; her once-capable mind is rendered dysfunctional by trauma. At times, she can barely hold herself together. One such instance occurs during a Potions class when Hermione looks across the room to see Pavarti Patil turn to say something to someone who isn't there. Hermione recognizes this act as Pavarti sharing a joke with her friend Lavender Brown, who died during the Battle of Hogwarts, which sends Hermione out of the classroom and "[retching] into the nearest sink."[25] Hermione experiences moments like these repeatedly, and her frustration at her inability to process these feelings, as it seems other Hogwarts students have done, only exacerbates her condition.

The mental block Hermione experiences undermines her self-perception as one who always knows how to find the correct answer, which rattles her self-confidence and makes it difficult for her to address her trauma. "Psychological trauma" like Hermione experiences is, as Herman notes, an affliction of the powerless. At the moment of trauma, the victim is rendered helpless by overwhelming force."[26] Hermione is a character unfamiliar with the feeling of powerlessness until a traumatic encounter with Bellatrix Lestrange. The feeling

---

[22] J. K. Rowling, *Harry Potter and the Prisoner of Azkaban*, (New York: Scholastic Inc., 1995), 346.
[23] Onyx_and_Elm, "Breath Mints/Battle Scars," *Archive of Our Own*, chap. 1 October 24, 2020, https://archiveofourown.org/works/15370968/chapters/35668776.
[24] Onyx_and_Elm, "Breath Mints," chap. 1.
[25] Onyx_and_Elm, "Breath Mints," chap. 4.
[26] Herman, *Trauma*, 33.

that remains after the encounter leads Hermione to relive that feeling of helplessness repeatedly, whether it involves flashbacks to the event or the physical pain that radiates from the scar on her arm, and it is the major obstacle on her road to recovery. She must become the "author and arbiter of her own recovery" if she is to process the trauma in a meaningful way.[27] But she cannot do this with her friends, who appear relatively well-adjusted. It is the pressure to behave normally that contributes to her spinning her emotional wheels.[28] She desperately wants to behave the way she feels, raw and unrefined, but "society gives women little permission either to withdraw or to express their feelings," particularly in the wake of traumatic events.[29]

It is only with the unfriendly Draco Malfoy that Hermione begins to find comfort. In this rendering, Draco is isolated upon his return to Hogwarts, branded a Death Eater, and hated by everyone, save his three closest Slytherin friends. Through mandated magical journal entries, readers learn that Draco is also experiencing residual physical and emotional trauma from his war experiences. Though initially antagonistic, Draco and Hermione's interactions become intimate upon realizing that they both feel like they are cracking under the pressure of living with unresolved trauma. Without the pretense of decorum, the two open up to each other and eventually learn to share the burden of trauma, a significant step since both Draco and Hermione have lost their families, and together learn how to find new meaning for their pain.[30]

The journal entries found at the beginning of each chapter of "Breath Mints/Battle Scars" are readers' sole opportunity to glimpse inside Draco's mind and, through them, his initial resistance to the process and the positive steps he takes as the story and his relationship with Hermione progresses becomes clear. These entries track the reconstruction of Draco Malfoy from angry and withdrawn to begrudgingly hopeful. This act of writing recalls Herman's theory of the trauma recovery process. Readers can follow Draco's progress as he recognizes his ability to regulate his emotions and establish safety while with loved ones, reconstructs the narrative of his experiences during the War, namely by confronting the lingering resentment towards his father, and reestablishes his sense of community by developing a romantic relationship with Hermione and friendships with Harry and other wizards. With Hermione's aid, Draco becomes a supervisor for other young wizards who are required to submit journal entries as part of their trauma recovery, which models and emphasizes the importance of this act both for the people within

---

[27] Herman, *Trauma*, 133.
[28] Herman, *Trauma*, 199-200.
[29] Herman, *Trauma*, 65.
[30] Herman, *Trauma*, 228.

the story and the fans reading it.[31] As Herman notes, "[those] who recover most successfully are those who discover some meaning in their experience that transcends the limits of personal tragedy."[32]

This act of rehabilitation also positions Draco as a metaphoric placeholder for lost support systems in the minds of fan fiction authors who may feel alienated from their communities due to harmful ideologies. In the books, Draco's antagonistic view toward others outside of Slytherin is rooted in his family's pride in its pure-blood superiority. For most of the series, he is a deeply unlikeable character, smugly swaggering around the castle, mocking students at one turn and hurling hateful slurs at others at the next. The brief glimpses of his family confirm that this behavior is deeply ingrained and encouraged by his father, Lucius, and, later, his aunt, Bellatrix. It is only subtly and momentarily in *Half-Blood Prince* and *Deathly Hallows* that Rowling creates any amount of sympathy for Draco whatsoever. However, in these small pockets of sympathy, fans have found a wealth of possibilities for rehabilitation. The relationship that develops between Draco and Hermione challenges the beliefs held by the Malfoy family concerning pure-blood supremacy, as Hermione's Muggle-born background is a canonical point of tension between the two. Draco's relationship with Hermione undermines the Malfoys' pride in their pure-blood status and highlights the fragility of such ideals both within the wizarding world and the real world at large. Not only is Hermione's very existence diversifying the physical space at Hogwarts and a metaphorical space in the Malfoy family, but her proximity to Draco also forces him to confront his family's problematic beliefs and begin to unlearn them. Draco's evolution from being angry and impetuous to confronting his problematic past offers cautiously optimistic hope for his future with Hermione which signals growth and change and prompts readers to view Draco as a more empathetic figure. By mapping this opportunity for rehabilitation onto a character who ultimately has no such redemption arc in the canonical texts, fan fiction authors may also metaphorically map the opportunity for rehabilitation onto characters within their own lives who are resistant to such change and growth, including themselves. In acknowledging the complicated weight of previous generations' worth of harmful behavior and ideology, Draco, and the author through him, reassesses and reshapes his identity to create room to pursue a more promising future unburdened by guilt and shame.

However, this reading is further complicated when Hermione's character is read as being a woman of color. Though "Breath Mints/Battle Scars" does not explicitly portray Hermione as such, it aligns with other works, ironically

---

[31] Onyx_and_Elm, "Breath Mints," Epilogue.
[32] Herman, *Trauma*, 73.

including the canonical text, that creates opportunities to read Hermione as being specifically Black. When *Harry Potter and the Cursed Child* cast a Black woman as Hermione in 2016, Rowling once again engaged in ret-con by claiming that the ambiguity of Hermione's race was intentional. While *Cursed Child*, a pseudo-fan fiction itself, portrays a more diverse wizarding world, it fails to engage with that diversity meaningfully. A Black Hermione creates more visible diversity, yet this inclusion of diversity does nothing to confront or correct the traumatizing ideals of pure-blood supremacy in the way "Breath Mints/Battle Scars" does, as Draco has a child with Astoria Greengrass, another pure-blooded witch, and Hermione's relationship with Ron challenges no status quo as the Weasleys are already seen as tainted by Arthur's long history with Muggle Relations at the Ministry of Magic. "Breath Mints/Battle Scars" then consciously addresses the problematic social structures inherent to the *Potter* series and takes on the mantel of a fix-it fic by demonstrating the fragility of those structures built by the pure-blood families in the text and by Rowling.

A trauma-informed reading of "Breath Mints/Battle Scars" then lays the groundwork for establishing how the steps for recovery often appear in *Potter* fan fiction by viewing the process through the lens of Hermione and Draco, two survivors of both physical and emotional trauma. "The goal of recounting the trauma story," Herman notes, "is integration, not exorcism. In the process of reconstruction, the trauma story does undergo a transformation, but only in the sense of becoming more present and more real."[33] Hermione's and Draco's acceptance of their trauma into the trajectory of their own lives frees them from the burden of expectations of how one should behave in the face of a traumatic event and transforms their experiences into a "hope that restorative love may still be found in the world."[34]

However, I argue that the emphasis on the aspirational outcome of the emotionally difficult recovery process in "Breath Mints/Battle Scars" is possible due to the heteronormative nature of their relationship. The neat resolution to the story is grounded in the heteronormative standards for resolutions that Rowling built into the series. For other fan fiction "ships," especially queer pairings, the journey becomes more complex, as fans not only have to navigate the treacherous waters of trauma recovery, but they must also do so against the backdrop of non-normative romantic relationships that have no official canonical representation and the inherent tensions that arise given the absence of those pairings in Rowling's texts. WolfStar fics then become a compelling foundation for this complicated intersection, for many of the fics are canon-compliant. The significance of reading WolfStar fics within Herman's

---

[33] Herman, *Trauma*, 181.
[34] Herman, *Trauma*, 211.

theoretical framework here is rooted in Herman's observation that those who suffer the most persistent and present threat of trauma are those who reside in marginalized communities, which here extends to include the LGBTQ+ community.[35] Spotlighting queer identities both in the *Harry Potter* fandom and in the discourse surrounding trauma recovery is a necessary step for fans to reestablish a safe space for all who participate in the fandom.

One of the most well-known stories in the *Harry Potter* fan fiction fandom, "All the Young Dudes," is a Marauders-era fic that follows the adventures of Remus, Sirius, James Potter, and Peter Pettigrew during their time at Hogwarts and in the subsequent First Wizarding War. Over the course of nearly twenty years, beginning with Lupin's acceptance to Hogwarts at age eleven, readers see how these four boys begin to form a near-inextricable connection with one another, a connection that they do not necessarily share with their families away from Hogwarts. As additional characters are brought into the fold, such as Lily Evans and Marleen McKinnon, the "found family" trope responds to the vulnerabilities felt by the LGBTQ+ community, particularly post-2016.

At the beginning of "All the Young Dudes," Remus Lupin is living in an orphanage in London, battling a case of lycanthropy with no magical assistance.[36] Lupin, as a child and later as an adolescent, is angry and temperamental, something he attributes to his abusive upbringing at the orphanage. Herman notes that for those who endured childhood trauma, it is common to "oscillate between uncontrolled expressions of rage and intolerance of aggression in any form," and this is evident in Remus's behavior in his early years at Hogwarts when he takes on the role of both perpetrator and victim of increasingly humiliating acts of bullying.[37] He acts on these impulses in the hopes of making connections with his fellow housemates, James, Sirius, and Peter, and in doing so, finds himself reaching for strands of a social system to which he can finally belong. This system cannot be a tight knit one, however, without Remus confronting his trauma and sharing his narrative with those who claim to be his friends.

Part of Lupin's inability to fully integrate into the Hogwarts community is because he is forced to hide his lycanthropy from his friends, afraid that, should they discover his condition, he would be forced to leave the school, which is the only friendly home he has ever had. His relationship with his identity as a werewolf parallels the feelings Lupin must confront when he develops a romantic attraction to his best friend, Sirius Black. His anxiety about people discovering his secret, both that he is a werewolf and that he is gay, is rooted in

---

[35] Herman, *Trauma*, 16, 248–249.
[36] MsKingBean89, "All the Young Dudes," *Archive of Our Own*, chap. 25, November 12, 2018, https://archiveofourown.org/works/10057010/chapters/22409387.
[37] Herman, *Trauma*, 56.

his fear of abandonment. As a child, Lupin believes his abandonment at the orphanage was due to his lycanthropy and that, upon his father's suicide, his Muggle mother believed raising a child like him would be "a bit much for her."[38] This feeling of abandonment recalls how trauma survivors, particularly those who are children, "[lose their] basic sense of self" when a "secure sense of connection with caring people" is damaged or absent.[39] It is not until he is well into his teenage years and engaged in a secret relationship with Sirius that Remus feels grounded in a sense of belonging and becomes comfortable sharing both parts of his secret identity with his friends; indeed, he is shocked when they are nothing but supportive of him. When Lupin thanks James Potter for his support, Potter promises they are "still marauders," emphasizing that the relationship between the friends had not and would not change given Lupin's revelation.[40] It is then that he sees his friends can become a family anchored in a sense of safety, acceptance, and connection and can begin to rebuild his sense of self.

The other half of the WolfStar relationship has his own issues regarding his identity. At first, Sirius Black seems the opposite of Remus Lupin in nearly every way. Where Lupin is a penniless orphan at the beginning of the book, Sirius is an obscenely wealthy heir to the "Noble and Most Ancient House of Black," one of the sacred pure-blood wizarding families, and is afforded the privilege that accompanies it.[41] His heritage, however, comes with its own set of difficulties and is the foundation of the trauma that initially binds Lupin and Sirius together. Much like Lupin, Sirius's identity struggles are paralleled in his relationship with his family. Upon arriving at Hogwarts, Sirius is sorted into Gryffindor and becomes the first Black family member in centuries sorted outside of Slytherin. This development is immediately a source of much tension between Sirius and his family. His older cousins, Bellatrix and Narcissa, begin "hissing" at him as he makes his way to the Gryffindor table. Later, his mother sends a letter that calls him a "blood traitor."[42] His mother is both emotionally and physically abusive, and it is not unusual for Sirius to return to Hogwarts after a holiday with scars to prove it. She repeatedly reminds Sirius that he "is not [their] only son," and when he refuses to join the ranks of Voldemort's growing forces, the Black family disowns him.[43] His disinheritance is caused by his unwillingness to engage with his family's growing association

---

[38] MsKingBean89, "All the Young Dudes," chap. 25.
[39] Herman, *Trauma*, 52.
[40] MsKingBean89, "All the Young Dudes," chap. 115.
[41] MsKingBean89, "All the Young Dudes," chap. 16.
[42] MsKingBean89, "All the Young Dudes," chap.3, chap. 12.
[43] MsKingBean89, "All the Young Dudes," chap. 12.

with Lord Voldemort, as well as his rejection of the Black family values of superiority and bigotry, and sets him apart as unable to continue the Black family legacy, an action that recalls anxieties about gay men who are unlikely to carry on their family name in a traditional way.

Despite Sirius' resistance to his family's pressures to join Voldemort, he cannot help but maintain some residual affection for them, particularly his younger brother, Regulus Black. Upon learning that Regulus has pledged his allegiance to Voldemort, Sirius is upset for days and blames himself for not being more protective of his brother. Sirius grasps at the lingering threads of his relationship with his family, seeking out one last time "the first source of comfort and protection" that affords him "attachment and meaning" to a community.[44] In finding nothing but the emotionally stagnant dynamic he has always encountered, Sirius experiences the same difficult situation as Remus: the "[shattering of] the construction of the self that is formed and sustained in relation to others," leaving "a sense of alienation" that affects his friendship with the other Marauders and resistance to sharing the brutal truth about his emotional trauma.[45]

The effects of Sirius' identity loss and disconnection are mirrored in Sirius' internalized homophobia. The first development in his and Lupin's relationship is a kiss that Remus initiates but that Sirius refuses to discuss until much later.[46] When the relationship becomes physical, Sirius refuses to acknowledge any potential emotional developments and continues to have physical relationships with multiple girls in Gryffindor. It is not until Lupin comes out to their friends that Sirius confronts their situation, seemingly surprised that Lupin identifies as gay. "You said you weren't," Sirius tells Lupin, "Like I said *I* wasn't. Thought we were both on the same page, that's all."[47] A moment later, Sirius tells Lupin that "[he] can care about [him] and […] not scream it from the rooftops."[48] At this moment, Sirius' fear of accepting his own identity is rooted in the trauma he experienced from his own family during his disinheritance. When Sirius voices his concerns about the possibility of a future with Remus, it is an acknowledgment of his familial trauma as well.[49] Sirius, whose entire life was mapped out for him, is shunned by his family and loses all direction only to find a new family in his friends. In realizing the safety afforded by the existence of his new familial community and deciding to pursue a public, romantic relationship

---

[44] Herman, *Trauma*, 52, 51.
[45] Herman, *Trauma*, 51, 52.
[46] MsKingBean89, "All the Young Dudes," chap. 86.
[47] MsKingBean89, "All the Young Dudes," chap. 115.
[48] MsKingBean89, "All the Young Dudes," chap. 115.
[49] MsKingBean89, "All the Young Dudes," chap. 115.

with Remus, Sirius packs away the traumatic memories of his family to rewrite the narrative of his identity and reengage with a supportive community.

The resolution to "All the Young Dudes" reflects the possibilities that can come with confronting and processing compounded emotional trauma to reclaim one's identity. The ending, which takes place before the events of *The Order of the Phoenix*, sees an adult Remus and Sirius confronting the years of trauma that they encountered because of their families, the war, and, ultimately, each other. Despite finding joy in his tenure as a professor at Hogwarts a year earlier, Remus is sullen and withdrawn, unable to shake the guilt of surviving the war when so many of his friends were killed. After spending over a year on the run after his escape from Azkaban, Sirius is still not fully present in the world around him and is begged by a friend to "be *here*; a real, flesh and blood person. Not a dog. Not a ghost."[50] When Sirius and Remus confront their trauma with themselves and each other, they find relief in the shared mourning of the lives and opportunities lost to them by the First Wizarding War, an essential act in Herman's recovery process.[51] With this act, they affirm each other and are finally able to, using Herman's terms once more, resolve their recovery by re-establishing safety and connection with the other, which enables them to work together to reactivate the Order of the Phoenix to fight Voldemort again.

These two examples exemplify how *Harry Potter* fan fiction can be used as a foundation for trauma recovery work for authors, particularly those who have experienced emotional trauma relating to identity, to explore their responses to those experiences and to provide opportunities for readers to do the same. By mapping the anxious process of coming out to oneself and to family and friends, the author of "All the Young Dudes" provides space for an emotional catharsis that Rowling never realizes in the series. The author of "Breath Mints/Battle Scars" provides the same release by allowing fans to feel how difficult the grieving process can be, even for one as strong as Hermione Granger. These stories allow complicated emotions to occupy space within the narrative without compromising character development. Based on the response to these stories and many others, the complications these characters encounter within fan fiction encourage far more nuanced and complex readings than the ones initially suggested by Rowling. The fact that trauma recovery, in all its messy forms, takes the forefront in so much *Potter* fan fiction demonstrates the fandom's prioritization of this process within themselves as

---

[50] MsKingBean89, "All the Young Dudes," chap. 187.
[51] Herman, *Trauma*, 69.

well by "[constructing] narratives that reclaim and normalize their identities for themselves, their community, and for society."[52]

Ultimately, there is an unprecedented need to engage with fan fiction, particularly *Harry Potter* fan fiction, as a critical site for intervention that lies at the intersection of many disciplinary fields. *Harry Potter*'s wide-reaching cultural influence was unique to its era. However, its novelty still finds root in younger generations' insistence on confronting the social issues embedded in and caused by the series. This fan awareness creates multiplicities of opportunities for engagement by scholars and fans alike and is reminiscent of the ideals embedded in the *Potter* series. By rallying together to create a community predicated upon empathy and acceptance for its participants, the *Harry Potter* fandom models behavior performed by Rowling's characters themselves throughout the series. Whereas Rowling seems to have forgotten the qualities her characters embody–curiosity, acceptance, persistence, and bravery–the fans have not. *Potter* fix-it fics prioritize tolerance and inclusion, transforming the work by taking these ideals to new levels. The presence of such relevant discussions of trauma and recovery in the fan fiction community speaks to the efforts of fans working to reclaim the enduring values of *Harry Potter* that made it so beloved nearly twenty-five years ago, safe from the original creator's disparaging influence. In doing so, this richly diverse community is creating an alternative wizarding world, a metaphorical Room of Requirement, that provides refuge for all those who seek it out.

Bibliography

Algahamdi, Alaa. "The Past is Present and Future: Recurring Violence and Remaining Human in J. K. Rowling's *Harry Potter* Series." *IAFOR Journal of Arts & Humanities* 5 (Spring 2018): 59-76. https://doi.org/10.22492/ijah.5.1.04.

Borah, Rebecca. "Apprentice Wizards Welcome." In *The Ivory Tower and Harry Potter*, edited by Lana A. Whited. Columbia: University of Missouri Press, 2002.

Duggan, Jennifer. "Transformative Readings: Harry Potter Fan Fiction, Trans/Queer Reader Response, and J. K. Rowling." *Children's Literature in Education* 53 (2022): 147-168. https://doi.org/10.1007/s10583-021-09446-9.

——. "Who writes Harry Potter fan fiction? Passionate detachment, 'zooming out,' and fan fiction paratexts on *AO3*." *Transformative Works and Cultures* 34 (2020). https://doi.org/10.3983/twc.2020.1863.

Dym, Brianna, Jed R. Brubaker, Casey Fieslet, and Bryan Seamaan. "Coming Out Okay: Community Narratives for LGBTQ Identity Recovery Work." *Proceedings of the AC on Human-Computer Interaction* 3, no. 154 (2019): 1-28 https://doi-org.ezproxy.bsc.edu/10.1145/3359256.

---

[52] Dym et al., "Coming Out Okay," 21.

Gierzynsky, Anthony and Kathryn Eddy. *Harry Potter and the Millenials: Research Methods and the Politics of the Muggle Generation.* Baltimore: The Johns Hopkins University Press, 2013.

Herman, Judith. *Trauma and Recovery–From Domestic Abuse to Political Terror.* New York: Basic Books, 1992.

Jenkins, Henry. "'Cultural acupuncture': Fan Activism and the Harry Potter Alliance." *Transformative Works and Cultures* 10 (2012). https://doi.org/10.3983/twc.2012.0305.

MsKingBean89. "All the Young Dudes." *Archive of Our own* https://archiveofourown.org/works/10057010/chapters/22409387.

Onyx_and_Elm. "Breath Mints/Battle Scars." *Archive of Our own.* https://archiveofourown.org/works/15370968/chapters/35668776.

Rowling, J. K. "The Fringe Benefits of Failure, and the Importance of Imagination." Convocation speech, Harvard University, 5 June 2008, Cambridge, MA. https://news.harvard.edu/gazette/story/2008/06/text-of-j-k-rowling-speech/.

——. *Harry Potter and the Deathly Hallows,* New York: Scholastic Inc., 2007.

——. *Harry Potter and the Prisoner of Azkaban,* New York: Scholastic Inc., 1999.

——. (@jkrowling). "If sex isn't real." *Twitter,* June 6, 2020. https://twitter.com/jk_rowling/status/1269389298664701952.

——. (@jkrowling). "People who menstruate." *Twitter,* June 6, 2020. https://twitter.com/jk_rowling/status/1269382518362509313.

——. "2016 PEN/Allen Foundation Literary Service Award: J. K. Rowling." Speech, New York City, 20 May 2016. PEN America. https://pen.org/multimedia/2016-penallen-foundation-literary-service-award-j-k-rowling/

Chapter 6

'I have my version and you have yours': Fan Fiction and *Supernatural* Fans' Road to Damascus

Anna Caterino
University of Milan

Abstract: In this article, Caterino investigates the ways that fix-it fics rebuke the show, *Supernatural*, and how the show-writers and actors undermined the role of fans and fan fiction in keeping the series alive for fifteen seasons. She considers how the shows queerbaiting pushed fans to use fix-it fics as a means of reclaiming the identities of characters whose evident same sex attractions were ignored in favor of committing the characters to toxic masculinity and heteronormative existences.

Keywords: queerbaiting, toxic masculinity, heteronormativity, fandoms, paratextuality, homophobia, *Supernatural*, fandoms, fans, fix-it fics, tags, *AO3*.

***

In its 200th episode, "Fan Fiction," *Supernatural* (2005-2020) once more reprises its tradition of metatextual narratives to remark on the writers' knowledge about fan practices and theories.[1] The story takes place at the fictional St. Alphonso Academy in Michigan, where a group of girls intends to stage *Supernatural: The Musical*, an adaptation of the *Supernatural* novels written by Chuck Shurley, played by Rob Benedict, and the girls' post-canon interpretation. Upon their arrival, Sam and Dean Winchester, played by Jared Padalecki and Jensen Ackles, are shocked to hear about the project. Their reaction allows the show to make a series of statements on authorial intent, audience interpretation and reception, and jokes on shipping portmanteaus such as 'Destiel' and 'Samstiel.' By the end of the episode, however, both brothers grant their support and encourage the girls to pursue their interest in writing, notwithstanding Dean Winchester's clarification, "I have my version and you

---

[1] Laura E. Felschow, "'Hey, Check It Out, There's Actually Fans': (Dis)empowerment and (Mis)representation of Cult Fandom in *Supernatural*," *Transformative Works and Cultures* 4 (2010). https://doi.org/10.3983/twc.2010.0134.

have yours."² Further validation comes in the episode's final scene, in which Chuck Shurley describes the stage production as "not bad"³ and smiles.

Although the show's approach appears to be positive, the way *Supernatural* deals with fan practices is not entirely celebratory to the point that years later, some fans still feel tempted to "bail halfway through."⁴ While the episode provides a "tacit endorsement of 'transformative work' or 'fan fiction,'"⁵ it also takes its distance from fans' analyses and perspectives, marking them as something other and inaccurate at best. Unlike his predecessors, screenwriter Robbie Thompson uses metatextuality to tackle the controversial topic of Destiel, the slash ship of Dean Winchester and Castiel, played by Misha Collins. However, the show's portrayal of its fandom remains negative. The girls in "Fan Fiction" are not interested in exploring problematic content or the potential of an incestuous relationship between the two brothers. They want to see themselves represented on screen and ascribe their sexualities to the characters. Nevertheless, they are grouped with characters like Becky Rosen, played by Emily Perkins. Like Becky in season five, they are "overwhelmed, eager and needing the approval of the Author God"⁶ and compared to a "misguided loser"⁷ who posed as a threat⁸ and served as a reminder "to sit back and let the big boys run the show."⁹

The overlap seemingly justifies fans' insistence on being disrespected by the writers for over a decade and their refusal to admit that *Supernatural*'s lack of subversion of the status quo coexists with the show's queercoding. Destiel was never the result of a "standard way of using camera angles and shot-reverse-shot or the requirements of physically staging a scene."¹⁰ Neither was it a

---

² *Supernatural*, season 10, episode 5, "Fan Fiction," directed by Phil Sgriccia, written by Robbie Thompson, featuring Jensen Ackles, and Jared Padalecki, aired November 11, 2014, The CW, 36:52.
³ "Fan Fiction," 41:25.
⁴ Shinelikethunder, "congratulations to the CW's Supernatural...," *Tumblr*, November 8, 2022, https://shinelikethunder.tumblr.com/post/700318812697919488/congratulations-to-the-cws-supernatural-season.
⁵ Erin M. Giannini, "'I so miss being an atheist': God, The Darkness and the Show That Wouldn't Die," in *Supernatural Out of the Box: Essays on the Metatextuality of the Series*, ed. Lisa Macklem and Dominick Grace (Jefferson: McFarland, 2020), 8.
⁶ Judith May Fathallah, *Fan Fiction and the Author* (Amsterdam: Amsterdam UP, 2017), 168.
⁷ Cait Coker and Candance Benefiel, "The Hunter Hunted: The Portrayal of the Fan as Predator in 'Supernatural,'" in *Supernatural, Humanity and the Soul: On the Highway to Hell and Back*, ed. Susan A. George and Regina Hansen (New York: Palgrave Macmillan, 2014), 109.
⁸ Giannini, "God, The Darkness and the Show That Wouldn't Die," 29.
⁹ Coker and Benefiel, "The Hunter Hunted," 108.
¹⁰ Ivan Askwith et al., "Industry/Fan Relations: A Conversation," in *The Routledge Companion to Media Fandom*, ed. Melissa A. Click and Suzanne Scott (New York and London: Routledge, 2018), 375.

byproduct of the presence of "two hot men [who] must be slashed"[11] or LGBTQ+ fans' desire to see themselves respectfully depicted on screen. It was embedded within the narrative since Castiel's introduction in "Lazarus Rising" and continued the pre-existing exploration of Dean Winchester's queerness. Even so, the ship has historically been a repeated source of conflict, leading to ongoing disputes between shippers, actors, and producers because of the latter's refusal to "make good on same-sex subtext"[12] and acknowledge that "subtext [is] based in T-E-X-T."[13] The lack of paratextual confirmation, as well as Dean Winchester's skeptical and judgmental looks at the camera[14] in "Fan Fiction," do not undermine the show's queercoding. However, they test fans' patience as the writing choices are perceived as a mockery of fans.

Supernatural's refusal to comply with the ever-growing percentage of LGBTQ+ characters in broadcasted television series has since led fans to seek out fan content on social media sites such as *Tumblr* and nonprofit fan fiction archives like *Archive of Our own* (*AO3*). The rejection of the show's canon has become particularly common in the aftermath of the show's final episodes. These not only "spat in the face of [the show's] own themes,"[15] but also failed to canonize Destiel despite the love confession in the antepenult episode "Despair" and the lack of need to cater to a conservative audience given that the show was coming to an end.[16] By a curious twist of fate, the overall dissatisfaction with the ending has led to a fandom renaissance. In the aftermath of November 5, 2020, when #Destiel trended above the American presidential election for hours, many people began to partake in fandom activities. Further engagement was also prompted by the airing of the Latin American dub of "Despair," renamed "La Verdad," in which the confession was

---

[11] Julie Wilkinson, "The Epic Love Story of *Supernatural* and Fanfic," in *Fic: Why Fanfic Is Taking Over the World*, ed. Annie Jamison (Dallas: Smart Pop, 2013), 309.

[12] Eliel Cruz, "Fans Take *Supernatural* to Task for Queer Baiting," *Advocate*, para. 14, July 17, 2014. https://www.advocate.com/bisexuality/2014/07/17/fans-take-supernatural-task-queer-baiting.

[13] Sadie Gennis, "*Supernatural* Has a Queerbaiting Problem that Needs to Stop," *TV Guide*, para. 6, November 17, 2014, https://www.tvguide.com/news/supernatural-queer baiting-destiel-1089286.

[14] "Fan Fiction," 13:56.

[15] Deirdre T., "*Supernatural*'s Legacy: The Trauma of Silence," *Buzzfeed*, November 23, 2020, para. 10, https://www.buzzfeed.com/deirdre-t/supernaturalas-legacy-the-trauma-of-silence-1b17yhc5ye.

[16] N. Micarelli, "Casual Homophobia at *Supernatural* Conventions Just Won't Die," *The Mary Sue*, November 8, 2021, https://www.themarysue.com/casual-homophobia-at-supernatural-conventions-just-wont-die.

both romantic *and* reciprocated.[17] By August 2021, the number of fan fiction on *AO3* tagged as Castiel/Dean Winchester surpassed the '100000+ works' mark, making it the first slash pairing ever to reach that milestone.[18] Of these works, almost 12600 were written after Castiel told Dean "I love you"[19] on TV.[20]

One of the most common genres is the fix-it fic, which authors use to reclaim and "reimagine [the] queer possibilities"[21] that mainstream media often disallows. Fans seek to explore the kind of positive LGBTQ+ representation they wish to consume.[22] In doing so, they abandon canonical depictions of queerness centered on shame and violence in favor of new models based on happiness. Fans thus reclaim the 'happily ever after' that is nowadays considered fundamental for good representation.[23] Consequently, the characters' sexual identities are often voiced out loud, and their storylines are deprived of any trait that is labeled as 'problematic.' These choices allow fans to challenge the source material and the status quo, succeeding where the series failed. It follows that this chapter will analyze the fix-it fic phenomenon within the *Supernatural* fandom, particularly the Destiel subsection of it, concerning the accusations of queerbaiting, the dismissal of authorial intent, and the striving for more positive representation. Above all, it will focus on fan fiction's power to construct identities and provide validation to the point that canonical events and not fans' productions become secondary and irrelevant.

Supernatural's Tentative Adherence to the Status Quo

Supernatural follows the story of the Winchester brothers as they travel across America, saving people and hunting monsters. Throughout the first season,

---

[17] Eliza Quinn, "*Supernatural* 15x18 Spanish Dub Confession Scene," *YouTube*, Video. November 25, 2020, https://www.youtube.com/watch?v=0Jsb6S1IkJw.
[18] "DeanCas100k," *Fanlore*, last modified August 2, 2021, https://fanlore.org/wiki/DeanCas100k.
[19] *Supernatural*, season 15, episode 18, "Despair," directed by Richard Speight Jr., written by Robert Berens, featuring Jensen Ackles, Misha Collins, aired November 5, 2020, The CW, 38:13.
[20] Perlukafarin, "I can't get over dean/castiel…," *Tumblr*, August 4, 2021, https://perlukafarin.tumblr.com/post/658597441676935168/i-got-curious-about-this-too-so-i-went-through.
[21] Michael McDermott, "The Broken Promise of Queerbaiting: Happiness and Futurity in Politics of Queer Representation," *International Journal of Cultural Studies* 24, no. 5 (2020): 859. https://doi: 10.1177/1367877920984170.
[22] McDermott, "The Broken Promise of Queerbaiting," 844-859.
[23] Eve Ng, "Reading the Romance of Fan Cultural Production: Music Videos of a Television Lesbian Couple," *Popular Communication* 6, no. 2 (2008): 103-121. https://doi:10.1080/15405700701746525.

their mythic quest is combined with their search for their missing father, John Winchester, played by Jeffrey Dean Morgan. Despite John's death at the beginning of season two, the consequences of his militaristic upbringing and White hegemonic masculinity haunt the rest of the narrative. The familial trauma and the cycles of violence he initiated shape the Winchesters' microcosm and prevent the actualization of queer authenticity. In turn, the narrative also exposes the dangers of the kind of masculinity embodied by the Independent Marlboro Man. Under such circumstances, it becomes evident that the show's main focus is the dysfunctional and codependent relationship that binds the two brothers, their trauma, and their overall inability to escape the family home – embodied by the show's most iconographic symbol: the 1967 Chevrolet Impala.[24]

Contemporary audiences, accustomed to more explicit and diverse representation, mistake the show's compliance to the status quo for blind support, regardless of the "feminist and/or queer readings"[25] that *Supernatural* allows. Dean Winchester is read as "aggressively straight [and] explicitly queerphobic,"[26] a "male-power-fantasy-wanna-be,"[27] and the protagonist of a "hypermasculine cw show"[28] that was trying to appeal to a male demographic. However, Dean is written as queer since the show's first season. Episodes like "Skin" and "Dream a Little Dream of Me," for example, expose his status as a pariah and his inability to comply with societal standards. Similarly, episodes like "Scarecrow" associate pie with the "domestic Americana and the American apple-pie life."[29] Thus, Dean's inability to consume his favorite food becomes indicative of his inability to enter a heterosexual lifestyle. In doing so, *Supernatural* deviates from the masculine and heterosexual standard without disavowing the cultural landscape of post-9/11 America. It retains the

---

[24] Thomas Knowles, "The Automobile as Moving Castle," in *The Gothic Tradition in Supernatural*, ed. Melissa Edmundson (Jefferson: McFarland, 2016), 25-36.
[25] Rhonda Nicol, "'How is this not rape-y?': Dean as Anti-Bella and Feminism without Women in *Supernatural*," in *Supernatural, Humanity and the Soul. On the Highway to Hell and Back*, ed. Susan A. George and Regina Hansen (New York: Palgrave Macmillan, 2014), 165.
[26] Deancritblog, "I will never understand how this fandom…," *Tumblr*, November 11, 2021, https://deancritblog.tumblr.com/post/667585107135201280/i-will-never-understand-how-this-fandom-took-an.
[27] Bundibird, "Someone go wake Eric up…," *Tumblr*, February 14, 2021, https://bundibird.tumblr.com/post/643134532923621376/someone-go-wake-eric-up-hes-running-late-hes.
[28] Castiels-pussy, "Knock knock Kripke are you there…," *Tumblr*, February 8, 2021, https://castiels-pussy.tumblr.com/post/642553082730954752/knock-knock-kripke-are-you-there-the.
[29] Kelli Wilhelm, "'Where's the pie?' Nostalgic and Apocalyptic Foodways in *Supernatural*," in *Supernatural Out of the Box: Metatextuality in the Series*, ed. Lisa Macklem and Dominick Grace (Jefferson: McFarland, 2020), 107-119.

preoccupation with masculinity,[30] "masculine fortitude,"[31] and the "foundational drama"[32] that characterizes the mediatic content produced at the beginning of the new millennium.

The monster-of-the-week narrative is also misinterpreted. While monsters are used as a metaphor to deconstruct childhood trauma and abuse, fans often think they are stand-ins for minorities and consequently claim that 'hunting' is an extension of White supremacy and ableism.[33] The show's social criticism[34] and its reference to paranoic ideologies[35] are hereby overlooked. Episodes like "Wendigo," "Bugs," and "Route 666" are labeled as 'problematic' and condemned to offer a haven for all. The only exception is the case in which they are used to mediate minorities' experiences and propose a different point of view.

The show's themes are repeatedly overanalyzed and condemned, while authorial intent is dismissed entirely in favor of a black-and-white narrative with no middle ground. Some may consider fan fiction as "secondary and derivative,"[36] but it allows corrective measures that reintroduce unproblematic content and "the full dignity that heteronormative media disallows"[37] by relying on explicit and overtly progressive storylines. As such, fix-it fics occasionally verge toward contemporary media, such as *Heartstopper* (2022-), in which the protagonists "don't take drugs, drink alcohol, have sex, swear or even argue with their parents."[38] Such a stance is taken mainly by teenagers

---

[30] Eve Bennett, *Gender in Post-9/11 American Apocalyptic TV. Representations of Masculinity and Femininity at the End of the World* (New York and London: Bloomsbury Academic, 2019), 1-10.

[31] Susan Faludi, *The Terror Dream: What 9/11 Revealed about America* (London: Atlantic Books, 2008), 8.

[32] Faludi, *The Terror Dream*, 208.

[33] Suncaptor, "One thing I do think is important to talk about in supernatural…," *Tumblr*, August 12, 2022, https://www.tumblr.com/suncaptor/692362692361699328/one-thing-i-do-think-is-important-to-talk-about-in?source=share.

[34] Annika Gonnerman, "'You Don't Have to Be a Monster. You Have a Choice': *Supernatural*, Free Will and the Deterministic Concept of Monstrosity," in *Supernatural Out of the Box: Essays on the Metatextuality of the Series*, ed. Lisa Macklem and Dominick Grace (Jefferson: McFarland, 2020), 90-103.

[35] Linnie Blake, "All Hell Breaks Loose: *Supernatural*, Gothic Neoliberalism and the American Self," in *Horror Studies* 6, no. 2 (2015): 232, *Supernatural*, Gothic Neoliberalism and the American Self," *Horror Studies* 6, no. 2 (2015): 225-238. https://doi: 10.1386/host.6.2.225_1.

[36] Fathallah, *Fan Fiction and the Author*, 190.

[37] Taylor Boulware, "Fascination/Frustration: Slash Fandom, Genre, and Queer Uptake." Order No. 10289659, University of Washington, 2017, 112, https://www.proquest.com/dissertations-theses/fascination-frustration-slash-fandom-genre-queer/docview/1942503674/se-2.

[38] Rachel Aroesti, "No Drugs, Booze, Sex or Swearing: Will *Heartstopper* Rewrite the Young Love Rulebook?" *The Guardian*, March 18, 2022, https://www.theguardian.com/tv-and-

and young adults who are not the original target of the show, not because Kripke was trying to cater to a male audience,[39] but because they were born after the show's first seasons aired on television. Acquainted as these fans are with more explicit representation and politically correct media, they urge fan fiction writers to provide a 'sanitized,' utopist, and escapist reality for all.

Only one of the writers who worked for the show is praised for his repeated attempts to challenge the status quo and provide the audience with more explicit representation. Indeed, Robert Berens is generally considered "not just another straight guy potentially catering to fans."[40] As the author of "Despair," he is sometimes considered to be the sole person responsible for the "homosexual declaration of love"[41] at the end of the episode. Together with Misha Collins, he is worthy of praise because of their fight for the scene and the consequent defiance of a narrative imposed by a "kind of very macho"[42] show. Contrary to fans' beliefs, the scene does not exist in a vacuum, and season fifteen alone features a variety of episodes in which the relationship between Dean Winchester and Castiel is marked as something other than friendship. Notoriously, the first half of the season is dedicated to Dean and Castiel's break-up and its consequences, building up and climaxing with "The Trap." While friends do quarrel, the storyline is introduced by "Raising Hell," an episode that once more marks Destiel as a romantic pairing. Here, Dean and Castiel's relationship is described as the only act of free will capable of defying the power of the Father/God.

On a closer look, the confession also loses its relevance and progressiveness in light of its blink-and-you'll-miss-it nature and ambiguity. The inconsequentiality of the scene is reinforced using the "bury your gays" trope, for which LGBTQ+ characters are erased "from the narrative entirely if the depiction goes beyond subtext to include acknowledged queer identities."[43]

---

radio/2022/mar/18/no-drugs-booze-sex-or-swearing-will-heartstopper-rewrite-the-young-love-rulebook.

[39] Lynn Zubernis and Katherine Larsen, *Fandom at the Crossroads: Celebration, Shame and Fan/Producer Relationships* (Cambridge: Cambridge Scholars), 2.

[40] Castiellesbian, "I feel like I need a glossary of terms...," *Tumblr*, December 1, 2020, https://castiellesbian.tumblr.com/post/636325192563621888/i-feel-like-i-need-a-glossary-of-terms-or-a.

[41] Hasnaa, "Misha and the Cast of *Supernatural* Talk about Destiel Going Canon," *YouTube*, Video, December 5, 2020, 0:41, https://www.youtube.com/watch?v=xdPzG1yqjEU.

[42] Seriously, "Misha Collins Révèle Tout Sur la Relation Dean/Castiel #SHORT," *YouTube*, Video, April 1, 2022, 0:28, https://www.youtube.com/shorts/FEwSuGqAKg0.

[43] Elizabeth Bridges, "A Genealogy of Queerbaiting: Legal Codes, Production Codes, 'Bury Your Gays' and *The 100* Mess," *Journal of Fandom Studies* 6, no. 2 (2018): 116. https://doi:10.1386/jfs.6.2.115_1.

Castiel confesses his love and promptly dies. Two episodes later, in the series finale, Dean dies after he is impaled on a rebar by vampire mimes, making it the second occurrence of the "bury your gays" trope within the span of three episodes.

Berens' resistance to both the status quo and Eric Kripke's show that supposedly "fetishizes toxic masculinity"[44] does not rely on the "positive affects"[45] that contemporary LGBTQ+ audiences seek. Even so, it offers fans validation of their interpretation of the show, and a more acceptable and explicit deviation from the norm. As such, it is a closer product of 'convergence culture' and distances itself from other screenwriters' overall disinterest in fans' "officially ridiculous"[46] claims. At the same time, it does nothing to subvert the status quo. It only reaffirms it.

Slash Fiction and the Road to Damascus

Throughout its run, *Supernatural* had several queer characters, and most of them ended up dead. The show seemingly failed its queer fandom repeatedly, even more so because it ended "unapologetically, cruelly, and yes, homophobically,"[47] and contradicted fans' hopes of seeing themselves "treated with dignity, respect, and love."[48] Citing other instances of homophobia, *Tumblr* user Izupie comments on the lack of canonical ships and happy endings, saying "you know something big went down in your fandom when there is a disproportionately large number of fix-it fics on *AO3*."[49] For this reason, fix-it fics are seen as the result of people's dissatisfaction with a show's canon and writing choices. In the context of *Supernatural*, such a list should also include the reappropriation of queer subtext, which is commonly perceived as "gaslighting [and] literal psychological abuse,"[50] and the show's overall lack of diversity.

The reintroduction of queer identities and the production of fan content centered on them goes beyond Destiel, as fans produce slash content for most of the characters, regardless of their canonical sexual orientation and the show's themes. Of all the combinations of queer ships that fans come up with,

---

[44] Omegaphobe, "Eric Kripke 2005…," *Tumblr*, March 12, 2022, https://omegaphobe.tumblr.com/post/678560116859174912/eric-kripke-2005-im-gonna-make-a-show.
[45] McDermott, "The Broken Promise of Queerbaiting," 854.
[46] Zubernis and Larsen, *Fandom at the Crossroads*, 181.
[47] T., "*Supernatural's* Legacy," para. 11.
[48] T., "*Supernatural's* Legacy," para. 9.
[49] Izupie, "You know something big went down…," *Tumblr*, July 15, 2022, https://izupie.tumblr.com/post/687101122263040000/you-know-something-big-went-down-in-your-fandom.
[50] Deanwasalwaysbi, "They really were just gaslighting us…," *Tumblr*, January 27, 2021, https://deanwasalwaysbi.tumblr.com/post/641484116212252672/they-really-were-just-gaslighting-the-fandom-for-a.

however, Destiel is by far the most popular and one of the few that is rooted in the show. To this date, there are 4,464 works written by Destiel fans that are tagged as fix-it on *AO3*.[51] However, the number does not include the works tagged as post-episode, post-canon, or any variation thereof, such as post episode: s15e18 "Despair," and fan fiction with no tag at all that can nevertheless belong to that category. The tag to use is the author's choice, even though *AO3* does suggest pre-filled tags when writers fill out the field. Not all of the above-mentioned cases feature stories that deal with the aftermath of the show's shortcomings and the final episodes. Despite the plot variations dictated by each author's prerogatives, these fan productions are centered on Dean Winchester and Castiel coming together and receiving their happily ever after.

Control over the narrative is hereby reclaimed in an act of defiance of the Author God, both in the case of Destiel and in other slash pairings. Their success is often considered to be a victory over "cisheteronormative values and problematic depictions of queerness"[52] in entertainment media. Still, fans' production of slash fiction is not necessarily seen as a form of progressivism. Occasionally, stories reinforce the pre-existing status quo rather than challenge it,[53] highlighting people's refusal to overtly engage in social activism[54] in their free time. A wide array of slash fiction serves as "wish fulfillment"[55] insofar as it is written by heterosexual women for whom the image of "intertwined male bodies is erotic in and of itself."[56] The sexual component and the erotic fantasies, however, are not the only reasons behind the production of fan fiction, even though it is the one aspect that the writers of *Supernatural* focused on the most in their metatextual narratives. Because of this trend, Becky Rosen was repeatedly depicted as a cliché who remains "relentlessly gendered"[57] and focuses obsessively on semi-naked masculine bodies and sexual acts. Such a

---

[51] "4,464 Works in Fix-It," *Archive of Our Own,* https://archiveofourown.org/tags/Fix-It.
[52] Diana Floegel, "'Write the story you want to read': World Queering Through Slash Fiction Creation," *Journal of Documentation* 76, no. 4 (2020): 785-805. https://doi: 10.1108/JD-11-2019-0217.
[53] Cornel Sandvoss, *Fans: The Mirror of Consumption* (Cambridge: Polity Press, 2005), 156.
[54] Henrik Linden and Sara Linden, *Fans and Fan Cultures. Tourism, Consumerism and Social Media* (Cambridge: Palgrave Macmillan, 2017), 217.
[55] Anissa M. Graham, "A New Kind of Pandering. *Supernatural* and the World of Fanfiction," in *Essays on Participatory Fandom in the 21st Century,* ed. Kristin M. Barton and Jonathan Malcolm Lampley (Jefferson: McFarland, 2014), 136.
[56] Roz Kaveney, "Gen, Slash, OT3s, and Crossover–The Varieties of Fan Fiction," in *The Cult TV Books: From Star Trek to Dexter. New Approaches to TV Outside the Box,* ed. Stacey Abbott (London: I.B. Tauris, 2010), 245.
[57] Kristina Busse, "Geek Hierarchies Boundary Policing, and the Gendering of the Good Fan," *Participations: Journal of Audience and Reception Studies* 10, no. 1 (2013): 82, https://www.participations.org/10-01-06-busse.pdf.

portrayal, made as a joke, "from the comfort of the writers' room, a serious position of power"[58] reduces the overall role played by fan fiction in self-exploration, which emerges in the production of fix-it fics.

When the source material fails to deliver positive representation, the study and deconstruction of LGBTQ+ relationships in fan fiction leads to "a productive alignment with gay activism."[59] The lack of marketing and capitalistic value of fan productions allow authors to produce queer positive narratives that do not depend on the standards dictated by cis and heterosexual media. This freedom also leads to the possibility of taking the characters out of their original narrative to focus on one aspect exclusively, either by removing characters that seem irrelevant to the journey or ignoring socio-cultural conflicts that are no longer felt close in time. As a result, Destiel fan fiction does not necessarily feature a version of Dean Winchester who moves past his life as a hunter, nor does it involve a separation of the two brothers, something that the show presented as the characters' ultimate objective.

The focus on the LGBTQ+ experience, too, is taken out of its original historical moment. This action allows authors and readers to mediate the "process of coming out to themselves"[60] as people's sexual identities and struggles are ascribed to the characters, validating their own experiences. Because of this approach, Dean Winchester and Castiel are allowed to be gay, bisexual, transexual, or even asexual, notwithstanding the potentiality of discourse that may emerge from such interpretations[61] and the limitations imposed by the show's original hyper-masculine and homophobic world. In doing so, the "joyful and cathartic"[62] narratives defy the imposition of contentedness dictated by entertainment media[63] by allowing the authors to write content that is catered first and foremost to themselves and other LGBTQ+ individuals. Consequently, the sense of community and "collective identity"[64] that fan fiction creates is reinforced. Fans "rewrite and reinterpret events in the story to suit the desire of

---

[58] Felschow, "(Dis)empowerment and (Mis)representation of Cult Fandom in *Supernatural*," para. 6.6.

[59] Mark Duffett, *Understanding Fandom. An Introduction to the Study of Media Fan Culture* (London and New York: Bloomsbury, 2013), 294.

[60] Duffett, *Understanding Fandom*, 294.

[61] Alwaysanoriginal, "I keep seeing posts that are…," *Tumblr*, July 23, 2022, https://alwaysanoriginal.tumblr.com/post/690624076003393536/i-keep-seeing-posts-that-are-like-interpretations.

[62] Floegel, "World Queering Through Slash Fiction Creation," 792.

[63] Diana Floegel and Kaitlin L. Costello, "Entertainment Media and the Information Practices of Queer Individuals," *Library and Information Science Research* 41, no. 1 (2019): 31-38. https://doi: 10.1108/JD-11-2019-0217.

[64] Henry Jenkins, *Textual Poachers. Television Fans and Participatory Culture* (New York and London: Routledge, 1992), 157.

the writer,"[65] modeling them after "positive imagery [...] motivated by the impulse to orient itself towards the future"[66] rather than the show's original discourses inherited by the AIDS crisis for which homosexuality was tied to monstrousness and shame.[67]

This approach is tied to the correction of canon and the production of content that aims to depict LGBTQ relationships as respectable. These stories are set after the events of the show, and every problem is expressed out loud, in a rather didactic manner, to exemplify healthy relationships both in the case of Dean and Castiel[68] and other queer pairings. For this reason, the characters are often written in situations that force them to explicitly address "their many, many years of trauma and misunderstandings"[69] and apologize for past instances of dismissal, deferral, or violence that the show left unaddressed. For example, this occurred in the infamous case of "Goodbye Stranger," in which Dean Winchester's question, "what broke the connection?"[70] never received a proper answer. The show, in short, might not allow any of the characters to voice all their thoughts and truths, "but fanfic writers do"[71] because of their awareness of the main prerogatives of the show's largely female and LGBTQ+ audience.

Conclusions

This chapter sets out the fix-it fic genre within the *Supernatural* fandom, particularly within the Destiel subsection of it. The show has long entered popular culture as the last behemoth of queerbaiting, racism, and misogyny. Even though its narrative partially resists such an interpretation, fans are on an ongoing quest to fix the source material. This push for social change and more positive and flattering representation is visible in the number of stories that are labeled or can be labeled as fix-it fic. This genre aims to challenge the show's

---

[65] Marianne MacDonald, "*Harry Potter* and the Fan Fiction Phenom," *The Gay and Lesbian Review Worldwide* 13, no. 1 (2006): 28. https://glreview.org/article/article-1032/.
[66] Dion Kagan, *Positive Images: Gay Men and HIV/AIDS in the Culture of 'Post Crisis'* (London: I.B. Tauris, 2018), 202.
[67] Harry M. Benshoff, *Monsters in the Closet: Homosexuality and the Horror Film* (Manchester: Manchester UP, 1997), 3.
[68] Rainbowtyrant, "Ok so I did it with the previous fic...," *Tumblr*, March 7, 2023, https://www.tumblr.com/rainbowtyrant/711158071715643392/ok-so-i-did-it-with-the-previous-fic-i-read.
[69] Profoundbondfanfic, "Heart Shaped Box," *Tumblr*, March 10, 2023, https://profoundbondfanfic.tumblr.com/post/711436515627171840/heart-shaped-box.
[70] *Supernatural*, season 8, episode 17, "Goodbye Stranger," directed by Thomas J. Wright, written by Robbie Thompson, featuring Jensen Ackles and Misha Collins, aired March 20, 2013, The CW, 36:23.
[71] Orphicdean, "The show might not allow..." *Tumblr*, July 22, 2022, https://orphicdean.tumblr.com/post/690480228666048512/the-show-might-not-allow-dean-to-speak-but-fanfic.

White, heteronormative, and masculine point of view through the reappropriation and imposition of explicitly queer narratives. These pieces of fan fiction are centered on happiness and honesty, discarding the show's coding and its embrace of discourses that emerged in the 1980s during the AIDS crisis. As such, fan-produced content is closer to "contemporary expectations"[72] and actively manages to fulfill them. There is, however, a downside to this. Fan fiction writing as a "social activity"[73] aims to please and attempts to maintain a careful and respectful tone to avoid falling into any 'problematic' content. Characters are always forward in what they say, their feelings are never mediated by anything, and neither is sexual attraction, which, within the show, was often coded through violence. While not a problem per se, the overtly politically correct content falls back onto itself by depicting a limited number of experiences and thus reveals itself as "a temporary fix,"[74] even in fan fiction. The connotations of the term fix-it evoke a series of expectations for fans that ultimately lead them to embrace a black-and-white mentality for the sake of purity culture. The condemnation of the deviation from the respectful norm in favor of embracing more complex storylines or simply a different approach to inherently multifaceted experiences may ultimately lead to vitriolic exchanges and possible mob mentality or the creation of a new status quo. The right not to lean into specific tropes is not reprehensible nor a disheartening instance of people humanizing corporations[75] instead of siding with minorities and taking on the role of "instigators of political and social change."[76] Rather, it may simply be the proposition of different approaches to the norm and different means by which to challenge it.

Bibliography

"4,464 Works in Fix-It." *Archive of Our own.* Accessed March 13, 2023. https://archiveofourown.org/tags/Fix-It.

Alwaysanoriginal. "I keep seeing posts that are…" *Tumblr.* July 23, 2022. https://alwaysanoriginal.tumblr.com/post/690624076003393536/i-keep-seeing-posts-that-are-like-interpretations.

---

[72] McDermott, "The Broken Promise of Queerbaiting," 849.
[73] Jenkins, *Textual Poachers*, 157.
[74] Jonina Anderson-Lopez et al., "Tug of War: Social Media, Cancel Culture, and Diversity for *Girls* and *The 100*," *Kome* 9, no. 1 (2021): 84. https://doi: 10.17646/KOME.75672.59.
[75] Deanhisnippleisout, "why do people get personally upset when…," *Tumblr*, March 8, 2023, https://deanhisnippleisout.tumblr.com/post/711194780318711808/is-this-because-corporations-are-considered-people.
[76] Linden and Linden, *Fans and Fan Cultures*, 19.

Anderson-Lopez, Jonina, R.J. Lambert and Allison Budaj. "Tug of War: Social Media, Cancel Culture, and Diversity for *Girls* and *The 100*." *Kome* 9, no. 1 (2021): 64-84. https://doi: 10.17646/KOME.75672.59.

Aroesti, Rachel. "No Drugs, Booze, Sex or Swearing: Will *Heartstopper* Rewrite the Young Love Rulebook?" *The Guardian*. 2022. Accessed February 1, 2023. https://www.theguardian.com/tv-and-radio/2022/mar/18/no-drugs-booze-sex-or-swearing-will-heartstopper-rewrite-the-young-love-rulebook.

Askwith, Ivan, Britta Lundin and Aja Romano. "Industry/Fan Relations: A Conversation." In *The Routledge Companion to Media Fandom*, edited by Melissa A. Click and Suzanne Scott, 365-380. London and New York: Routledge, 2018.

Bennett, Eve. *Gender in Post-9/11 American Apocalyptic TV. Representations of Masculinity and Femininity at the End of the World*. London: Bloomsbury Academic, 2019.

Benshoff, Henry M. *Monsters in the Closet: Homosexuality and the Horror Film*. Manchester: Manchester UP, 1997.

Blake, Linnie. "All Hell Breaks Loose: *Supernatural*, Gothic Neoliberalism and the American Self." *Horror Studies* 6, no. 2 (2015): 225-238. https://doi: 10.1386/host.6.2.225_1.

Boulware, Taylor. "Fascination/Frustration: Slash Fandom, Genre, and Queer Uptake." Order No. 10289659, University of Washington, 2017. https://www.proquest.com/dissertations-theses/fascination-frustration-slash-fandom-genre-queer/docview/1942503674/se-2.

Bridges, Elizabeth. "A Genealogy of Queerbaiting: Legal Codes, Production Codes, 'Bury Your Gays' and *The 100* Mess." *Journal of Fandom Studies* 6, no. 2 (2018): 115-132. https:// doi: 10.1386/jfs.6.2.115_1.

Bundibird. "Someone go wake Eric up…" *Tumblr*. February 14, 2021. https://bundibird.tumblr.com/post/643134532923621376/someone-go-wake-eric-up-hes-running-late-hes.

Busse, Kristina. "Geek Hierarchies Boundary Policing, and the Gendering of the Good Fan." *Participations: Journal of Audience and Reception Studies* 10, no. 1 (2013): 73-91. https://www.participations.org/10-01-06-busse.pdf.

Castiellesbian. "I feel like I need a glossary of terms…" *Tumblr*. December 1, 2020. https://castiellesbian.tumblr.com/post/636325192563621888/i-feel-like-i-need-a-glossary-of-terms-or-a.

Castiels-pussy. "Knock knock Kripke are you there…" *Tumblr*. February 8, 2021. https://castiels-pussy.tumblr.com/post/642553082730954752/knock-knock-kripke-are-you-there-the.

Coker, Cait, and Candence Benefiel. "The Hunter Hunted: The Portrayal of the Fan as Predator in *Supernatural*." In *Supernatural, Humanity and the Soul: On the Highway to Hell and Back*, edited by Susan A. George and Regina Hansen, 97-110. New York: Palgrave Macmillan, 2014.

Cruz, Eliel. "Fans Take *Supernatural* to Task for Queer Baiting." *Advocate*. 2014. Accessed January 25, 2023. https://www.advocate.com/bisexuality/2014/07/17/fans-take-supernatural-task-queer-baiting.

Deancritblog. "I will never understand how this fandom…" *Tumblr*. November 11, 2021. https://deancritblog.tumblr.com/post/667585107135201280/i-will-never-understand-how-this-fandom-took-an.

Deanhisnippleisout. "Why do people get personally upset when…" *Tumblr.* March 8, 2023. https://deanhisnippleisout.tumblr.com/post/711194780318711808/is-this-because-corporations-are-considered-people.

Deanwasalwaysbi. "They really were just gaslighting us…" *Tumblr.* January 27, 2021. https://deanwasalwaysbi.tumblr.com/post/641484116212252672/they-really-were-just-gaslighting-the-fandom-for-a.

Duffett, Mark. *Understanding Fandom. An Introduction to the Study of Media Fan Culture* London: Bloomsbury, 2013.

Faludi, Susan. *The Terror Dream: What 9/11 Revealed about America.* London: Atlantic Books, 2008.

Fanlore. "DeanCas100k." Last modified August 2, 2021. https://fanlore.org/wiki/DeanCas100k.

Fathallah, Judith May. *Fan Fiction and the Author.* Amsterdam: Amsterdam UP, 2017.

Felschow, Laura E. "'Hey, Check It Out, There's Actually Fans': (Dis)empowerment and (Mis)representation of Cult Fandom in *Supernatural.*" *Transformative Works and Cultures* 4 (2010).

Floegel, Diana, and Kaitlin L. Costello. "Entertainment Media and the Information Practices of Queer Individuals." *Library and Information Science Research* 41, no. 1 (2019): 31-38. https://doi: 10.1016/j.lisr.2019.01.001

Floegel, Diana. "'Write the story you want to read': World Queering Through Slash Fiction Creation." *Journal of Documentation* 76, no. 4 (2020): 785-805. https://doi: 10.1108/JD-11-2019-0217.

Gennis, Sadie. "*Supernatural* Has a Queerbaiting Problem that Needs to Stop." *TV Guide.* 2014. Accessed January 25, 2023. https://www.tvguide.com/news/supernatural-queerbaiting-destiel-1089286.

Giannini, Erin M. "'I so miss being an atheist': God, The Darkness and the Show That Wouldn't Die." In *Supernatural Out of the Box: Essays on the Metatextuality of the Series*, edited by Lisa Macklem and Dominick Grace, 28-41. Jefferson: McFarland, 2020.

Gonnerman, Annika. "'You Don't Have to Be a Monster. You Have a Choice': *Supernatural*, Free Will and the Deterministic Concept of Monstrosity." In *Supernatural Out of the Box: Essays on the Metatextuality of the Series*, edited by Lisa Macklem and Dominick Grace, 90-103. Jefferson: McFarland, 2020.

Graham, Anissa M. "A New Kind of Pandering. *Supernatural* and the World of Fanfiction." In *Fan CULTure: Essays on Participatory Fandom in the 21st Century*, edited by Kristin M. Barton and Jonathan Malcolm Lampley, 131-145. Jefferson: McFarland, 2014.

Hasnaa. "Misha and the Cast of Supernatural Talk about Destiel Going Canon," *YouTube.* Video. December 5, 2020. https://www.youtube.com/watch?v=xdPzG1yqjEU.

Izupie. "You know something big went down…" *Tumblr.* July 15, 2022. https://izupie.tumblr.com/post/687101122263040000/you-know-something-big-went-down-in-your-fandom.

Jenkins, Henry. *Textual Poachers. Television Fans and Participatory Culture.* London and New York: Routledge, 1992.

Kagan, Dion. *Positive Images: Gay Men and HIV/AIDS in the Culture of 'Post Crisis.'* London: I.B. Tauris, 2018.

Kaveney, Roz. "Gen, Slash, OT3s, and Crossover–The Varieties of Fan Fiction." In *The Cult TV Books: From Star Trek to Dexter. New Approaches to TV Outside the Box*, edited by Stacey Abbott, 243-247. London: I.B. Tauris, 2010.

Knowles, Thomas. "The Automobile as Moving Castle." In *The Gothic Tradition in Supernatural*, edited by Melissa Edmundson, 24-36. Jefferson: McFarland, 2016.

Linden, Henrik, and Sara Linden. *Fans and Fan Cultures. Tourism, Consumerism and Social Media.* New York: Palgrave Macmillan, 2017.

MacDonald, Marianne. "*Harry Potter* and the Fan Fiction Phenom." *The Gay and Lesbian Review Worldwide* 13, no. 1 (2006): 28-30. https://glreview.org/article/article-1032/.

McDermott, Michael. "The Broken Promise of Queerbaiting: Happiness and Futurity in Politics of Queer Representation." *International Journal of Cultural Studies* 24, no. 5 (2020): 844-859. https://doi: 10.1177/1367877920984170.

Micarelli, N. "Casual Homophobia at *Supernatural* Conventions Just Won't Die." *The Mary Sue*. 2021. Accessed January 25, 2023. https://www.themarysue.com/casual-homophobia-at-supernatural-conventions-just-wont-die.

Ng, Eve. "Reading the Romance of Fan Cultural Production: Music Videos of a Television Lesbian Couple." *Popular Communication* 6, no. 2 (2008): 103-121. https://doi: 10.1080/15405700701746525.

Nicol, Rhonda. "'How is this not rape-y?': Dean as Anti-Bella and Feminism without Women in *Supernatural*." In *Supernatural, Humanity and the Soul. On the Highway to Hell and Back*, edited by Susan A. George and Regina Hansen, 155-167. New York: Palgrave Macmillan, 2014.

Omegaphobe. "Eric Kripke 2005…" *Tumblr*. March 12, 2022. https://omegaphobe.tumblr.com/post/678560116859174912/eric-kripke-2005-im-gonna-make-a-show.

Orphicdean. "The show might not allow…" *Tumblr*. July 22, 2022. https://orphicdean.tumblr.com/post/690480228666048512/the-show-might-not-allow-dean-to-speak-but-fanfic.

Perlukafarin. "I can't get over dean/castiel…" *Tumblr*. August 4, 2021. https://perlukafarinn.tumblr.com/post/658597441676935168/i-got-curious-about-this-too-so-i-went-through.

Profoundbondfanfic. "Heart Shaped Box." *Tumblr*. March 10, 2023. https://profoundbondfanfic.tumblr.com/post/711436515627171840/heart-shaped-box.

Quinn, Eliza. "*Supernatural* Spanish Dub Confession Scene." *YouTube*. Video. November 25, 2020. https://www.youtube.com/watch?v=0Jsb6S1IkJw.

Rainbowtyrant. "Ok so I did it with the previous fic…" Tumblr. March 7, 2023. https://www.tumblr.com/rainbowtyrant/711158071715643392/ok-so-i-did-it-with-the-previous-fic-i-read-and.

Sandvoss, Cornel. *Fans: The Mirror of Consumption.* Cambridge: Polity Press, 2005.

Seriously. "Misha Collins Révèle Tout Sur la Relation Dean/Castiel #SHORT." *YouTube*. Video. April 1, 2022. https://www.youtube.com/shorts/FEwSuGqAKg0.

Shinelikethunder. "Congratulations to the CW's Supernatural…" *Tumblr*. November 8, 2022. https://shinelikethunder.tumblr.com/post/700318812697919488/congratulations-to-the-cws-supernatural-season.

Suncaptor. "One thing I do think is important to talk about in supernatural…" *Tumblr.* August 12, 2022. https://www.tumblr.com/suncaptor/692362692361699328/one-thing-i-do-think-is-important-to-talk-about-in?source=share.

Supernatural. Season 8, episode 17. "Goodbye Stranger." Directed by Thomas J. Wright, written by Robbie Thompson, featuring Jensen Ackles and Misha Collins. Aired March 20, 2013, The CW.

———. Season 10, episode 5, "Fan Fiction." Directed by Phil Sgriccia, written by Robbie Thompson, featuring Jensen Ackles, and Jared Padalecki. Aired November 11, 2014, The CW.

———. Season 15, episode 18, "Despair." Directed by Richard Speight Jr., written by Robert Berens, featuring Jensen Ackles, Misha Collins. Aired November 5, 2020, The CW.

T., Deirdre. "*Supernatural*'s Legacy: The Trauma of Silence." *Buzzfeed.* 2020. Accessed February 2, 2023. https://www.buzzfeed.com/deirdre-t/supernaturalas-legacy-the-trauma-of-silence-1b17yhc5ye.

Wilhelm, Kelli. "'Where's the pie?' Nostalgic and Apocalyptic Foodways in *Supernatural.*" In *Supernatural Out of the Box: Essays on the Metatextuality in the Series*, edited by Lisa Macklem and Dominick Grace. Jefferson: McFarland, 2020.

Wilkinson, Julie. "The Epic Love Story of *Supernatural* and Fanfic." In *Fic: Why Fanfic Is Taking Over the World*, edited by Annie Jamison. Dallas: Smart Pop, 2013.

Zubernis, Lynn, and Katherine Larsen. *Fandom at the Crossroads: Celebration, Shame and Fan/Producer Relationships.* Cambridge: Cambridge Scholars, 2012.

Chapter 7

"'This is all I ever wanted for you, Will. For both of us.' 'It's beautiful.'": *Hannibal* Post-Canon Fics and Queer Futurity

Jamie MacGregor
Independent Scholar

Abstract: In this article, MacGregor uses the fix-it fic to examine queer futurity, specifically through the lens of the television show *Hannibal*. They argue that imagining utopias create positive futurity and offers a hopeful outlook for queer relationships, specifically between the characters Hannibal and Will Graham. Looking specifically at the finale, MacGregor suggests that fix-it fics create Utopias to demonstrate that positive futurities afford queer characters a hopeful future, and satisfying relationships, despite heteronormative ideas of futurity within society.

Keywords: queer futurity, positive futurity, negative futurity, utopia, *Hannibal*, hope, *AO3*, tags, fix-it fics.

***

Queer theory, much like any field of study, has several very distinct schools of thought, often in conversation with each other. In the wake of the AIDS epidemic, there was a turn towards antirelationality and negativity, with one of the foundational texts being Lee Edelman's 2004 book, *No Future: Queer Theory and the Death Drive*.[1] Edelman argues that futurity is based on heterosexual reproduction and that it was not meant for queer people. However, this stance was not without criticism. In his 2009 book, *Cruising Utopia: The Then and There of Queer Futurity*,[2] José Esteban Muñoz directly addresses Edelman's work, saying that while he admires the argument, "antirelationality approaches

---

[1] Lee Edelman, *No Future: Queer Theory and the Death Drive* (Durham, NC: Duke University Press, 2004).
[2] José Esteban Muñoz, *Cruising Utopia: The Then and There of Queer Futurity*, 10th Anniversary Edition (New York: New York University Press, 2019).

to queer theory are romances of the negative."[3] Instead, Muñoz argues that hope, futurity, and images of utopia are essential for queer people since they can help build a new and better world.

Despite now having a cult following, Bryan Fuller's *Hannibal* (2013-2015)[4] was threatened with cancellation every season before it was announced on June 22, 2015, that the third season would be its last. The show's final episode, 'The Wrath of the Lamb,'[5] and its subsequent cancellation can be read with Edelman and Muñoz in mind as it struggles to pick a side – negativity or futurity. However, the literal cliffhanger ending, which finally saw Will accepting his relationship with Hannibal, forced fans to turn to fan fiction for closure and allowed for a reconciliation of these opposing readings. Thus, a range of fix-it fics, referred to as 'post-fall' fics, spawned on *Archive of Our own* (*AO3*), creating, among others, the 'Post-Fall' and 'Post-Episode s03e13 The Wrath of the Lamb' tags, with the latter being one of the most popular additional tags. These fics explore Will and Hannibal's relationship after the final episode, allowing fans to give Hannibal and Will any future they want, and imagine thousands of utopias where they could be allowed to be together. In other words, these fics are a specific form of the fix-it fic. Thus, fans then create the queer utopia they want to see as they draw attention to the reality that our current society is often hostile to queer people and relationships.

First, I will introduce the pairing of Will and Hannibal to provide some background before discussing the final episode of *Hannibal*. I will examine the finale using Edelman's concept of negative futurity and then Muñoz's idea of queer futurity, which I argue is a much more productive way of reading the text because of the hopeful tone of the ending. Moreover, a reading using Muñoz better accounts for the popularity of fix-it fics after the show, focusing on Will and Hannibal's future. Finally, I will argue that it is through the category of 'post-fall' fix-it fics that queer futurity is fully realized and becomes a form of activism in its own right. I will discuss the 'post-fall' fix-it fics of MissDisoriental, specifically a *Hannibal* fan fiction writer with five stories of over 14,000 kudos individually. Their two post-fall fix-it fics, "The Shape of Me Will Always be You"[6] and "The Very Secret Diary of Will Graham,"[7] are among the most popular *Hannibal* fics on *AO3*, and they choose to write in the first person, which is, broadly speaking, less common in fan fiction.

---

[3] Muñoz, *Cruising Utopia*, 11.
[4] Bryan Fuller, *Hannibal*, performed by Mads Mikkelsen and Hugh Dancy (2013-2015; Sony Pictures Television), TV Show.
[5] *Hannibal*, season 3, episode 13, "The Wrath of the Lamb," directed by Michael Rymer, written by Bryan Fuller, aired August 27, 2015 on *NBC*.
[6] MissDisoriental, "The Shape of Me Will Always be You," *Archive of Our Own*, July 23, 2016, https://archiveofourown.org/works/5367389/chapters/85748575.
[7] MissDisoriental, "The Very Secret Diary of Will Graham," *Archive of Our Own*, November 23, 2018, https://archiveofourown.org/works/11159646/chapters/24904593.

Much like many popular fandom ships, the series' main ship, Hannigram or Murder Husbands (Will Graham and Hannibal Lecter), accidentally came around. Though a small number of fics were published on *AO3* tagged Hannibal Lecter/Will Graham before the show's premiere, two were published in 2013 prior to the pilot episode and acknowledged the series. In "there's beauty in your venom," by the author postcardmystery, who says in their note that the fic "was written pre-series, so this is no longer how [they] would necessarily characterize Will or Hannibal"[8] [9] and author ohfreckle, expresses excitement for the series in their fic, "You'll only see my reflection."[10] However, Fuller did not initially intend for Graham and Lecter to become romantic. He says that this happened naturally because of the chemistry between Mads Mikkelsen (Hannibal) and Hugh Dancy (Will) and that he "was aware of the fan community wanting a sexualization between the characters and [he] was entertained by that greatly and got a kick out of it certainly."[11] Indeed, *AO3* suggests that fans were shipping the two characters from episode one, with the first fic appearing on April 5, 2013, just one day after the series premiered in the U.S. It is hard to ignore the homoerotic subtext that exists in the show between the two main characters. Though it is not said as much in the text, Fuller has also said that he sees Hannibal as pansexual and that "Will Graham is a heterosexual character, but sexuality is fluid."[12] The show does seem to have been influenced by fan interaction to a degree, though; in an interaction between Freddie Lounds (the reporter behind 'Tattlecrime' who is determined to show the world that Will is a killer) and Will, it is revealed that Freddie wrote an article calling Will and Hannibal 'murder husbands,'[13] a ship name that was popularized by the fandom prior to this.

Thomas Harris is the original creator of Hannibal Lecter, who first appeared in the novel *Red Dragon*[14] in 1981 along with Will Graham. Lecter would later appear in three more novels by Harris, including the famous *The Silence of the Lambs*. Fuller has gone as far as to describe the show as being fan fiction of

---

[8] postcardmystery, "there's beauty in your venom," *Archive of Our Own*, March 17, 2013, https://archiveofourown.org/works/725049.
[9] This was presumably added after the series had started airing.
[10] ohfreckle, "You'll only see my reflection," *Archive of Our Own*, April 1, 2013, https://archiveofourown.org/works/744755.
[11] Ryan Lattanzio, "'Hannibal': Bryan Fuller Teases a Pansexual Mads Mikkelsen for Possible Season 4," *IndieWire*, July 11, 2020, https://www.indiewire.com/2020/07/hannibal-season-4-pansexual-mads-mikkelsen-1234572817/.
[12] Lattanzio, "'Hannibal': Bryan Fuller Teases…" 2020.
[13] *Hannibal*, season 3, episode 9, "…And the Woman Clothed with the Sun," directed by John Dahl, written by Bryan Fuller, aired July 30, 2015, on City.
[14] Thomas Harris, *Red Dragon* (New York, NY: G. P. Putnams, 1981).

Harris'[15] novels, namely *Red Dragon* (though he does pull from all of the novels), while also sharing fan art and engaging in conversation with fans on *Twitter*. As a creator, Fuller is very supportive of all work from fans, saying that "this fanbase that has taken this show, made it their own and created parallel worlds of fan fiction to this work of fan fiction."[16] Indeed, Fuller's adaptation acts as an 'official' fix-it fic of Harris' novels, which were notably homophobic and transphobic. Jeff Casey notes that the novels "participate in the conflation of queerness, disability, and criminal violence,"[17] which is something that *Hannibal* consciously avoids.

In Mary Kate Messimer's article, "Did You Just Smell Me?': Queer Embodiment in NBC's *Hannibal*," she argues that *Hannibal* is "an expression of Hollywood's erasure of queerness in film,"[18] which is why it seems to end with the death of both main characters. She also links *Hannibal* and Lee Edelman's *No Future: Queer Theory and the Death Drive*, an emblematic text of the antirelationality turn that queer theory took in the early 2000s in the wake of the AIDS crisis. Edelman argues that, for politics and society, the source of futurity is heteronormativity and the figure of the Child. Therefore, to embrace queerness is to reject the concept of futurity, as it was never meant for queers. He also asserts that stepping outside of the realm of politics is necessary since any attempt to reform it will not be enough; consequently, we must embrace negativity and the death drive.[19] Edelman asserts that by embracing the death drive, we can therefore embrace queer desire and negative futurity, which can be a source of Lacanian *jouissance* beyond the restrictive limitations of society. However, this is an unsatisfying answer to a complicated problem. It would be much more productive to create a future in which queer people can safely live – *Hannibal* seems to hint at this with the post-credit scene that suggests Hannibal and Will survive. This is fully realized in post-fall fix-it fics, which, by their very nature, only exist when fans feel that something needs fixing.

---

[15] Ross Scarano, "Bryan Fuller Knows You're Reading into '*Hannibal*'s' Homoeroticism, and He Thinks It's Hilarious," *Complex*, September 16, 2014, https://www.complex.com/pop-culture/2014/09/bryan-fuller-hannibal-interview-slash-fiction.
[16] Laura Prudom, "'*Hannibal*' Finale Postmortem: Bryan Fuller Breaks Down That Bloody Ending and Talks Revival Chances," *Variety*, August 29, 2015, https://variety.com/2015/tv/news/hannibal-finale-season-4-movie-revival-ending-spoilers-1201581424/.
[17] Jeff Casey, "Queer Cannibals and Deviant Detectives: Subversion and Homosocial Desire in NBC's *Hannibal*," *Quarterly Review of Film and Video*, 32, 6 (2015): 550-567. https://doi.org/10.1080/10509208.2015.1035617.
[18] MaryKate Messimer, "'Did You Just Smell Me?': Queer Embodiment in NBC's *Hannibal*," *The Journal of Popular Culture* 51, no. 1 (2018): 175-193. https://doi.org/10.1111/jpcu.12632.
[19] Edelman, *No Future*, 2014.

For Messimer, *Hannibal* showcases negative futurity; for the purposes of this chapter, though, I am particularly interested in her assertion that "The Wrath of the Lamb" is a literal depiction of this rejection of futurity and embrace of the death drive. Will is at odds with his identity and his feelings for Hannibal for most of the show, but in the last episode, he embraces acceptance:

> HANNIBAL: See. This is all I ever wanted for you, Will. For both of us.
>
> WILL: It's beautiful. [20]

The two then share a tender embrace that seems to tease a kiss before Will tips them off the cliff and into the sea below. Fuller decided not to have Hannibal and Will kiss before the fall as he said, "we really went for it... but it felt like it became something else in that moment and sort of verged on fan service that felt inauthentic to me for this adaptation."[21] While it is not accurate to accuse the show of queerbaiting, Fuller's reasoning here is questionable as it leads to fans' concerns because he fails to explain *why* a kiss between Hannibal and Will felt 'inauthentic.' However, in a discussion of whether Hannibal and Will's relationship is queerbaiting or gay subtext, Jeff Casey argues that by teasing a kiss Fuller creates potentiality as "this is not a dead end, but a beginning. The show invites us to innovate within this otherwise arid conceptual space."[22] Thus, fans can fully conceptualize the murder husbands' relationship in post-fall fix-it fics.

As the couple falls off the cliff, the camera slowly pans toward the bottom, and there are no bodies. Then, the credits roll, and the viewer is left wondering if the murder husbands survived. In embracing Hannibal and his queerness as a result, Will rejects heteronormativity, leaving his wife and stepchild behind. However, he throws himself and Hannibal off the cliff — he does not see a future for them and embraces negativity and the death drive, as Edelman suggests. Messimer agrees with this reading, saying:

> Will and Hannibal embrace, but in doing so, they also embrace the death drive; in accepting his queer desire, Will recognizes that there is no place in society for him to be with Hannibal. The violent, penetrative killing of the Red Dragon and the men's tumble into the abyss can be

---

[20] *Hannibal*, season 3, episode 13.
[21] Alex E. Jung, "Bryan Fuller on That *Hannibal* Finale and the Show's Campy, Sensual Undertones," *Vulture*, August 30, 2015, http://www.vulture.com/2015/08/bryan-fuller-hannibal-finale-campy-sensual.html.
[22] Jeff Casey, "Afterthoughts on 'Queer Cannibals and Deviant Detectives,' Inspired by *Hannibal* Season 3," *Quarterly Review of Film and Video*, 35:6 (2018): 583-600.

read as literal representations of Edelman's jouissance…The violent consummation of their strange relationship forces them to realize that there is no acceptance and no future for them within society.[23]

The show's unexpected cancellation also reinforces this link between queerness and the death drive, as season three was more explicitly queer than the previous two, filled with romantic lines and even the confirmation that Hannibal loves Will. Unfortunately, fans would never see their relationship play out due to the show's cancellation. Fuller's original plan for the series was for seven seasons, which later changed to just six. Given its success, it was a surprise to many when NBC did not renew the series for a fourth season. Cast members have been quoted as saying they were surprised by the cancellation and were much more worried about being renewed for seasons two and three. Mikkelsen explains, "The third season, after that, we were *pretty sure* we're getting a fourth. That was not the feeling after the first or the second. But the third [season], we were pretty sure."[24]

This all reads as a rather bleak ending, though Messimer argues that there is hope in negative futurity, for she mentions the potentiality behind Will and Hannibal's relationship, "viewers do not see a kiss, leaving the men's love suspended in an extended moment of utopian possibility; it does not happen, but it could, it might, it seems to be happening."[25] Messimer argues further that their "embrace of the abyss" allows them to escape the limitations of society and embrace "the utopian and infinite possibilities of what is real."[26] However, this presence of hope is notably lacking in Edelman's *No Future*, a criticism that Muñoz also leveled at the text,[27] yet Messimer fails to address this hopelessness. While there is hope to be found in the final episode of *Hannibal*, it is inaccurate to attribute this to Edelman's concept of negative futurity, which fails to offer a future. Instead, I argue that it is more productive to view the episode with Muñoz's idea of queer futury in mind, particularly because of the afterlife that *Hannibal* has in fan fiction, especially in post-canon fix-it fics, as Muñoz argues, writing that: "[q]ueerness is essentially about the rejection of a here and now and an insistence on potentiality or concrete possibility for another

---

[23] Messimer, "Did You Just Smell Me," 190.
[24] Will Lavin, "'*Hannibal*'s Mads Mikkelsen says show's popularity on Netflix has 'revitalised' fourth season talks," *NME*, January 29, 2021, https://www.nme.com/news/tv/hannibals-mads-mikkelsen-says-shows-popularity-on-netflix-has-revitalised-fourth-season-talks-2868300.
[25] Messimer, "Did You Just Smell Me," 189.
[26] Messimer, "Did You Just Smell Me," 190.
[27] Muñoz, *Cruising Utopia*. 92.

world."[28] Critiquing Edelman, Muñoz also argues that he fails to take race and class into account.[29] Essentially, middle-class gay men are not denied a future in the same way as queer people of color. This is equally a criticism that may be leveled at *Hannibal* since the queer characters are all white and affluent, a fact that remains true in most fix-it fics following the show. However, some authors choose to delve more into the fact that Will grew up poor, which is only mentioned in passing during the show. In post-canon fix-it fics, writers create the future that Will and Hannibal were not allowed to have, and the hope that is present in these fics gives readers a safe space to explore queer desire. There is also the sense that if Will and Hannibal, who are literal murderers, are allowed a happy ending, then there is hope for anyone. Therefore, it is through this hope that both reading and writing fix-it fics are forms of personal advocacy and activism.

In *Cruising Utopia: The Then and There of Queer Futurity*, Muñoz draws from the German idealist tradition, particularly Ernst Bloch and his treatise *The Principle of Hope*, to argue that "queerness exists for us as an ideality that can be distilled from the past and used to imagine a future. The future is queerness's domain."[30] Essentially, the world that we currently live in is hostile to queerness, so thinking of utopia allows us to critique the present and hope for a better future. In essence, creating utopias could be a form of activism as it aims to change the future for the better. Muñoz says that:

> we must dream and enact new and better pleasures, other ways of being in the world, and ultimately new worlds. Queerness is a longing that propels us onward...Queerness is the thing that lets us feel that the world is not enough, that indeed something is missing.[31]

Muñoz argues that the way that we find hope and these queer utopias is through 'cruising' art. Here, 'cruising' refers not to the traditional meaning of looking for gay sex but to the practice of "carefully cruising for the varied potentialities that may abound."[32] Given the hopeful tone of "The Wrath of the Lamb," it is a more helpful framework for analyzing the episode – particularly when considering post-canon fan fiction. Through fix-it fics, Muñoz's concepts of queer futurity and cruising for utopia are fully realized. Post-canon fan fiction for *Hannibal* exists because of the potentiality at the end of the final

---

[28] Muñoz, *Cruising Utopia*, 1.
[29] Muñoz, *Cruising Utopia*, 94.
[30] Muñoz, *Cruising Utopia*, 94.
[31] Muñoz, *Cruising Utopia*, 94.
[32] Muñoz, *Cruising Utopia*, 18.

episode, which allows fans to imagine thousands of futures and utopias for the murder husbands.

Hopeful fans will note the song that plays over the end credits of "The Wrath of the Lamb," "Love Crime" by Siouxsie, which contains the lyrics, "I will survive, live and thrive."[33] These lyrics are heard for the first time when the camera pans over the cliff. Fans are then treated to a post-credit scene with Bedelia DuMaurier (Gillian Anderson), Hannibal's therapist, sitting at a dinner table set for three. The camera shows the elaborate meal on the table before pulling back to show that Bedelia is missing a leg, implying that Will and Hannibal are about to dine on her flesh. Though we never see this pan out because of the cancellation, and Fuller has remained relatively quiet about what he had planned next, he has confirmed that Will and Hannibal survived the fall. Thus, the couple's relationship is left in a state of potentiality that allows fans to imagine how their future may have looked. There are lots of interpretations in fix-it fics of Hannibal and Will's life after the fall. However, the most popular seems to be the couple living happily together (usually in a country with no extradition treaty to the U.S.) after sorting out the various problems in their relationship, resulting in a truly utopian ending.

In the essay "Sex, Utopia, and the Queer Temporalities of Fannish Love," Alexis Lothian argues that fan fiction writers engage in queer utopia all the time, "making sexual and emotional fantasies narratively real with an explicit detail."[34] This is particularly true of fix-it fic writers as they are constantly imagining queer utopias while also offering explicit content that is free of societal judgments, allowing readers the space to explore their sexuality in varied ways, as well as see what a queer utopia might look like for them. This act itself could be viewed as a form of activism as it is attempting to show a world that allows queer people to have a happy ending. *Hannibal*'s literal cliffhanger ending has resulted in a whole sub-category of fix-it fics dedicated to exploring Will and Hannibal's life after the show, and the fandom is still very active even eight years after *Hannibal*'s finale. In a fully licensed *Hannibal* fan art book, published by Printed in Blood in 2022 and funded entirely by donations on Kickstarter, Bryan Fuller contributed a foreword, saying:

---

[33] Siouxsie, "Love Crime From The Wrath of the Lamb," recorded on 2015, produced by Brian Reitzell, track 16 on *Hannibal Season 3 Volume 2 Original Television Soundtrack*, by Brian Reitzell, Lakeshore Records, 2015, compact disk.

[34] Alexis Lothian, "Sex, Utopia, and the Queer Temporalities of Fannish Love," in *Fandom, Second Edition: Identities and Communities in a Mediated World*, edited by Jonathan Gray, Cornel Sandvoss, and C. Lee Harrington (New York, NY: New York University Press, 2017), 238-252.

The love story of Hannibal Lecter and Will Graham, anatomical and metaphysical, has evolved beyond the television narrative. It is now written by every image and every imagination. It belongs to all of us. This is our becoming. This is our story and because of our Fannibal Family, it will survive, live and thrive. This is our design.[35]

With a total of 35,900 works in the '*Hannibal* (TV)' tag of *AO3*,[36] it is safe to say that Hannibal and Will's story has evolved well beyond that of the television show precisely because of the potentiality that exists in the finale. Moreover, though the show has always had an active fandom, there was an exponential increase in the number of fics uploaded/updated in 2020 (4590 fics) and 2021 (4592 fics) compared to 2019 (2671 fics).[37] This rise in popularity corresponds with *Hannibal* being added to Netflix, but also with the Covid-19 pandemic, a time when people were seeking hope and futurity that could not be found in day-to-day life, so many turned to fiction and then fan fiction. The benefit of *AO3* is that the archive is searchable through the use of tags, defined by the site as "a keyword or phrase that provides information about a work, and can be made by anyone creating content such as works or bookmarks on the *Archive of Our own*."[38] Within this, *AO3* identifies different types of tags, but I will be discussing 'additional tags,' defined as tags that "cover any details not specified by other categories."[39] Tagging practices are not universal and are up to the author's discretion, but they are a defining feature of *AO3* and the easiest way for authors to attract readers, so they are fairly widely used. Also, alongside ongoing uploads, authors can and do delete their work, meaning that while *AO3* is the most complete archive, it is subject to change. Thus, all the information and figures provided are accurate at the time of writing.

---

[35] Bryan Fuller, "Foreword," in *Hannibal Artbook* (Los Angeles, CA: Printed in Blood, 2022), 5.
[36] *Hannibal* (TV), on *Archive of Our Own*, https://archiveofourown.org/tags/Hannibal%20(TV)/works. This number is accurate as of March 17, 2023 and includes fics that are only visible to members of *AO3*.
[37] This data can be found by filtering work in *Hannibal* (TV) by Date Updated from January 1 to December 31 of the relevant year in the format of 'From: year-month-day, To: year-month-day.'
[38] *Archive of Our Own*, FAQ, "What is a tag?," https://archiveofourown.org/faq/tags?language_id=en#whatisatag.
[39] *Archive of Our Own*, FAQ, "What are the different types of tags?," https://archiveofourown.org/faq/tags?language_id=en#tagtypes. The other categories that this refers to are: Rating, Archive Warnings, Category, Fandom, Relationships, and Characters.

In the search panel, *AO3* lists up to ten of the most used tags. Some of the most popular additional tags in '*Hannibal* (TV)' are somewhat surprising given the nature of the show, with 'Fluff' coming in at the top, followed by 'Hannibal Lecter Loves Will Graham' and 'Murder Husbands.' However, the seventh most common tag, 'Post-Episode: s03e13 The Wrath of the Lamb,' is by far the most important for my argument. This tag is just one of many used by fans to explore Will and Hannibal's relationship after the end of the series. Others include Post-Season/Series 03, Post-Canon, Post-Canon Fix-It, Post-Finale, Post-Fall (Hannibal), and Curtain Fic. However, the most popular tag among these is 'Post-Episode: s03e13 The Wrath of the Lamb' with 2,762 fics tagged.[40] Though *AO3* does group tags with the same meaning, it is done manually by 'tag wranglers,' so searching 'Post-Episode: s03e13 The Wrath of the Lamb' will only show fics with the related tags, and may not show every post-fall fix-it fic on the archive. For numbers, I will only be using the 'Post-Episode: s03e13 The Wrath of the Lamb' tag since this is the most widely used, but it should be noted that this is not the entire picture simply because finding ever post-fall fix-it fic would involve going through every work tagged '*Hannibal* (TV)' that was published after the finale to verify the content, which includes over 28,774 fics published from August 27, 2015 to now, and is not a viable option for one researcher. However, having been involved in the *Hannibal* fandom since 2013 and having read many fics, I will be using my own experience and observations to supplement my argument.

At the time of writing, the most popular *Hannibal* fic, by a large margin, describes itself as "a post-canon Hannigram fix-it fic."[41] MissDisoriental's "The Shape of Me Will Always be You" has a total of 34,316 kudos, has been translated into approximately ten languages, and has multiple fan videos, animations, fan arts, and podfics made for it. Kudos are a feature specific to *AO3* that allows readers to let a writer know that they enjoyed a fic. Notably, readers can only leave kudos on a fic once, and they cannot give kudos on every chapter.[42] This alone shows just how popular post-canon fix-it fics are in the *Hannibal* fandom, as this fic is part of a series called "Love Crime Series," which has a total of 791,829[43] words dedicated to imagining Will and Hannibal's life after the fall. Putting this word count into context, the entire *Lord of the Rings* series

---

[40] "Post-Episode: s03e13 The Wrath of the Lamb," on *Archive of Our Own*, https://archiveofourown.org/tags/PostEpisode:%20s03e13%20The%20Wrath%20of%20the%20Lamb/works.
[41] MissDisoriental, "The Shape of Me," 2016.
[42] *Archive of Our Own*, FAQ, "What is Kudos?" https://archiveofourown.org/faq/comments-and-kudos?language_id=en#whatiskudos.
[43] MissDisoriental, "Love Crime Series," *Archive of Our Own*, November 20, 2022, https://archiveofourown.org/series/2101557.

has 576,459 words.[44] The popularity of this fic alone is enough to speak to a demand among readers for queerer utopias. The fic does involve some angst, in keeping with the tone of the series, but also includes the tag 'hurt/comfort,' so it does have more hope than the show. The ending of "The Shape of Me Will Always be You" leads to the next story in the series, but Will and Hannibal are clearly happy and looking forward to their life together. This ending is not unique, as most post-fall fics are fix-it fics with a happy ending for Will and Hannibal, who are usually living comfortably in another country with fake identities, a life that is afforded to them because of Hannibal's vast fortune. However, "The Shape of Me Will Always be You" is unusual because it combines first- and second-person narration. The benefit of this is that the reader may feel more involved in the story, meaning that as well as imagining a future for Hannibal and Will, they may also imagine a better future for themselves. Despite suggesting in their author note that the second story in the series might be in the third person, MissDisoriental chose to write "The Seventh Sense,"[45] the follow-up to "The Shape of Me Will Always be You," using a similar blend of first and second person. This involvement of the reader may encourage readers to imagine, and perhaps take steps to create, a queer utopia for themselves in the real world, as well as engage in utopias based on the fiction that fix-it fic authors create. Though it is not quite as popular as its predecessor, "The Seventh Sense" is still in the top twenty '*Hannibal* (TV)' fics when sorted by kudos, proving that this style is very popular with readers. Moreover, MissDisoriental has yet another post-canon fix-it fic in the top twenty '*Hannibal* (TV)' fics, though it is much shorter and appears to exist outside of their "Love Crime Series." The tone of "The Very Secret Diary of Will Graham"[46] is more light-hearted than MissDisoriental's other post-fall fics, being tagged specifically as 'crack,' fandom slang that refers to a story with an unbelievable or ridiculous premise.[47] These stories tend to include far more humor and be less serious than others, and we assume the unbelievable premise is that Will would never write a diary. Since it is written as a diary, "The Very Secret Diary of Will Graham" keeps the first-person narration as if Will is writing it. Though Hannibal will occasionally write things, his additions are still in the first-person. This again adds to the reader's investment as they are brought closer to

---

[44] "Word Counts of the Most Popular Books in the World," *Foster Grant*, August 3, 2017, https://blog.fostergrant.co.uk/2017/08/03/word-counts-popular-books-world/#:~:text=The%20Fellowship%20of%20the%20Ring,including%20The%20Hobbit)%20–%20576%2C459%20words.

[45] MissDisoriental, "The Seventh Sense," *Archive of Our Own*, November 20, 2022, https://archiveofourown.org/works/28649502/chapters/70227522.

[46] MissDisoriental, "The Very Secret Diary of Will Graham," 2018.

[47] "Crack," *Fanlore*, February 27, 2023, https://fanlore.org/wiki/Crack.

the characters and the story, much like in "The Shape of Me Will Always be You." The light-hearted tone of Will's diary also perhaps adds more to the sense of a queer utopia as it is a generally more upbeat story; it is a world where Will can easily fix and overcome the problems in his and Hannibal's relationship simply by reading *Cosmopolitan*. Nevertheless, the fic is still, at its core, about imagining a better future for Hannibal and Will – one where they are finally allowed to be happy together, and this is a running theme of *Hannibal* fan fiction in general, but particularly post-fall fix-it fics.

Many post-canon fix-it fics also focus on Hannibal and Will's daily life together, which is particularly interesting as Muñoz, drawing on Roland Barthes, says that the utopian may be found in the quotidian.[48] The importance of the every day, according to Muñoz, is that it can provide "a looking back at a no-longer-conscious that provides an effective enclave in the present that staves off the sense of 'bad feelings' that mark the affective disjuncture of being queer in straight time."[49] Essentially, it can be a temporary escapism from a world that is hostile to queerness. However, this utopia doesn't have to be completely otherworldly as it is arguably through the every day that it becomes more plausible. Muñoz also argues that a turn back to 'a no-longer-conscious' is the route to the 'not-yet-here' and that the root of this turn to the past critiques the present due to a 'desire for futurity.'[50] Using this framework, where "The Wrath of the Lamb" contains a utopian impulse, post-canon fix-it fics are performative since they have an explicit desire for the utopian – it *does* utopia and futurity rather than simply suggesting it or hoping for it, making it a queer sort of activism. Thus, *Hannibal*'s finale may suggest queer futurity, but it is only through post-fall fix-it fics that this futurity is fully realized.

As Muñoz says, the world, as it is, is hostile to queerness. Queer people are frequently not afforded happiness or even a future. Therefore, it is essential that we have hope as we look for and create our own queer utopias. In doing so, we make the present more livable and stive to improve the future. Art is one way that we may 'cruise' for these utopias, and I have argued that the last episode of *Hannibal* has the potentiality for this; however, it is in post-fall fix-it fics that this potentiality is realized. I primarily discussed the work of MissDisoriental, simply because she is one of the most popular writers in the fandom, and the popularity of their fix-it fics speaks to a desire in the Hannibal fandom for a queer utopia for Hannibal and Will, but also for the reader due to the use of

---

[48] Muñoz, *Cruising Utopia*, 22.
[49] Muñoz, *Cruising Utopia*, 24. For a detailed explanation and analysis of queer vs. straight time, see J. Jack Halberstam, *In a Queer Time & Place: Transgender Bodies, Subcultural Lives* (New York, NY: NYU Press, 2005).
[50] Muñoz, *Cruising Utopia*, 30.

first-person narration. Moreover, I would encourage further reading than just these fics since there is a wide array of fix-it fics where Will and Hannibal get to have their happy ending. By imagining a utopia for these characters, readers are also engaging with what queer futurity may look like for others in the real world and thus take part in their own form of activism.

Bibliography

Archive of Our own, FAQ. "What is a tag?." https://archiveofourown.org/faq/tags?language_id=en#whatisatag.

———. "What are the different types of tags?." https://archiveofourown.org/faq/tags?language_id=en#tagtypes.

———. "What is Kudos?." https://archiveofourown.org/faq/comments-and-kudos?language_id=en#whatiskudos.

Casey, Jeff. "Queer Cannibals and Deviant Detectives: Subversion and Homosocial Desire in NBC's *Hannibal*." *Quarterly Review of Film and Video*, 32:6 (2015): 550-567. https://doi.org/10.1080/10509208.2018.1499346

———. "Afterthoughts on 'Queer Cannibals and Deviant Detectives,' Inspired by *Hannibal* Season 3." *Quarterly Review of Film and Video*, 35:6 (2018): 583-600.

"Crack." *Fanlore*, February 27, 2023. https://fanlore.org/wiki/Crack.

Edelman, Lee. *No Future: Queer Theory and the Death Drive*. Durham, NC: Duke University Press, 2004.

Fuller, Bryan. "Foreword" In *Hannibal Artbook*. Los Angeles, CA: Printed in Blood, 2022.5.

Halberstam, J. Jack. *In a Queer Time & Place: Transgender Bodies, Subcultural Lives*. New York, NY: NYU Press, 2005.

Hannibal. Written by Bryan Fuller. Performed by Mads Mikkelsen and Hugh Dancy. 2013-2015, Sony Pictures Television. TV Show.

———. Season 3, episode 9, "…And the Woman Clothed with the Sun." Directed by John Dahl. Written by Bryan Fuller. Aired July 30, 2015 on *City*.

———. Season 3, episode 13, "The Wrath of the Lamb." Directed by Michael Rymer. Written by Bryan Fuller. Aired 27 August, 2015 on *City*.

"*Hannibal* (TV)." *Archive of Our own*. https://archiveofourown.org/tags/Hannibal%20(TV)/works.

Harris, Thomas. *Red Dragon*. New York, NY: G. P. Putnams, 1981.

Jung, E. Alex. "Bryan Fuller on That Hannibal Finale and the Show's Campy, Sensual Undertones." *Vulture*, August 30, 2015. http://www.vulture.com/2015/08/bryan-fuller-hannibal-finale-campy-sensual.html.

Lattanzio, Ryan. "'*Hannibal*': Bryan Fuller Teases a Pansexual Mads Mikkelsen for Possible Season 4." *IndieWire*, July 11, 2020. https://www.indiewire.com/2020/07/hannibal-season-4-pansexual-mads-mikkelsen-1234572817/.

Lavin, Will. "'Hannibal's' Mads Mikkelsen says show's popularity on Netflix has 'revitalised' forth season talks." *NME*, January 29, 2021. https://www.nme.com/news/tv/hannibals-mads-mikkelsen-says-shows-popularity-on-netflix-has-revitalised-fourth-season-talks-2868300.

Lothian, Alexis. "Sex, Utopia, and the Queer Temporalities of Fannish Love." In *Fandom, Second Edition: Identities and Communities in a Mediated World*. Edited by Jonathan Gray, Cornel Sandvoss, and C. Lee Harrington (New York, NY: New York University Press, 2017), 238-252.

Messimer, Kate. "'Did You Just Smell Me?': Queer Embodiment in NBC's *Hannibal*." *The Journal of Popular Culture* 51, no. 1 (2018): 175-193. https://doi.org/10.1111/jpcu.12632.

MissDisoriental. "The Shape of Me Will Always be You." *Archive of Our own*. July 23, 2016. https://archiveofourown.org/works/5367389/chapters/85748575.

———. "The Very Secret Diary of Will Graham." *Archive of Our own*. November 23, 2018. https://archiveofourown.org/works/11159646/chapters/24904593.

———. "Love Crime Series." *Archive of Our own*. November 20, 2022. https://archiveofourown.org/series/2101557.

———. "The Seventh Sense." *Archive of Our own*. November 20, 2022. https://archiveofourown.org/works/28649502/chapters/70227522.

Muñoz, José Esteban. *Cruising Utopia: The Then and There of Queer Futurity*, 10th Anniversary Edition. New York: New York University Press, 2019.

ohfreckle. "You'll only see my reflection." *Archive of Our own*. April 1, 2013. https://archiveofourown.org/works/744755.

postcardmystery. "there's beauty in your venom." *Archive of Our own*. March 17, 2013. https://archiveofourown.org/works/725049.

Prudom, Laura. "'*Hannibal*' Finale Postmortem: Bryan Fuller Breaks Down That Bloody Ending and Talks Revival Chances." *Variety*, August 29, 2015. https://variety.com/2015/tv/news/hannibal-finale-season-4-movie-revival-ending-spoilers-1201581424/.

"Post-Episode: s03e13 The Wrath of the Lamb." *Archive of Our own*, https://archiveofourown.org/tags/Post-Episode:%20s03e13%20The%20Wrath%20of%20the%20Lamb/works.

Scarano, Ross. "Bryan Fuller Knows You're Reading into 'Hannibal's' Homoeroticism, and He Thinks It's Hilarious." *Complex*, September 16, 2014. https://www.complex.com/pop-culture/2014/09/bryan-fuller-hannibal-interview-slash-fiction.

Siouxsie. "Love Crime From The Wrath of the Lamb." Recorded 2015. Produced by Brian Reitzell. Track 16 on *Hannibal Season 3 Volume 2 Original Television Soundtrack*, by Brian Reitzell. Lakeshore Records, 2015. Compact disk.

"Word Counts of the Most Popular Books in the World." *Foster Grant*, August 3, 2017. https://blog.fostergrant.co.uk/2017/08/03/word-counts-popular-books-world/#:~:text=The%20Fellowship%20of%20the%20Ring,including%20The%20Hobbit)%20–%20576%2C459%20words

Chapter 8

Fixing 'The Fixer': Fan Fictional Representations of *Wentworth*'s Joan Ferguson in Lesbian Relationships

Kristy Smith
York University

Abstract: In this article, Smith uses the fix-it fic to examine one of the main characters, Joan, in the television series *Wentworth*. She demonstrates how fanfiction writers provide Joan with the emotional and sensual qualities that she is deprived of in the show through exploring the complexities of sapphic desire and the female gaze to frame fix-it fics as a means of reparative reading. In the case of Joan's character, Kristy argues that this theoretical lens allows fans to create a world for Joan where lesbianism is rooted in happiness and contentment, rather than in the traumatic rejection that defines Joan's character throughout the series.

Keywords: sapphic, female gaze, lesbian, reparative, trauma, rejection, fanon, *Wentworth*, AO3, tags, fix-it fics.

***

As a medium historically enjoyed by queer readers and writers, fix-it fics offer useful insight into how fans reimagine canonical stories as a way of *doing better* for LGBTQ+ characters. This chapter will explore how the canonically lesbian character Joan Ferguson, the infamous Governor-turned-prisoner on the television show *Wentworth*, is conceptualized in lesbian fix-it fics.[1] Nicknamed 'The Fixer' and 'The Freak' for her manipulative demeanor and sadistic impulses, other characters believe Joan to be a psychopath, positioning her as a primary villain on the show. She is often framed through a lens of monstrosity in both the plot and artistic direction of the show – a characterization commonly

---

[1] Reg Watson, *Wentworth*, performed by Pamela Rabe (2013-2021; Foxtel), TV Show.

imposed on queer characters.[2] Audiences learn that a traumatic childhood and the death of a prisoner she fell in love with fifteen years before becoming the Governor of Wentworth Correctional Center have made her internalize her militaristic father's message that 'emotions lead to mistakes,' a mantra that comes up several times throughout the show. However, Joan's fans see glimpses of hopefulness, affection, and a desire to connect with the women in her life. This chapter will explore how Joan fans imagine her speculative romantic and sexual relationships with two other characters: Vera Bennett, her Deputy Governor during her employment at Wentworth during seasons two and three, and Brenda Murphy, a correctional officer she seems close to after she is incarcerated at Wentworth as a prisoner at the beginning of season four. Through these character relationships, fix-it fic writers pick up canonical threads to weave myriad stories in which Joan is an emotional and sexual agent imbued with sensuality and eroticism, thereby becoming active participants in reimagining this often-misunderstood character.[3] I will examine how fix-it fic writers engage with questions of intimacy in Joan's relation(ship)s in fics that simultaneously comply with canon and disrupt it to create a new fanon imaginary. Through a sapphic female gaze, I consider how fix-it fic writers invite audiences to think differently about the complexities of sapphic desire. Although Joan does commit monstrous acts to some of the women she seems to care for, a sapphic gaze unveils the nuance of her emotional entanglements and makes visible her repressed desire for an intimate connection that often catalyzes acts of monstrosity. While hundreds of fics depict Joan's relationships with Vera and Brenda, I will focus on two in particular: "If Only You Knew" by MsYukari and "Feels Like Home" by DefyingNormalcy. I frame my analysis of these stories as fix-it fics most prominently through the work of Henry Jenkins[4] and Lesley Goodman,[5] who conceptualize fix-it fics as a response stemming from fans' fascination and frustration with the source text in pursuit of making right what the source text did "wrong". Additionally, I apply Neha Hazra's[6]

---

[2] Harry M. Benshoff. "The Monster and the Homosexual" in *The Dread of Difference: Gender and the Horror Film*, 2nd edition, ed. Barry Keith Grant (NY: University of Texas Press, 2015), 116-142.
[3] Henry Jenkins. *Textual Poachers: Television Fans and Participatory Culture. 2nd edition.* (PA: Routledge, 1992).
[4] Henry Jenkins, "Textual Poachers" in *The Fan Fiction Studies Reader*, eds. Karen Hellekson and Kristina Busse (Iowa City: University of Iowa Press, 2012), 26-43.
[5] Lesley Goodman, "Disappointing Fans: Fandom, Fictional Theory, and the Death of the Author," *The Journal of Popular Culture* 48, no. 4 (2015): 662-676. https://doi.org/10.1111/jpcu.12223.
[6] Neha Hazra, "Queerer than Canon: Fix-it Fanfiction and Queer Readings," *Seattle University Undergraduate Research Journal* 5, no. 16 (2021): 105-124. https://scholarworks.seattleu.edu/suurj/vol5/iss1/16.

examination of queer fan fiction as a form of reparative reading as imagined by Eve Sedgwick.[7] This framework is beneficial for unpacking elements of Joan's character because audiences know that Joan is a lesbian, but the portrayal of her lesbian identity in the show is rooted in repression, rejection, and trauma. This chapter is organized chronologically per the sequence of *Wentworth*, in which I provide context about the show and characters and explain fans' perceptions of the two ships that I investigate. Then, I will examine the fix-it fics that stem from these moments through the lens of fandom studies scholarship.

Throughout the show, audiences see that Joan has a propensity to become fixated on women at her job through infatuation and obsession. Through flashbacks, audiences see that Joan became infatuated with a young pregnant prisoner, Jianna Riley while working at Blackmoor prison. She cared for Jianna throughout her pregnancy and the birth of her son Shayne and was forced to watch a social worker remove Shayne from Jianna's care. After finding Jianna hanging in the stairwell, for the next seventeen years, Joan believes that she had died from suicide. During her time as Governor of Wentworth, she learns that Jianna died because the other prisoners lynched her after they learned of their illicit relationship. When Joan arrives at Wentworth, she similarly becomes infatuated with prisoner Doreen Anderson, presumably because of the similarities she shares with Jianna: she is Indigenous, she is around the same age that Jianna was, and she becomes pregnant while incarcerated. During a private moment, Joan tries to kiss Doreen but is interrupted when Doreen's water breaks and her labor begins. After the baby is born, Joan overhears Doreen telling fellow prisoner Bea Smith about Joan's attempt to kiss her and calls her a freak. While not many fans have shipped Joan with Doreen through fan fiction, these examples are characteristic of Joan's failed attempts to connect with the women she cares for. Fans are demonstrably interested in her turbulent relationship with Vera, as at the time of writing, there were 668 fics with the relationship tag "Vera Bennett/Joan Ferguson" on *Archive of Our own (AO3)*. Fans see the missed opportunities for Joan to connect emotionally and sexually with other women, and they can both grapple with and look beyond her villain persona to do better for her character. Ultimately, this chapter will illuminate how fans honor Joan's lesbian-ness in their fan fictional storytelling, a part of her character that remains buried under a façade of monstrosity in *Wentworth*.

---

[7] Eve Kosofsky Sedgwick, "Paranoid Reading and Reparative Reading, or, You're So Paranoid You Probably Think this Essay is About You," in *Novel Gazing: Queer Readings in Fiction*, ed. Eve Sedgwick (Durham: Duke UP, 1997), 123-151.

Examining "The Fixer" in Fix-It Fics

Fix-it fic writers who believe Joan Ferguson deserved better than what *Wentworth*'s canonical storyline gave her often do so from a place of discontent. They seek to honor this complex character and her lesbian sexuality that is made clear in canon but never embodied beyond experiences of trauma and rejection. Building upon Jenkins'[8] suggestion that fans combine fascination and frustration in creatively reimagining the source text, Goodman ascertains that "this fannish anger explains the genre of fan fiction known as the "fix fic" or "fix-it fic," an attempt to make right that the source text made 'wrong'... such a model of fan fiction suggests that the fictions themselves serve as an outlet for and resolution to fan's frustration by allowing fans to play out what they *wish* had happened."[9] Joan and Vera's ship name in the fandom is "Freakytits": a nod to the prisoners' moniker for Joan, "The Freak," and the unfortunate nickname given to Vera by prisoners, "Vinegartits," after she slips and falls in a pool of vinegar in the canteen. For Freakytits shippers, fans are often frustrated that Joan and Vera seem to share elements of homoerotic and homoromantic chemistry. However, their tension never materializes in a sexual or romantic relationship. Perhaps this frustration is exacerbated by the knowledge that this chemistry was created organically and intentionally by Kate Atkinson and Pamela Rabe, the actresses who play Vera and Joan. In an interview, Pamela Rabe shed light on how Freakytits became such a popular ship in the fandom:

> With some fans even shipping the pair as an end game couple, Pamela smiled when speaking with us at Metro.co.uk: 'It was born out of the relationship that Kate and I found in the very first scenes we shot. We enjoyed each other as fellow performers and a dynamic was set up. It was interesting and oddly co-dependant as a mentorship relationship. They found a level of trust and shared secrets. Kate and I get off on performing with each other so the fact we enjoy each other's company probably fed into the writer's room. So, in time yes, it became very deliberate and we're all very aware of it and enjoy playing with that.[10]

---

[8] Jenkins, *Textual Poachers*, 14-15
[9] Goodman, "Disappointing Fans," 663-664.
[10] Duncan Lindsay, "*Wentworth* Prison Star Pamela Rabe Addresses Ferguson and Vera Chemistry – It's Very Deliberate!,'" last modified August 12, 2020. https://metro.co.uk/2020/08/12/wentworth-prison-star-pamela-rabe-addresses-ferguson-vera-chemistry-deliberate-13121340.

Freakytits shippers apply the chemistry they see between Joan and Vera to "colonize" the text and rework them "to become open to feminine pleasures"[11] through creating stories and communities that are uniquely female and sapphic. Ria Narai conceptualizes female-centered fan fiction as a genre that incorporates femslash but refuses to draw a strong distinction between sexual and nonsexual relationships between women.[12] Narai's definition of this genre echoes throughout Freakytits fan fiction as a whole: some fics depict a sexual relationship, while others depict a romantic one. However, some leave the connection between Joan and Vera open to readers' interpretation. Narai's conception of homoaffection as a practice of centering female narratives and relationality holistically describes a consistent thread that weaves throughout Freakytits fix-it fics regardless of whether the writers situate Joan and Vera in a sexual and romantic relationship. Narai applies Eve Sedgwick's refusal to contain relationships between women within societal binaries that are often applied to men to her conception of homoaffection. Sedgwick offers a reading of femaleness and femininity that transcends binaries and honors the relational complexity of womanhood, stating, "the diacritical opposition between the homosocial and the homosexual seems to be much less thorough and dichotomous for women, in our society, than for men."[13] Joan and Vera's relationship in the show consistently illustrates this nuance and others through highly charged moments of love, hate, tenderness, violence, friendship, mentorship, halted attempts to kill each other, and successful attempts to save each other. Fix-it fic writers interpret these emotional entanglements and expand upon them to further develop specific moments or bring these hints of sapphic chemistry to fruition through writing complete stories. These moments can be quite small: Vera looking at Joan in a particular way that connotes interest, Joan delicately removing a stray piece of lint from Vera's shoulder, or the two of them leaning in close to whisper to each other. *Wentworth* fan fiction writers are skilled at taking these intimate moments and creating romantic and erotic stories through a female gaze that satisfies fans' desires for Joan and Vera to be together. In the next section, I offer some general information about *Wentworth* and additional context for Joan and Vera's relationship in the show to introduce the first fic examined in this chapter, MsYukari's "If Only You Knew."

---

[11] Jenkins, *Textual Poachers*, 14-15
[12] Ria Narai, "Female-Centered Fan Fiction as Homoaffection in Fan Communities," *Transformative Works and Cultures*, no. 24 (2017). https://doi.org/10.3983/twc.2017.01014.
[13] Sedgwick, "Paranoid Reading and Reparative Reading," 123-151.

Wentworth Seasons 1 through 3, The Governor and her Deputy

Wentworth is an Australian television show that first premiered in 2013 and was introduced as a reimagining of *Prisoner Cell Block H*, which ran in Australia from 1979 to 1986. Indeed, *Wentworth* is a form of fan fiction itself. *Wentworth* begins with Bea Smith's arrival at Wentworth Correctional Center after being charged with the attempted murder of her abusive husband. From the first episode, *Wentworth* distinguished itself as an entirely different show from *Prisoner Cell Block H* by killing off a prominent character in the original series, Governor Meg Jackson. Audiences meet Joan Ferguson in the first episode of season two when she takes over as the Governor of Wentworth, preceded by her reputation for successfully abolishing drugs and bringing order to several prisons in Victoria, earning her the moniker "The Fixer." Standing at six feet tall with her hair styled into a large bun, she is portrayed as formidable and intimidating. From the outset, Joan establishes herself as a force to be reckoned with. Corinne E Hinton highlights how Joan presents herself as an assertive and unemotional leader to fulfill her need for control, order, and obedience. Hinton characterizes Governor Ferguson as 'the masculinized boss bitch' as one part of her monstrous personae that develops throughout seasons two and three of *Wentworth*, stating, "the masculinized boss bitch performs constructions of masculinity visually and/or discursively to secure her professional power untethered to the trappings of femininity."[14] Soon after Joan's arrival, she connects with Vera Bennett, her Deputy Governor. Standing nearly a foot shorter than the Governor, Vera's soft feminine features and shy nature starkly contrast Joan's characterization as the 'masculinized boss bitch.' Joan offers to mentor her after learning that Vera has been passed over for the Governorship several times. Vera quickly expresses her appreciation, and audiences can see that Joan and Vera appear to be opposites in how they present themselves to the world.

Audiences quickly realize that Governor Ferguson's methods for managing the prison are unorthodox, and throughout seasons two and three, she makes clear her ability to manipulate others to achieve her ends. While Vera's colleagues continually caution her about Joan's cruelty, she ignores their warnings. Joan provides Vera with ongoing praise, validation, and confidence in her professional abilities, and it is evident that this is the first time Vera has felt supported and appreciated. Their mentor/mentee dynamic continues until

---

[14] Corinne E. Hinton, "From 'Fixer' to 'Freak': Disabling the Ambitious Madwoman in *Wentworth*," in *Screening the Gothic in Australia and New Zealand: Contemporary Antipodean Film and Television*, eds. Jessica Gildersleeve and Kate Catrell (Amsterdam: Amsterdam University Press, 2022), 234.

prisoners take siege of the prison, and Vera is taken hostage with a syringe of blood held to her neck. When Joan refuses to negotiate with the prisoners to protect Vera's safety, Vera is pricked with the needle and contracts Hepatitis C. Vera later learns of Joan's refusal to negotiate and feels betrayed, and Joan eventually senses the tension and invites Vera to her home that night. Over dinner, Joan seems like she is about to disclose romantic feelings for Vera, but Vera interrupts and accuses Joan of not caring about her. Joan hesitantly places her hand over Vera's and insists that she does care, but when Vera discloses her Hepatitis C status, Joan, a germaphobe, compulsively pulls her hand away and wipes it on her napkin. This moment signifies the beginning of the end of Vera's unconditional loyalty to Joan. This scene is particularly interesting to fans and a cause for much frustration. Several fix-it fic writers have used this moment as a prompt to imagine how this scene might have ended differently. They typically fix this scene by depicting Joan and Vera honestly discussing how they feel and finding a resolution. Writers tend to explain Joan's reasoning for not negotiating with the prisoners, thereby humanizing her as a flawed woman who made a bad decision rather than the villainess she is portrayed to be in the show.

The Fix-it Fic: "If Only You Knew"

In her fic "If Only You Knew," MsYukari fixes this canonical scene by giving readers insight into Joan's inner thoughts during the siege and her attempt to connect with Vera despite her social ineptitude. When Joan pulls her hand away from Vera's after she discloses her Hepatitis C status, MsYukari's description of this moment provides explicit reasoning as to why she does this, perhaps inspiring fans to see Joan's rejection of Vera with greater empathy:

> She pulled her hand away as if she'd been burned, rubbing her hand on her napkin to try and get rid of any germs. She knew it was an irrational reaction, but she couldn't help it then. She wanted to say something, but she was stunned into silence.
>
> *What am I doing?! That look in her eyes, I've destroyed things between us!*
>
> She kept rubbing her hands on the napkin, an almost uncontrollable urge and it was embarrassing for someone else to see. Especially in such

a private and intimate setting between them. She watched helplessly as Vera walked out the door.[15]

By imagining this canonical scene through Joan's perspective, MsYukari mobilizes a level of vulnerability that fans do not see from Joan at this point in the show. Joan's inability to express her feelings for Vera, her standoffishness, and her refusal to take responsibility for Vera being harmed catalyze the destruction of their mentor/mentee relationship. By framing this moment through Joan's perspective, MsYukari prepares the reader for an intimate moment between the characters. Vera tries to leave Joan's apartment, and Joan responds with determination to show Vera how much she truly does care for her:

> "Oh Vera, if only you knew." She cupped Vera's cheek and kissed her. She kissed softly at first, and then with a growing intensity as she pulled Vera against her. Her tongue licked her lips, seeking entrance and she moaned softly as Vera's tongue rolled over hers.
>
> Vera gently bit her lip, pulling back to look into her eyes. Her breathing was ragged, and Joan leaned down again to kiss her neck. "Joan, what are we doing?"
>
> Her mouth skimmed her throat, moving up to her ear. "Mending our relationship," she whispered.[16]

Here, MsYukari showcases the concept of fixing it quite literally as Joan expresses that she wants to fix the relationship between them and begins to do so with a passionate kiss, which starkly contrasts with Joan's compulsion to withdraw her hand in disgust moments prior. Fixing this scene responds to fannish anger that Joan ruined her relationship with Vera in this moment, and MsYukari illustrates the combination of fascination and frustration that Goodman[17] characterizes as a primary motivation for writing fix-it fics. The remainder of the fic describes Joan and Vera having sex for the first time. The tone of their sexual encounter is sweet and affectionate, yet MsYukari stays true to Joan's canonical character by keeping Joan in control of their intimacy. "If Only You Knew" concludes with a somewhat awkward post-coital conversation between them where both women are nervous about expressing their feelings. Ultimately, fans are left with hope for the couple as Joan assures Vera that she

---

[15] MsYukari, "If Only You Knew," *Archive of Our Own*, last modified May 18, 2020, https://archiveofourown.org/works/24248548
[16] MsYukari, "If Only You Knew."
[17] Goodman, "Disappointing Fans," 662-676.

has always wanted her. This fic serves as a reparative reading of a scene that sparks the destruction of Joan and Vera's relationship in canon. Freakytits shippers may be understandably frustrated by Joan and Vera's ongoing inability to communicate with each other throughout the trajectory of *Wentworth*, and MsYukari repairs this issue by imagining a scenario in which these characters talk about their feelings regardless of how uncomfortable it may be for them.

Freakytits writers demonstrate Narai's application of Eve Sedgwick's and Adrienne Rich's conception of the lesbian continuum that all women exist on a sapphic spectrum.[18] MsYukari addresses this in her fix-it as Vera is canonically heterosexual, but her admiration of and dedication to Joan give fans hope for the pairing. MsYukari and other writers often write stories where Vera has never experienced intimacy with another woman, nor has she wanted to, until she meets Joan. This common theme permeating Freakytits fan fiction speaks to the female, sapphic gaze that *Wentworth* fans desire and perhaps feel is missing from the show. It is significant as well that writers largely conform to the show's portrayal of Vera as heterosexual – up until the point where she meets Joan. They frame her attraction to Joan as an interruption to Vera's heterosexuality, and this mirrors what many fans have publicly shared on social media: that they never questioned their heterosexuality until watching Pamela Rabe's performance as Joan Ferguson. In this vein, it is not only lesbians and bisexual women who watch Joan and Vera through a sapphic gaze, but fans who consider(ed) themselves to be straight as well. Regardless of how female Freakytits fans identify, Narai's concept of homoaffection visibly characterizes this ship's fix-it fics themselves, as well as the connection between readers and writers on *AO3* and fandom communities on other social media platforms.

Wentworth Seasons 4 through 9, The Prisoner, and her Screw

At the end of season three, Joan is arrested for numerous crimes and sent to a psychiatric institution. She eventually returns to Wentworth, escorted by a new character: correctional officer Brenda Murphy. Joan is placed in the protected isolation unit for her safety and is expected to continue taking a regime of antipsychotic medication. Audiences first see a connection between Joan and Brenda when the nurse administers Joan's medication, and rather than checking to ensure she has swallowed the pills as is her professional duty, Brenda allows Joan to spit them into her hand. Brenda discreetly provides Joan with a pencil after Vera, who has taken over as the Governor, refuses to let Joan

---

[18] Adrienne Rich, "Compulsory Heterosexuality and Lesbian Existence," *Journal of Women's History* 15, no. 3 (2003): 11-48. https://doi.org/10.1353/jowh.2003.0079.

have one. While audiences do not see Joan and Brenda interact much throughout season four, if they watch closely, Brenda consistently looks at Joan in a way that suggests a sexual attraction. In season five, Joan is released into the general population after being held responsible for the death of Bea Smith, a prisoner who was well loved by the other inmates. When Joan enters the yard for the first time since Bea's death, she is attacked by several women and impressively takes down every single one of them. Brenda, the only officer present, watches Joan win each fight with admiration. Not only does she not intervene, but she prevents other officers who arrive during the fights from intervening.

Brenda ultimately resigns from Wentworth after Vera blackmails her into doing so. After terrorizing both inmates and staff alike and subsequently being lynched by prisoners, Joan escapes in a wooden box, being shipped out of prison but is buried alive by correctional officer Will Jackson. Vera later becomes aware of this murder attempt and accompanies Will and Jake Stewart, another officer to ensure Joan's body is still buried. Fans are led to believe that the body in the box *is* Joan, but Vera begins receiving threatening text messages demanding money from someone with an incriminating photograph of the three of them at the burial site. The blackmailer is revealed to be Brenda, and her appearance is noticeably queer-coded in a way that contrasts her appearance earlier in the show. When Brenda later arrives to collect the payment with her hair styled in Joan's signature bun, she is shot dead by a former colleague who mistook her for Joan. In season eight, the audience learns that Joan is, in fact, alive and that Brenda has rescued her and hidden her from the authorities in her home. The revelation that Joan was living with Brenda up until her death leaves fans with an important question: what happened during the months that Joan and Brenda lived together before Brenda was killed?

The Fix-it Fic: "Feels Like Home"

Joan and Brenda ultimately became a ship known as "Screak," a combination of the words "screw" for Brenda, a term prisoners use in reference to correctional staff, and "freak" to refer to Joan. Screak shippers see the potential of a healthy relationship between Joan and Brenda as an alternative to the canonically, and at times, within fanon, the toxic dynamic between Joan and Vera. At the time of writing, the relationship tag Joan Ferguson/Brenda Murphy on *AO3* was at 185 stories. Many Screak fix-it fics fill in the canonical gaps, mobilizing Sheenagh Pugh's thinking that fans write fan fiction because they want more of their source material or want more from it.[19] The most common fix in Screak fics is simple: Brenda survives. To explore the absence of Joan and

---

[19] Sheenagh Pugh, *The Democratic Genre* (Bridgend: Seren, 2005).

Brenda's dynamic while cohabitating, DefyingNormalcy published "Feels Like Home," a forty-chapter fic that documents and expands upon their imagined relationship. She introduces the story as a fix-it fic quite explicitly in the introductory notes of the first chapter: "This fic blissfully ignores the canon of the series from the end of season six onwards in order to focus on how the relationship between Brenda and Joan might have developed under different circumstances."[20] Staying true to the character traits that audiences can discern in canon, the story begins after Joan has taken residence in Brenda's home to hide from the authorities after her prison escape. Joan feels indebted to Brenda for her willingness to harbor her as a fugitive and feels she must be useful during her time in her home. The story follows the canonical thread of Brenda blackmailing Vera with the photograph she took of Vera and her colleagues at the burial site. DefyingNormalcy diverges from canon by making this attempt at extortion successful. Before Brenda arrives at Vera's house, DefyingNormalcy offers readers insight into Joan's perspective of their relationship:

> Brenda had been a lifeline to Joan when she'd run out of hope. A friend in an otherwise lonely existence. A voice of reason and support amongst a sea of resentment and violent opposition. When Joan had first made the move to elicit the former officer's support, she'd never imagined their arrangement far outlasting their relationship as prisoner and officer. She never imagined ending up as Brenda's unexpected but graciously welcomed and cared for housemate. She certainly never imagined the friendship which had grown, surprisingly, not just out of the need to settle a shared score, but out of trust, respect, and understanding.[21]

The first few chapters establish this growing friendship and treat readers to glimmers of the mutual desire building between Joan and Brenda. DefyingNormalcy brings the plans that Joan had in canon to fruition – a plan to escape to Rio de Janeiro, Brazil – before being found and incarcerated once more in season eight. In "Feels Like Home," Joan *does* relocate to Brazil and reconnects with Brenda. In the fifth chapter, DefyingNormalcy describes Joan's feelings, "there was joy in anonymity. A lightness, even. Yet she'd found these things at the cost of leaving behind the only true reciprocal connection she'd forged in her adult life."[22] In this excerpt, DefyingNormalcy speaks to a frustration shared among fans of Joan in that audiences never get to see her in a healthy lesbian relationship. For Screak fans especially, this frustration is

---

[20] DefyingNormalcy, "Feels Like Home," *Archive of Our Own*, last modified May 21 2022, accessed February 20, 2023, https://archiveofourown.org/works/38384824/chapters/9592308
[21] DefyingNormalcy, "Feels Like Home," 1.
[22] DefyingNormalcy, "Feels Like Home," 5.

further compounded by their observation that Brenda seems to be the only person in Joan's life who genuinely cares for her and advocates for her despite her crimes. In canon, Vera tries to punish Joan for sending four inmates to the medical unit who tried to attack her, and Brenda confirms that Joan acted in self-defense to prevent her from going to the slot. When Vera admonishes Brenda for not intervening, Brenda crassly remarks that she is not paid enough to risk getting her neck broken. DefyingNormalcy applies this fascination with Joan and Brenda's canonical relationship to explore their romance. Over time, Joan and Brenda communicate through written letters and eventually begin speaking once Joan procures an untraceable cell phone. During one of their phone calls, DefyingNormalcy offers a fix to another problem that has never been solved in canon: Vera, Will, and Jake were never arrested for their knowledge of or contributions to Joan's attempted murder. Within fandom communities, Joan fans have continually expressed their frustration that Vera, Will, and Jake – often referred to as "the three stooges" in public fandom spaces – are never held accountable for their crimes. In "Feels like Home," Joan anonymously sends a photograph of the three perpetrators to the police. Rather than sending Brenda's photograph, Joan takes one herself with a hidden camera to protect Brenda from becoming further involved. DefyingNormalcy's choice here illustrates Joan's love and care for Brenda, thereby disrupting the canonical portrayal of Joan as a monster incapable of caring for others. This Screak fix-it fic, as well as others, responds to fans' desires for Joan to develop a healthy romantic relationship grounded in trust and care, perhaps a desire that Vera cannot fulfill due to their turbulent history. The remainder of this slow burn fic documents Joan and Brenda's growing love, intense sexual relationship, and Brenda's eventual permanent relocation to Rio to be with Joan.

Freakytits Versus Screak

At the time of writing, "Feels Like Home" has 2580 hits and 427 kudos – *AO3's* version of a "like" button. The fic has performed well within such a small section of the *Wentworth* fandom. I argue that this is partly because DefyingNormalcy creates a uniquely sapphic character relationship. Her descriptions of Joan and Brenda's emotional and physical intimacy resist the male gaze as conceptualized by Laura Mulvey.[23] While this love story is certainly unique, there are consistent moments between the characters that sapphic

---

[23] Laura Mulvey, "Visual Pleasure and Narrative Cinema," in *Film Theory and Criticism: Introductory Readings*, eds. Leo Braudy and Marshall Cohen (Oxford: Oxford Up, 1999), 833-844.

readers can find relatable.[24] Joan and Brenda are represented as equals within fanon, and always portrayed as lesbians. Queer women can see themselves in these stories and may observe similarities between Joan and Brenda's relationship and their own relationships in real life. Many Freakytits fix-it fics differ in this respect, as Joan and Vera are often described in somewhat heteronormative ways that may cater more towards a male gaze rather than a female or sapphic one. Joan is typically positioned, as Hinton[25] observes, as the 'masculinized boss bitch' in the bedroom and within her romantic relationships with Vera. Vera is often described as soft and feminine, and perhaps this dichotomy between the characters makes Freakytits more appealing to non-lesbian readers of different genders and sexualities.

While fans of Joan Ferguson enjoy myriad fan fictional stories and ships, they typically subscribe to either Freakytits *or* Screak. The two ships and the differences between them have contributed to what Derek Johnson calls 'fan-tagonism,' in which fans of a particular source text create conflicting 'truths' about the series.[26] Largely, Freakytits shippers position Vera as the only character worthy of Joan's affection, and take clues from their long, detailed storyline in *Wentworth* to construct fan fictional stories. Perhaps some Freakytits shippers do not see the subtle chemistry between Joan and Brenda that Screak shippers do, and perhaps they feel that Screak fix-it fic writers are creating meaning where there was none in canon. Perhaps some Screak shippers feel that the toxicity between Joan and Vera ruins Freakytits as a ship because they want to see Joan in a healthy relationship with a partner she can see as an equal. However, writers of both ships consistently mobilize a sapphic gaze to disrupt perceptions of Joan as a monster. They interpret subtle hints from *Wentworth* as to why Joan manipulates, threatens, and kills, and generally subscribe to three key reasons: to protect women that she cares for, to enact justice on behalf of women weaker than herself, and because she is experiencing mental illness without support and therefore struggles to form healthy connections with other people. Writers justify Joan's cruel actions by framing them through a place of care: where some audiences see a monster, Freakytits writers see a protector. Where some audiences see a psychopath, Screak writers see a traumatized, lonely woman trying to survive. Across fix-it fics from both ships, writers position Vera or Brenda as pivotal love interests who crack open

---

[24] Julie Levin Russo, "The Queer Politics of Femslash," in *The Routledge Companion to Media Fandom*, eds. Melissa A. Click and Suzanne Scott (NY: Taylor and Francis, 2018), 155-164.
[25] Hinton, "From 'Fixer' to 'Freak,'" 229-250.
[26] Derek Johnson, "Fan-tagonism: Factions, Institutions and Constitutive Hegemonies of Fandom," in *Fandom: Identities and Communities in a Mediated World*, eds. Jonathan Gray, Cornel Sandvoss, and C. Lee Harrington (NY: New York UP, 2007), 285-300.

Joan's hardened exterior and bring forth her vulnerability. In doing so, they humanize Joan Ferguson as a complex lesbian character who is not only capable of love but is *deserving* of love as well.

Conclusion

While passionate Freakytits and Screak shippers disagree on what truths they see in canon, they share a common desire to do better for Joan. Jenkins' and Goodman's assertion that fix-it fics stem from a combination of fans' fascination and frustration rings true for both ships that I have explored in this chapter: Freakytits fic writers channel their frustrations that Joan and Vera never became romantically or sexually involved into writing these stories and bringing their onscreen chemistry to fruition in fix-it fics. Screak fic writers use their frustration that Brenda was killed and that *Wentworth* never showed audiences what occurred between Joan and Brenda when Joan was hiding in Brenda's home to save Brenda's life through fix-it fics and give Joan a fulfilling relationship with the queer-coded character. Perhaps there is something fascinating about the fact that Joan is most often shipped with Vera and Brenda, because both characters saved her life in the show. While fans of both ships hold markedly different opinions about what Joan would or should have in a lesbian relationship, they come together through their shared fascination with Joan Ferguson. Several writers for both ships have referred to Joan as enigmatic, and the sensual energy that Pamela Rabe brings to her portrayal of the iconic character makes it easy to see why. While *Wentworth* aired its final episode in the autumn of 2022, fans' fascination with Joan is still thriving on *AO3* as fics continue to be published.

My analysis in this chapter contributes to a few critical undertheorized areas of scholarship: while *Wentworth* has enjoyed global popularity and introduced new audiences to Australian television, the fandom is quite small. At the time of writing, there were only 2,447 fics categorized under the *Wentworth* tab on *AO3*, and similarly, there is a lack of academic publications about the show and fandom as well. In focusing on Joan's character specifically, I also sought to explore elements of her character that are often marginalized in popular media: lesbians, mature women, women with mental illness(es), and villains, queer characters conceptualized through the lens of monstrosity. Joan Ferguson and the way that fix-it fic writers interpret her character are generative for thinking differently about what a sapphic gaze and homoaffection can offer in mobilizing empathy and desire as a catalyst for critically analyzing characters who are disliked by mainstream audiences and who reject prescriptive notions of femininity.

Bibliography

Benshoff, Harry M. "The monster and the homosexual." In *The Dread of Difference: Gender and the Horror film*, 2nd edition, edited by Barry Keith Grant, 116-142. NY: University of Texas Press, 2015.

DefyingNormalcy. "Feels Like Home." *Archive of Our own*. 2022. Last modified May 21, 2022. https://archiveofourown.org/works/38384824/chapters/95923084.

Goodman, Lesley. "Disappointing Fans: Fandom, Fictional Theory, and the Death of the Author." *The Journal of Popular Culture* 48, no. 4 (2015): 662-676. https://doi.org/10.1111/jpcu.12223.

Hazra, Neha. "Queerer than Canon: Fix-it Fanfiction and Queer Readings." *Seattle University Undergraduate Research Journal* 5, no. 16 (2021): 105-124. https://scholarworks.seattleu.edu/suurj/vol5/iss1/16.

Hinton, Corinne E. "From 'Fixer' to 'Freak': Disabling the Ambitious Madwoman in *Wentworth*." In *Screening the Gothic in Australia and New Zealand: Contemporary Antipodean Film and Television*, edited by Jessica Gildersleeve and Kate Catrell, 229-250. Amsterdam: Amsterdam University Press, 2022.

Jenkins, Henry. *Textual Poachers: Television Fans and Participatory Culture*. 2nd edition. PA: Routledge, 1992.

Jenkins, Henry. "Textual poachers." In *The Fan Fiction Studies Reader*, edited by Karen Hellekson and Kristina Busse, 26-43. Iowa City: University of Iowa Press, 2012.

Johnson, Derek. "Fan-tagonism: Factions, Institutions and Constitutive Hegemonies of Fandom." In *Fandom: Identities and Communities in a Mediated World*, edited by Jonathan Gray, Cornel Sandvoss, and C. Lee Harrington, 285-300. NY: New York UP, 2007.

Lindsay, Duncan. "*Wentworth* Prison Star Pamela Rabe Addresses Ferguson and Vera Chemistry – It's Very Deliberate!'" Last modified August 12, 2020. https://metro.co.uk/2020/08/12/wentworth-prison-star-pamela-rabe-addresses-ferguson-vera-chemistry-deliberate-13121340.

MsYukari. "If Only You Knew." *Archive of Our own*. 2020. Last modified May 18, 2020. https://archiveofourown.org/works/24248548.

Mulvey, Laura. "Visual Pleasure and Narrative Cinema." In *Film Theory and Criticism: Introductory Readings*, edited by Leo Braudy and Marshall Cohen, 833-844. Oxford: Oxford Up, 1999.

Narai, Ria. "Female-Centered Fan Fiction as Homoaffection in Fan Communities." *Transformative Works and Cultures*, no. 24 (2017). https://doi.org/10.3983/twc.2017.01014.

Pugh, Sheenagh. *The Democratic Genre*. Bridgend: Seren, 2005.

Rich, Adrienne. "Compulsory Heterosexuality and Lesbian Existence." *Journal of Women's History* 15, no. 3 (2003): 11-48. https://doi.org/10.1353/jowh.2003.0079.

Russo, Julie Levin. "The Queer Politics of Femslash." In *The Routledge Companion to Media Fandom*, edited by Melissa A. Click and Suzanne Scott, 155-164. NY: Taylor and Francis, 2018.

Sedgwick, Eve Kosofsky. "Paranoid Reading and Reparative Reading, or, You're So Paranoid You Probably Think this Essay is About You." In *Novel Gazing: Queer Readings in Fiction*, edited by Eve Sedgwick, 123-151. Durham: Duke UP, 1997.

Wentworth. Written by Reg Watson. Performed by Pamela Rabe. 2013-2021. Foxel. TV Show.

Part Three:
Fixing Other Genres

Chapter 9

The Fix-It Novel: How Commercial Authors Instrumentalize Fan Fiction's Subversive Potential

Amanda Boyce
Universität Trier

Abstract: In this article, Boyce notes that fans and the commercial creators are always in a struggle for power. They point out that when authors incorporate fans of their work in the work, they portray fans as extremists, and are ultimately threatened by new interpretations and approaches to their original creation. The hegemony of author versus authority redefines how much power the fan possesses. Boyce focuses on the fix-it-novel as a means of illuminating the fan fiction writer's voice within the boundaries of a fictional world, thus highlighting the ongoing tension between fans and commercial authors, while also demonstrating the power of fandom.

Keywords: fix-it-novel, commercial, hegemony, power, author, authority, fandom, marginalizing, reimagining, fix-it fics, tags, *AO3*.

***

In both the public sphere and the academia, the discourse around fan fiction has, over time, gone through multiple stages of scrutiny, from condemnation for its seemingly shameless cooption of someone else's intellectual property to glorification for its ostensibly indiscriminate inclusion of identities traditionally marginalized by mainstream media. More recent investigations of fan behavior have shown that patterns of marginalization may also transfer to fandom subculture, bursting the bubble of fandom as an indiscriminate space, as power negotiations exist there as well.[1] In accordance with this notion, Judith Fathallah situates fan fiction in a space between the extremes, especially when it comes to critically reflecting on their commercial source texts, stating that

---

[1] Victoria M. Gonzalez, "Swan Queen, Shipping, and Boundary Regulation in Fandom," *Transformative Works and Cultures*, vol. 22, (2016).

"*all* derivative and transformative text is, by its very form, *both* legitimating *and* critical of the primacy of its sources."[2]

Throughout its existence, fan fiction has the potential to initiate a continuous power struggle between commercial authors and fan fiction authors when it comes to meaning creation within their mutually dependent relationship. If there is no commercial text, there can be no fan fiction. If there is no fandom[3] to speak of, the text will be commercially less successful.[4] The fan fiction author's questioning of the hegemony of the commercial author through new interpretations and reimaginations has neither gone unnoticed nor unchallenged by commercial authors, as the discourse around fan fiction is migrating from a hidden subculture to a more prominent cultural status. Investigations of examples from television media and its depiction of fans and their writing have indicated that when commercial authors include (writing) fans of their narrative within their narrative, it is often in a derisive way. The obsessive aspects of fandom are singled out.[5] The ongoing exchange in this mutually dependent relationship has resulted in seemingly opposing sides forming, the commercial author vs. the fan author, in a struggle for supremacy, a struggle that is heavily influenced by the notion anchored within commercial writing that one text belongs to one author, lending them the authority over the 'true' meaning of their text. Assis explains, "[t]he etymological relation between 'author' and 'authority' implies the hierarchical authority inherent in the texts' addressor. The authority of the writer of the text stems from his perception as the source of the text [...]."[6] Fathallah postulates that the commercial author who sees their authority over the interpretation of their texts ostensibly threatened through fan authors' transformative work, then aims to reclaim their authority through these negative and castigating fan inclusions.[7]

One example of a more direct and unveiled act of challenging the commercial author's authority over the interpretation of ambiguous meaning and character and narrative trajectory comes in the shape of the fix-it fic. The fix-it fic is a sub-

---

[2] Judith Fathallah, *Fanfiction and the Author: How Fan Fic Changes Popular Cultural Texts* (Amsterdam: Amsterdam University Press, 2017), 201, emphasis in original.
[3] Though fandom and fan fiction writing are not the same, fan fiction writing is a major part of the more deeply involved fandom experience and is thus found to be one of the more instrumental aspects of keeping a text popular long after its original publication. Abigail De Kosnik, *Fandom as Free Labor* (New York: Routledge, 2013).
[4] Henry Jenkins, et al., *Spreadable Media: Creating Value and Meaning in a Networked Culture: with a New Afterword*, (New York: New York University Press, 2018).
[5] Fathallah, *Fanfiction and the Author*, 159.
[6] Amit Assis, "Author-ity," *Mafte'akh: Lexical Review of Political Thought, 2nd edition*, (2011):1, quoted in Fathallah, *Fanfiction and the Author*, 103.
[7] Fathallah, *Fanfiction and the Author*, 159.

genre within fan fiction writing that concerns itself with rewriting, "something about canon that the fan writing the fic wasn't happy with. This can be anything from explaining plot holes or inconsistent characterization to bringing a favorite character back from the dead."[8] Building on this understanding of the fix-it fic, a new type of genre novel is emerging: the fix-it novel. The Fix-it novel, this essay proposes, follows in a similar vein to the fix-it fic by centering its narrative on a fan fiction author and their writing but uses its position as a commercially published text to challenge perceived hegemonic structures in this context. While the issue of what makes a fan happy with a text may be a subjective matter of aesthetic taste, fix-it fics, and the discourse they create also present a forum for marginalized voices to criticize their counterparts' problematic treatment in commercial writing. By the time the BBC's *Sherlock*[9] ended its run with Sherlock Holmes and John Watson's romantic relationship remaining in the realm of plausible deniability, allegations of queerbaiting[10] had already arisen within the fandom.[11] The term queerbaiting and its usage within fandom points out the are-they-are-they-not[12] way in which mainstream media has traditionally dealt with queer characters and relationships by setting up expectations of queerness within a text, but ultimately never confirming them.[13] Rewriting their own, more inclusive story, and fixing the marginalization within the source text, then gives the fan author of the fix-it fic a vessel to make their criticism heard, understood, and discussed by others. However, even as

---

[8] Fanlore, s.v, "Fix-it," last modified March 13, 2023, 01:15, https://fanlore.org/wiki/Fix-it.
[9] *Sherlock*, directed by Mark Gatiss and Steven Moffat (2010-2017; UK: BBC One, 2017), DVD.
[10] In this paper, the term 'queer' will be used as an umbrella term. There are issues that may arise with using such broad terminology for a diverse group with different needs; however, in the context of this chapter, this variety of different identities is viewed as united under the common factor of marginalization based on their non-heteronormative understanding of various aspects of identity.
[11] Cassidy Sheehan, "Queer-baiting on the BBC's Sherlock: Addressing the Invalidation of Queer Experiences through Online Fan Fiction Communities" (Undergraduate Research Posters, Virginia Commonwealth University, 2015).
[12] The Motion Picture Production Code (also known as the Hays Code), in a move of the US film industry's self-censorship to circumvent state censorship, saw queer characters and relationships being excluded from open film discourse. Mark Duffett, *Understanding Fandom: An Introduction to the Study of Media Fan Culture*, (London: Bloomsbury Academic) 200, considers that censorship has led to a decades long tradition of queer-coded characters and storylines and, with it, both a kind of queer literacy among (queer) audiences and a tool for commercial writers to 'include' queer characters without alienating queerphobic audiences, as coding keeps undesired queerness in the realm of plausible deniability.
[13] Emma Nordin, "From Queer Reading to Queerbaiting: The Battle over the Polysemic Text and the Power of Hermeneutics" (Master's Thesis, Stockholms Universitet, 2015), 47.

Jenkins et al.[14] recognize fandom's power to influence the commercial success of their source text, and rendering criticism through altering a source text's storyline may be viewed as an expression of such power, this power is nevertheless limited. As most fan activities and the discourse they engender remain within fandom, the (marginalized) fan author's voice has a small chance of reaching a more mainstream audience to use this ostensive power to effect potential social change. The fix-it novel, on the other hand, this chapter proposes, aims to bridge exactly this gap between the marginalized fan author's voice and mainstream discourse.

The Fix-It Novel: Fan Fiction and Commercial Texts Colliding

As television texts acknowledge the existence of fandom and fan fiction authors, the past decade has also seen a steady increase in commercially published *novels* focused on fan fiction authors in a notably more positive and empowering manner than their television counterparts. Rainbow Rowell's YA novel *Fangirl*,[15] constitutes one of the first in-depth inclusions of a fan fiction author and their writing in a contemporary novel. Its fan-author protagonist, Cath, adamantly argues for fan fiction's emotional and craft-honing merit when confronted with accusations of plagiarism by her writing teacher, who also happens to be a commercially published author. However, due to Cath's shy nature, most of her arguments remain unspoken, a secret to be shared with the understanding reader, but effectively having no influence on the general perception of fan fiction by her novelist teacher or in the narrative world. Eventually, the YA novel ends with Cath not finishing her novel-length queer fan fiction piece but publishing her first original essay instead. This fan fiction author's happy ending lies in growing out of her fan-fic origins and ultimately graduating into commercial publishing, leaving the hegemonic structures between commercial author and fan author effectively unaltered. Other books feature much more vocal fan authors, including Anna Breslaw's YA novel, *Scarlett Epstein Hates It Here*,[16] in which title hero Scarlett writes real person fics[17] about her classmates, and TJ Klune's YA novel trilogy *The Extraordinaries*,[18] in which Nicky writes self-insert fics[19] about himself and the local superhero.

---

[14] Henry Jenkins, et al., *Spreadable Media*.
[15] Rainbow Rowell, *Fangirl*, (London: Macmillan, 2013).
[16] Anna Breslaw, *Scarlet Epstein Hates It Here* (New York: Penguin Random House, 2016).
[17] Real-person fic "is fanfiction written about actual people, rather than fictional characters." Fanlore, s.v. "RPF," last modified April 23, 2023, 4:44, https://fanlore.org/wiki/RPF.
[18] TJ Klune, *The Extraordinaries Trilogy* (New York: Tom Doherty Associates Book, 2020-22).
[19] Self-insert fics are fan fics that feature the "practice by authors of writing themselves into their own stories, either explicitly or in thinly-disguised form." Fanlore, s.v. "Self-insertion," last modified December 20, 2022, 6:47, https://fanlore.org/wiki/Self-insertion.

However, these texts focus mainly on the young fan author and their journey of making sense of their growing desires and the world through fan fiction writing. Breslaw's novel, like Rowell's, also includes a commercial author, in this case, Scarlett's estranged father, against whose writing Scarlett's fan fiction is pitted. Indeed, in this comparison, the YA novel does make a point of dragging her father's commercial writing from its self-perceived quality throne by pointing out the similarities to Scarlett's fan fiction writing. Nevertheless, similar to Cath in *Fangirl*, Scarlett's realizations remain in the personal sphere, with no effect on how others perceive her father's writing and commercial writing in general.

In contrast to these examples, the fix-it novel is more daring when it comes to depicting fan fiction authors and their writing, moving beyond the plea for fan fiction's mere acceptance, which we see in Rowell's text, and the personal development focus presented in Breslaw's and Klune's YA novels. Rather, the fix-it novel situates itself in a hybrid position between fan writing and commercial writing, attempting to consolidate both positions by making use of both the authorial power and reach of commercial writing and the subverting potential of fan fiction writing, specifically of that of the fix-it fic. While the fix-it fic aims to 'repair' what the fan author perceives as wrong, problematic, or unsatisfactory in canon, the fix-it novel, this chapter will demonstrate, additionally seeks to mend the increasingly weary relationship between fans and the commercial texts they consume. The fix-it novel incorporates both fan fiction *and* commercial writing examples in its narrative, challenging and aiming to renegotiate the hegemonic structures between fan authors and commercial authors by juxtaposing the two types of writing and their emotional merit and then pushing this discourse into the narrative's public sphere. This chapter suggests there are two main features of the fix-it novel, which will be discussed in more detail below, including 1) a narrative within a narrative with a two-character perspective and 2) a call for (commercial) change.

Illustrating how exactly this structure plays out in text, this chapter will examine two fix-it novels in more detail: Britta Lundin's YA novel *Ship It*[20] and Olivia Dade's novel *Spoiler Alert*[21]. Lundin's and Dade's novels can both be tied back to actual television fandoms, the CW's *Supernatural*[22] and HBO's *Game of Thrones*,[23] respectively, and two major issues that have arisen within these fandoms regarding marginalized identities. *Ship It* deals with the impact of queerbaiting, a vocal allegation within the *Supernatural* fandom, while *Spoiler*

---

[20] Britta Lundin, *Ship It* (New York: Freeform Books, 2018).
[21] Olivia Dade, *Spoiler Alert* (London: Piatkus, 2020).
[22] *Supernatural*, created by Eric Kripke (2005-20; USA: CW, 2021), DVD.
[23] *Game of Thrones*, created by David Bennioff and D.B. Weiss (2011-19; USA: HBO, 2020), DVD.

Alert deals with the treatment of female identities, with a focus on body diversity, specifically the big female body, addressing the disappointment of the *Game of Thrones* Braime[24] fandom. While both texts fall into the category of the fix-it novel, the analysis of their nuanced approaches aims to highlight the versatility of this emerging genre.

A Narrative within a Narrative with a Two-Character Perspective

Britta Lundin's YA novel, *Ship It*, predominantly satirizes the CW's long-standing urban fantasy series *Supernatural* with its own fictional television series called *Demon Heart*. *Demon Heart* tells the story of the titular Heart, a demon whose physical property of literally possessing a heart – as opposed to other demons in this setting – allows him to feel empathy with humans. Smokey, on the other hand, is a demon hunter whose guilt over opening the gates to hell propels him to hunt down any demon that escapes it, including Heart. However, eventually, the two characters reach a tentative truce,[25] and throughout its brief first season run, their relationship manages to garner a small but steadily increasing queer fandom that sees the potential for a star-crossed-lovers relationship between the two. Many aspects of their inter-being relationship can be seen as a mirror to Dean Winchester and Castiel's relationship from *Supernatural*, which, as evident in the amount of fan fiction pieces[26] still being written about the pairing, continues to be popular among the show's fans even years after the series finale. Here, too, Dean is a demon hunter and, though not a demon, but an angel, Castiel is similarly depicted as different from the rest of his brethren in his love for humans. After initial inter-being struggles, the two eventually form a close bond that many fans have interpreted as queer. This is a fact the series' commercial writers appear to have been aware of, as multiple references to it are made throughout the series.[27]

---

[24] Braime is the shipping name of Brienne of Tarth and Jaime Lannister from *Game of Thrones*, an expression of the desire to see these two characters in a relationship.
[25] Lundin, *Ship It*,17.
[26] In the 2022 "This Year's Top 100 Ship Stats," fan fiction website, *Archive of Our Own* (*AO3*), recorded 6,632 new fan fiction texts written in 2022, two years after the series' run ending, and 103,224 fan fiction texts in total, about the romantic pairing of Dean/Castiel alone, placing the pairing on the top 10 list of most written about character pairings.
Archive Of Our Own, s.v. "*AO3* Ship Stats 2022," last modified August 4, 2022, https://archiveofourown.org/works/40795074/chapters/102218811.
[27] Most notably so in season 10, episode 5 "Fan Fiction," in which the protagonists witness a school play based on a fictionalized version of the protagonists' demon hunting adventures. Both on and off stage, the Dean/Castiel pairing is referenced as the play explores their queer potential directly on stage, and the two female actors playing Dean

Demon Heart's commercial author is also portrayed as being aware of their fandom's queer reading of their two protagonists, with many of the paratexts leaning into it, with, for example, ambiguously romantic promotion photos that are perceived as showing Smokey and Heart gazing longingly into each other's eyes.[28] Interviews given by the commercial author of the series also remain intentionally vague about the expected textual queer outcome of the relationship, even when directly asked about it,[29] doing "whatever it damn well takes to get them to tune into the finale."[30] A strategy in line with queerbaiting, attempting to garner a queer audience, which, in the case of *Demon Heart*, is shown to be successful, as "[a] lot of people came to *Demon Heart* from other fandoms where they had gotten their hopes up about a gay ship and been disappointed."[31] However, both *Demon Heart* and *Supernatural* ultimately opt out of making the perceived queerness part of the series' canon, leaving the queer reading in its traditionally marginalized realm of plausible deniability. *Demon Heart* then becomes a stand-in not solely for *Supernatural*; rather, the slightly ambiguous connection to one particular fandom focuses the attention on the criticism of queerbaiting as a whole and the disappointment and the increasing distrust it generates within fans.

One of *Demon Heart*'s most prolific fans is *Ship It*'s sixteen-year-old protagonist Claire. Going by the name *heart-of-lightness* in online fandom spaces, she is well known and admired for her SmokeHeart slash[32] among other fans.[33] The queer potential between Smokey and Heart is what draws Claire to the show in the first place, her fan fiction becoming an expression of her queer desires, yet unrealized by even herself. Whenever Claire begins to question her sexuality, her thoughts spiral, and she is unable to find a clear answer for herself; instead, her mind eventually turns to SmokeHeart because "SmokeHeart always makes me feel better, like the world is manageable and love is real."[34] The solace she finds in the pairing intensifies her desire to see the queer ship be made part of the canon, which, in turn, becomes increasingly linked to her own queer journey. When Claire gets to travel from convention to convention with the cast

---

and Castiel are revealed to be a romantic couple. *Supernatural*, Season 10, episode 5, "Fan Fiction," created by Eric Kripke, aired November 11, 2014; USA: CW, 2021, DVD.
[28] Lundin, *Ship It*, 13.
[29] Lundin, *Ship It*, 69.
[30] Lundin, *Ship It*, 73.
[31] Lundin, *Ship It*, 18.
[32] Slash fiction is a subgenre of fan fiction writing "in which two (or more) characters of the same sex or gender are placed in a sexual or romantic situation with each other." Fanlore, s.v. "Slash," last modified October 17, 2022, 18:42, https://fanlore.org/wiki/Slash.
[33] Lundin, *Ship It*, 53.
[34] Lundin, *Ship It*, 18.

and crew of *Demon Heart*, she hatches a plan to make the series' author commit to SmokeHeart publicly. However, when pushed about the reasons for her planned actions, Claire is unable to admit her true feelings, even to herself, instead claiming that she is doing it, "[n]ot for me, [...] but for... for all the kids out there who are watching the show and didn't even know that someone like Smokey could be gay."[35] As Claire's frustration with both the series author and one of the lead actors grows over their unwillingness even to consider making SmokeHeart canon, Claire again turns to fan fiction to work through her feelings.[36]

It is Claire's fan fiction and her personal interactions with twenty-three-year-old Forest that sends *Demon Heart*'s lead actor on his own journey of queer acceptance. Landing his first lead role in a series with the part of Smokey, Forest is still unaccustomed to the demands of having a fandom. Wrongly assuming that the action-fantasy series' fans are mostly comprised of "fan*boys*,"[37] he is shocked to discover their largely female fanbase at his first fan convention, not to mention the queer one. When confronted at a Q&A by Claire about the SmokeHeart pairing, Forest publicly calls Claire crazy for suggesting it.[38] This incident again seems to draw a satirical line to *Supernatural*, as it is reminiscent of the dismissive and adverse reaction actor Jensen Ackles, who portrays Dean on *Supernatural*, had when asked about Destiel[39] at a fan convention.[40] Obsessed with wanting to be cast as the hyper-masculine action hero from his favorite game-turned-blockbuster, Forest is afraid to be associated with anything that might tarnish his reputation, including having one of his characters be called gay.[41] As he and Claire are forced to travel together on their convention tour, the two begin to build a fragile bond over multiple conversations, during one of which it is hinted that Forest's intense negative reactions to being associated with a gay character might stem from his own internalized homophobia.[42] Eventually prompted by curiosity, though, Forest reads one of Claire's SmokeHeart fan fiction pieces,[43] and his perception of queerness slowly begins to shift toward a more open stance. Instead of reacting

---

[35] Lundin, *Ship It*, 97.
[36] Lundin, *Ship It*, 139.
[37] Lundin, *Ship It*, 62, emphasis added.
[38] Lundin, *Ship It*, 70.
[39] The shipping name for the *Supernatural* characters Dean Winchester and Castiel.
[40] Aja Romano, "How 1 Question Triggered a 'Supernatural' Fandom Meltdown," last modified June 1, 2021, *Daily Dot*, https://www.dailydot.com/unclick/jensen-ackles-homophobia-supernatural-fandom/.
[41] Lundin, *Ship It*, 81.
[42] Lundin, *Ship It*, 127.
[43] Lundin, *Ship It*, 180.

with ire as before, he is curious about SmokeHeart fanart,[44] begins to imagine a queer relationship between two male fans when he sees them hugging,[45] and eventually even recognizes the queer potential in his own acting.[46] This queer possibility in Forest's acting is what situates his character in a position of relative power, as it may influence the interpretation of the television text, though not what is put in the script directly. A position, as Claire points out to him, he could, nevertheless, at the least use to "heal some old wounds"[47] caused to fans by other commercial texts that made use of queerbaiting by him speaking out publicly in favor of SmokeHeart.

While the satirical connection between *Demon Heart* and *Supernatural* leaves room for interpretation, Olivia Dade's *Spoiler Alert* makes it a point to have the relationship between HBO's hit series *Game of Thrones* (*GoT*) and its fictional facsimile *Gods of the Gates* (*GotG*) not be missed. The final words of Dade's acknowledgments for the novel are directed at the Braime fandom, which she states to have been a part of, with "some signs of that [noticeable] throughout this manuscript."[48] Indeed, there are multiple parallels found between *GoT* and *GotG*, besides the obvious reference in their preferred abbreviations. In *Spoiler Alter*, *GotG* is the recent television adaptation of a fictional novel series by the same title. Both the novels and the television series tell the story of Aeneas, a demi-god hero inspired by Virgil's ancient one, who enters a political marriage with Lavinia, a female character who, in the books, is described as "unattractive in terms of conventional beauty."[49] This translates in the television adaptation into the actor cast for the role of Lavinia not wearing any make-up and only "dull, unflattering clothing," which is perceived to "undercut the resonance of that story line, but echoes of it are still there in the show."[50]

This relationship is where the fictional fandom's interest lies. Although an arranged marriage, beautiful Aeneas and unattractive Lavinia come to appreciate each other on a level that goes beyond the surface of their physical appearances. It is a sentiment appreciated by fans who, for their validation, "desperately needed to read and watch the story of how a woman most considered homely or downright hideous could earn respect, admiration, desire, and eventually love from the man she desired and loved herself."[51] This

---

[44] Lundin, *Ship It*, 204.
[45] Lundin, *Ship It*, 216.
[46] Lundin, *Ship It*, 305.
[47] Lundin, *Ship It*, 341.
[48] Dade, *Spoiler*, 403.
[49] Dade, *Spoiler*, 156.
[50] Dade, *Spoiler*, 156.
[51] Dade, *Spoiler*, 156.

pairing mirrors the characters of *GoT*'s Jaime Lannister and Brienne of Tarth and their odd romantic pairing of a golden boy hero and a woman daring to live outside of the heteronormative understanding of feminine beauty and behavior. Although a morally ambiguous character, Jaime outwardly fits the description of a knight in shining armor. Brienne, on the other hand, while not explicitly described as hideous, her desire to live by a knightly code of conduct, her above-average height, and her prowess with the sword code her as conventionally masculine by heteronormative standards and so as unattractive as a romantic partner. Still, in episode five of the final season of *GoT*, their relationship finally grows into a romantic one. The mirroring of these two pairings is also present in both couples' unhappy endings. Jaime and Brienne break up in the same episode where they admit their feelings for each other, with Jaime abandoning both his character's carefully established redemptive arc and a sobbing Brienne.[52] As *GotG* moves beyond the novel series on which it is based, most of the major female storylines begin to derail, again a heavy satirical hint at *GoT*, and the interactions between Aeneas and Lavinia are reduced to superficial and misogynistic exchanges, with suggestions of Aeneas being unfaithful.[53]

In contrast to the teenaged and young adult protagonists in *Ship It*, *Spoiler Alert*'s fan fiction author April, a thirty-six-year-old self-described fat woman,[54] knows exactly what drew her to the romance of *GotG*'s Lavinia and Aeneas. Having struggled with self-worth all her life due to her parents and ex-partners shaming her for her size, the series' emotional merit for April lies in the appearance-transcending love between the two characters. Though Lavinia is not like April, the character's unconventional looks nonetheless give April hope that she, too, might find a partner who is accepting. Having found a like-minded community of Lavineas[55] fans in the series' fandom gives her the confidence to post a full-body picture of herself dressed up in a Lavinia cosplay to *Twitter*, which results, to April's dismay, though not surprise, in a string of fat shaming comments.[56] In response to someone tagging Marcus, the actor who embodies Aeneas in the television series, in one of those insulting comments in an attempt to get him to also engage in fat shaming, Marcus publicly asks April out on a date.[57] With the budding romance plot between in-shape Marcus and curvy-shaped April, *Spoiler Alert* recreates an echo of both the Lavineas

---

[52] *Game of Thrones*, Season 8, episode 5, "The Bells," created and written by David Bennioff and D.B. Weiss, aired May 12, 2019, USA: HBO, 2020, DVD.
[53] Dade, *Spoiler*, 66.
[54] Dade, *Spoiler*, 156.
[55] The shipping name for the characters Lavinia and Aeneas.
[56] Dade, *Spoiler*, 26.
[57] Dade, *Spoiler*, 27.

and the Braime pairing in their combination of desirable men with women deemed undesirable by society. After a misunderstanding on one of their dates ensues, in which April believes Marcus was trying to give her dieting tips,[58] April turns to her fandom community for solace by posting about her feelings and calling out fat shaming not only in commercial publishing but also in fan fiction.[59] More open to April's criticism because of their passion for the Lavineas pairing, her small fan community responds with compassion and promises of future accountability, most vocally among them April's long-standing online friend, who goes by the moniker of Book!AeneasWouldNever (BAWN).[60] BAWN even goes on to post a fan fiction piece about a misunderstanding between Lavinia and Aeneas similar to that of April and Marcus, though BAWN's narrative is told from the perspective of Aeneas' character. As she reads this fan fic, April revisits her conversation with Marcus. Reading from the perspective of Aeneas, so from the point of view of the person who inadvertently hurt their partner, enables April to consider Marcus' point of view, leading her to suspect that they actually had a misunderstanding after all, and so, eventually, she reaches out to Marcus again despite her hurt feelings.[61]

However, that BAWN's fan fic mirrors Marcus and April's misunderstanding is not a coincidence. BAWN, it turns out, is Marcus' alter-fandom-ego through which he has been expressing, over the past seven years of the series' run, first his passion for the Lavineas pairing and eventually his dismay about the misogynistic turn his character took in the television adaptation.[62] With this dual identity, Marcus becomes a hybrid character, embodying both the fan side and the commercial side of the argument. His access to the Lavineas fandom allows him to connect with April on a deeper level and to use their mutual love and knowledge of the ship to reach out to her through his writing. His position as actor and public figure, on the other hand, allows him to counteract some of the misogyny perpetuated through the later seasons of *GotG*, which he does by publicly asking April out on a date after she is fat shamed. In his position of actor, however, though adorned with some power, Marcus is constantly reminded of his dependency on the commercial authors in that position. He is disappointed by the failed chances of inclusion but cannot express these feelings publicly for fear of losing his career,[63] similar to Forest in *Ship It*.

---

[58] Dade, *Spoiler*, 147.
[59] Dade, *Spoiler*, 156.
[60] Dade, *Spoiler*, 166.
[61] Dade, *Spoiler*, 181.
[62] Dade, *Spoiler*, 6.
[63] Dade, *Spoiler*, 105.

Both of the examples presented here have honed in on two marginalized identities, the queer character and the 'unattractive' female character, and their representation in mainstream media. By presenting us with a fictional television text and its accompanying fandom, the fix-it novel can bring together the two opposing sides and establish the battlefield for competing over how representation of marginalized identities should happen. If not necessarily explicitly, the satirical connection of this fictional television text to a real-life counterpart and its issues with representation its fandom desires to see resolved is a basic principle of the fix-it novel. Because by connecting its narrative to an actual television text prominent in the public discourse and its perceived problematic representation, the fix-it novel's eventual call for action, as opposed to the reach of the intra-fandom discourse prompted by the fix-it fic, attempts to move itself into the mainstream discussion, contributing to the wider critical discourse of actual marginalization.

By having one of the two focus characters as a major player within the fandom, the fix-it novel gives a voice to those marginalized by the same texts they passionately follow. Both novels created fan author characters who are vocal and outspoken about their need for representation in the public discourse. These characters and the platform the fix-it novel provides allow for the traditionally disadvantaged side of the discussion to be heard articulately, as opposed to the mocking inclusions they are used to from television media. By having the second focus character be part of the production process of the problematic series, the fix-it novel highlights the need for the commercial end of the discussion to take action, as the marginalized fan alone is perceived to not be in a position of enough power to influence their identity's representation in the commercial text. In this way, the fix-it novel creates a space in which the novel's author may demonstrate, discuss, and seek to remedy the increasingly distrustful relationship between fan and commercial text while also highlighting the uneven power distribution in the argument between fandoms and commercial texts when it comes to the decision-making process of marginalized identity representation. Intriguingly, both analyzed examples chose actors as representatives for the side of the commercial text, even though from a pure executive power point of view, writers or showrunners might be the more obvious choice. The position of actor, though not the only possibility, is most likely chosen for two reasons. On the one hand, they embody hope for inclusion for the fan author as they portray at least one of the characters the fan author views as crucial for a successful inclusive representation of their marginalized identity. On the other hand, the position of power they hold is relative in so far that they may add nuance to the characters they play, which often influences interpretation. However, they do not have complete authority over their character and are still subject to the decisions made by the commercial writers and producers. In this way, the fix-it novel seeks to establish allyship between fans and actors against the perceived true antagonists, the commercial (television) authors.

A Call for (Commercial) Change

Ship It's central conflict revolves around the ambiguity of queer inclusion, of which the strategy of queerbaiting makes use. Due to this vague, non-commitment type of allusion to queer potential, queer fans are strung along by the hope of eventual open inclusion, and Claire is no exception and becomes attached to the series due to its queer potential. Her plans to make Jaime, *Demon Heart*'s commercial author, commit SmokeHeart to canon, however, are stalled by Jaime's evasiveness, both in answering her questions about the queer ship,[64] and in spending more than a few moments with her alone.[65] Jaime is using both his position as an adult and as the commercial author to suppress any meaningful interaction with her or exchange about queer inclusion. Eventually, Claire, driven into an emotional corner as the airing of the final episode of the season is approaching, forces Jaime into an interaction with her by hijacking Jaime's *Twitter* account and changing his profile picture into one supporting SmokeHeart.[66] Claire tries to appeal to Jaime's empathy by reminding him of his own underdog origins as a meek *Spiderman* fan.[67] However, instead of choosing to use his acquired power as a commercial author to uplift another disenfranchised identity, Jaime admits to using this power instead to garner an audience for his series by actively queerbaiting with no intention of ever making it canon.[68] Realizing that queerbaited fans like Claire are becoming increasingly difficult for him to handle as they demand actual representation, Jaime finally opts for the bury-your-gays trope by firing Forest from *Demon Heart* and killing off his character Smokey in an attempt to also bury the gay rumors around the character.[69]

The novel's ending makes it unequivocally clear that there is no hope left for Forest to return to *Demon Heart* and so for SmokeHeart to become canon.[70] The resolution of the conflict, and, with it, the hope for open queer inclusion instead, comes with a new job offer for Forest. In a final show of respect for his queer fans, Forest decides to publicly acknowledge SmokeHeart's potential, reassuring his fans that they are "not delusional" about the queer content of the

---

[64] Lundin, *Ship*, 91.
[65] Lundin, *Ship*, 100.
[66] Lundin, *Ship*, 268.
[67] Lundin, *Ship*, 283.
[68] Lundin, *Ship It*, 274.
[69] Lundin, *Ship It*, 292.
[70] Lundin, *Ship It*, 366.

series and that their "opinions are valid."[71] He and his co-star then proceed to act out a kiss scene in their roles of Smokey and Heart at a convention in front of their fans.[72] Though having no direct influence over the script as an actor, Forest nevertheless uses his position of relative power to at least validate his queer fans' desire for inclusion. Although this queer act presumably costs him the chance of playing the hyper-masculine action hero role,[73] Forest is rewarded with a part in a new series,[74] one that, to Claire's delight, promises to be queer inclusive.[75]

In *Spoiler Alert*, on the other hand, the commercial authors of *GotG*, Ron, and R.J. – another satirical line drawn to *GoT*'s showrunners David Benioff and D.B. Weiss – never appear in person, so there never is a chance for April to confront them directly. One of the in-narrative reasons for this is that the novel's storyline sets in when the final season of *GotG* wraps. With the series having officially ended, there is no chance for April to petition for better representation as there was with *Demon Heart* in *Ship It*. Thus, this novel's major conflict does not revolve around remedying *GotG*'s perceived failed representation of the 'undesirable' female character but around understanding how the commercial authors of this series and mainstream media have done injustice to female characters of all identities. April's geologist explanation of how landowners may deal with contaminated soil can be seen as a metaphor for how commercial authors may deal with decades' worth of legacy of failed inclusive representation. She explains, "[e]ither the owner will devote the enormous amount of time and effort and money necessary to dig up all the contamination and dispose of it elsewhere, or they won't."[76] If the owners decide against rooting out the contamination caused by damaging past decisions, April adds, then "the land can never be used for any purpose that would require digging below the surface level."[77]

Spoiler Alert seems to follow a parallel line of thought when it comes to female identities in media. If the systemic issues of sexism that underlie the representation of female identities are not examined and addressed, then those identities will continue to remain superficial and sexist caricatures. To illustrate this, instead of exclusively presenting the reader with fan fiction pieces like *Ship It* did, *Spoiler Alert* includes direct examples of multiple types of media texts and paratexts, such as messages exchanged between the actors,[78] DMs

---

[71] Lundin, *Ship It*, 356.
[72] Lundin, *Ship It*, 360.
[73] Lundin, *Ship It*, 354.
[74] Lundin, *Ship It*, 369.
[75] Lundin, *Ship It*, 373.
[76] Dade, *Spoiler*, 75.
[77] Dade, *Spoiler*, 76.
[78] Dade, *Spoiler*, 68.

exchanged between fan fiction authors,[79] and most interestingly in this context, sample scripts from commercial television and film texts.[80] The depicted commercial scripts exclusively present texts that promote misogynistic, yet common female stereotypes and plot devices, such as fridging,[81] the Manic Pixie Dream Girl,[82] and the Cherchez la Femme,[83] among others. In line with this and April's metaphor, the resolution of *Spoiler Alert*'s central conflict is ultimately found in a new commercially published film adaptation of *GotG*. In addition to reprising his role as Aeneas with his female co-stars from *GotG*, Marcus is also the producer of this film, lending him more power over decisions about their characters, with this adaptation promising to be better to its female characters than *GotG*. As such, it is fittingly described by April as "one big fix-it fic in response to *Gods of the Gates*."[84] Interestingly, the ultimate narrative reward for Marcus comes in the form of an email to him from E. Wade, the author of the fictional novel series *GotG* was based on. In this email, E. Wade validates Marcus' take on his character, also implying that she has read his and April's fan fiction while devaluing the version that the commercial television authors created.[85] The novel seems to spend its entire narrative deconstructing the idea of the commercial author-god figures of the series showrunners only to reestablish the concept on the penultimate page of the epilogue by imbuing the commercial novel author with the power of legitimization. With this decision, both commercial television authors and fan fiction authors are placed on the same power level by the novel author.

The fix-it novel's central conflict highlights the disadvantaged position of power fans find themselves in when fighting for their desire to exist in the mainstream media landscape. In the two examples of this chapter, this illustration is achieved via two different strategies. *Ship It* creates a commercial author character who is explicitly evasive about a critical conversation and downright hostile in a direct confrontation by creating an almost fantastical scenario in which a fan tours with the cast and crew of the commercial television text. *Spoiler Alert*, on the other hand, creates a more realistic picture, demonstrating how most fans find themselves out of reach of the commercial authors by never presenting the fan character with the ability to confront them in its narrative. The central conflict of the fix-it novel is resolved by attempting to consolidate both positions. By allying the character involved in the production process –in these two cases the actors and their newfound

---

[79] Dade, *Spoiler*, 43.
[80] Dade, *Spoiler*, 65.
[81] Dade, *Spoiler*, 168.
[82] Dade, *Spoiler*, 195.
[83] Dade, *Spoiler*, 123.
[84] Dade, *Spoiler*, 396.
[85] Dade, *Spoiler*, 399.

sensitivity for the needs of the marginalized group– with the fan character, the ending is able to offer hope for a new, more inclusive commercial text. In this way, the fix-it novel is both a call for action to commercial television authors and a show of solidarity to marginalized fans from the commercial novel author's corner of the discourse.

As commercial television authors attempt to hold on to their unquestioned authority in one corner, and fan authors seek to see their individualistic needs realized in commercial fiction in the other corner, the fix-it novel is emerging in a hybrid position between the two camps. Functioning as an intersection between commercial publication and barely veiled fan tribute situates the fix-it novel as a kind of cultural consolidator, seeking to not only fix what has ostensibly been problematically handled in the commercial source text but also to mend the relationship between fan and commercial text in general. In this sense, the fix-it novel fulfills a dual function, as it is arguing for fan fiction to be acknowledged as making use of the potential to express the emotional needs of a diverse viewership and, at the same time, highlighting how commercial (television) texts could also do so but choose not to. This disparity becomes poignantly evident in Claire's frank and ultimately fruitless exchange with *Demon Heart*'s commercial writer, Jaime. As the frustration with exploitative commercial writing grows, so will the discourse around this abuse of the power to represent, with the fix-it novel emerging as one such outlet.

Additionally, it needs to be considered that, although created for a smaller, more specific audience, with less money flow involved than in the production of a television series, novels are still commercially published products. As such, it is no surprise that the fix-it novel seems to attempt to reconcile the ideas of inclusive *and* commercial writing by highlighting the problematic structures of the current system with the help of the inclusion of fan fiction and then rewarding their characters with a hopeful future in which the two are not mutually exclusive. What the fix-it novel does categorically state, though, is that fan fiction writing hands the power to represent to underrepresented identities, such as curvy April or queer Claire, making fan fiction reading and writing a meaningful part of the process of the fan fiction author's self-discovery, self-expression, and, ultimately, self-empowerment. By having the happy ending involve the promise of more inclusive *commercial* texts, however, there is a suggestion of the limitations within which fan fiction writing operates when it comes to shifting or evoking mainstream opinion towards underrepresented identities because fan fiction writing happens predominantly in semi-private, subcultural spaces. Had the male leads of the novels not been actors actively involved in the creation process of the commercial texts and thus already situated in a position of relative commercial power, the promise of more inclusive commercial texts would most likely not have come to be. Ultimately, what the fix-it novel then inadvertently shows is that *who* uses their power to represent diverse identities still matters in the context of larger cultural change.

Bibliography

"*AO3* Ship Stats 2022." *Archive of Our own.* Last modified August 4, 2022. https://archiveofourown.org/works/40795074/chapters/102218811.

Breslaw, Anna. *Scarlet Epstein Hates It Here.* New York: Penguin Random House, 2016.

Dade, Olivia. *Spoiler Alert.* London: Piatkus, 2020.

De Kosnik, Abigail. *Fandom as Free Labor.* New York: Routledge, 2013.

Duffett, Mark. *Understanding Fandom: An Introduction to the Study of Media Fan Culture.* London: Bloomsbury Academic, 2013.

Fanlore. "Fix-it." Last modified March 13, 2023. *Fanlore.* https://fanlore.org/wiki/Fix-it.

———. "RPF." Last modified April 23, 2023. *Fanlore.* https://fanlore.org/wiki/RPF.

———. "Self-insertion." Last modified December 20, 2022. *Fanlore.* https://fanlore.org/wiki/Self-insertion.

———. "Slash." Last modified October 12, 2022. *Fanlore.* https://fanlore.org/wiki/Slash.

Fathallah, Judith. *Fanfiction and the Author: How Fan Fic Changes Popular Cultural Texts.* Amsterdam: Amsterdam University Press, 2017.

Game of Thrones. Season 8, episode 5, "The Bells." Directed by Miguel Sapochnik, written by David Bennioff and D. B. Weiss. Aired May 12, 2019 on HBO, 2020, DVD.

Gonzalez, Victoria M. "Swan Queen, Shipping, and Boundary Regulation in Fandom." *Transformative Works and Cultures*, vol. 22, (2016).

Jenkins, Henry, Sam Ford and Joshua Green. *Spreadable Media: Creating Value and Meaning in a Networked Culture: with a New Afterword.* New York: New York University Press. 2018.

Klune, TJ. *The Extraordinaries.* New York: Tom Doherty Associates Book, 2020-2022.

Lundin, Britta. *Ship It.* New York: Freeform Books, 2018.

Nordin, Emma. "From Queer Reading to Queerbaiting: The Battle over the Polysemic Text and the Power of Hermeneutics." Master's Thesis, Stockholms Universitet, 2015.

Romano, Aja. "How 1 Question Triggered a 'Supernatural' Fandom Meltdown." In *Daily Dot* (2013), Last modified June 1, 2021. https://www.dailydot.com/unclick/jensen-ackles-homophobia-supernatural-fandom/.

Rowell, Rainbow. *Fangirl.* London: Macmillan, 2013.

Sheehan, Cassidy. "Queer-baiting on the BBC's Sherlock: Addressing the Invalidation of Queer Experiences through Online Fan Fiction Communities." Undergraduate Research Posters, Virginia Commonwealth University, 2015.

Sherlock. Created by Mark Gatiss and Steven Moffat. Aired July 25, 2010 – January 15, 2017 on BBC One, 2021, DVD.

Supernatural. Season 10, episode 5, "Fan Fiction." Directed by Phil Sgriccia, written by Erick Kripke. Aired November 11, 2014, on The CW, 2021, DVD

Chapter 10

Real-Life Magic: *Harry Potter* and the Fan Film Canon

Jordan Hansen

Indiana University of Pennsylvania

Abstract: In this chapter, Hansen examines fan-film as a form of fix-it fic, offering fans a visual component that transcends traditional, written fix-it fics. Through this lens, Hansen examines the aspects of performativity, and how affective hermeneutics is more identifiable through the physicality of film. They argue that actors provide a deeper experience to the viewers that cannot be achieved through the written word. Using *Harry Potter* fan-films as a means of analysis, Hansen shows how the fan-film also provides viewers with an outlet for examining gender, race, and sexuality.

Keywords: fan-film, affective hermeneutics, performativity, physicality, acting, tags, *Harry Potter, Youtube, AO3*, fix-it fics.

***

While commercial adaptations, such as *Wide Sargasso Sea* and *The Lion King*, have been heavily analyzed for their connections to their source texts (*Jane Eyre* and *Hamlet*, respectively), there is less critical analysis for unofficial or noncommercialized adaptations such as fan fiction. Even less analyzed is the rise of the fan film, or a film version of fan fiction, typically created by private, non-profit content creators. Literary fan fiction is found on websites like *Archive of Our own (AO3)* or *Fanfiction.net*. However, fan films are delegated to creator platforms such as *TikTok* or *YouTube* because of their easy accessibility for creators and fans alike. This chapter aims to consider fan films as a unique extension of the fix-it fic process that includes a performance aspect beyond the typical reading material, as well as being the next step in literary and film adaptation. Additionally, it will consider how those films are analyzed through the lens of their source material regarding gender, sexuality, and race representation. For this chapter, I will examine several *TikTok* creators who create fan adaptations of *Harry Potter* characters and scenarios that may or may not be canon-compliant, as well as four film films on *YouTube*: the "Noble

House of Black" series by Sasha Sloan,[1] "Mudblood" parts 1-3 directed by Faraj Conrad,[2] "Voldemort: Origins of the Heir" directed by Gianmaria Pezzato,[3] and "Dumbledore and Grindelwald - The Greater Good - Secrets of Dumbledore Prequel" directed by Justin Zagri.[4] Through an analysis of these fan films, it is clear how fix-it fan fiction is a branch of adaptation studies which should be included in an analysis of gender, sexuality, and feminist conversations within specific subgenres. I argue that fan fiction, particularly fan films, has created a new source for literary criticism within adaptation studies that allows for deeper critical analysis of queer and feminist studies within specific popular culture areas. The goal is to understand how fan films create a new opportunity for film and literary criticism within the scope of adaptation studies and theorize how future creation of fan films can be used to understand their source material and adaptive possibilities through the lens of fixing the original source content.

In June 2016, *Harry Potter and the Cursed Child* debuted on the London stage, becoming the first theater production in Harry Potter's story and giving fans something akin to an epilogue to the original seven books (and eight films). In November of the same year, the first *Fantastic Beasts and Where to Find Them* film premiered in movie theaters, bracketing the original canon with a prequel meant to fill in plot gaps created by the author. For fans who have been following the stories anytime since their original publication through the premier of the final film, these extras provided by J.K. Rowling were meant to give fans both a sense of closure and serve as a form of explanation for how the world Rowling created began in the first novel. However, before these extras came into existence, and often despite them, fans have long since taken up the mantle of filling in these gaps themselves by writing fan fiction. Several websites contain hundreds of thousands of fan-created imaginings of Rowling's characters in all sorts of alternative storylines, ranging from those that closely follow the original canon to those that veer wildly off course. Interestingly, in recent years, fans have decided that simply writing these stories may or may not be enough.

Thanks to easy access to social media platforms like *TikTok* and public streaming services like *YouTube*, live-action fan fictions and fix-it fics have risen significantly in popularity due to their visual entertainment aspect, production

---

[1] Sasha Sloan, "The Noble House of Black," *YouTube* video, modified September 1, 2023, https://www.youtube.com/playlist?list=PLXRzEyWb-mn_qjkjmlp-uBEky2bZHlV7G.

[2] Conrad Faraj, "Mudblood," YouTube video, modified September 8, 2023, https://www.youtube.com/playlist?list=PLXMPSiuBPSUhsFzfLyH7FyM8UtfXJ93pZ.

[3] Gianmaria Pezzato, "Voldemort: Origins of the Heir" *YouTube* video, Jan 13, 2018, https://www.youtube.com/@tryanglefilms.

[4] Justin Zagri, "Dumbledore and Grindelwald - The Greater Good - Secrets of Dumbledore Prequel," *YouTube* video, December 3, 2013, https://www.youtube.com/watch?v=OGHBwk0s.

capabilities, and enhanced storytelling opportunities. Fan fiction writers are now able to produce stories that not only match the energy of the original canon productions and go beyond words on a computer or phone screen to bring those stories to life. There is also the added potential for content creators to break into a new form of content that aims to create a deeper understanding of popular culture topics, both for content creators and their audiences. While there is little theoretical exploration into fan films, there has been increasing debate not only on the merit of fan fiction as a literary source but also on the development of fan fiction study as a critical genre. Considering these creators' additions to the fan fiction canon, fan films act as fix-it fics that meet the same visual appeal as the original films while maintaining original content. These films provide rewrites and additional commentary on prequel and sequel events, allowing for fans to fill in the blanks left by the author and aid in a more inclusive understanding of the original canon. The purpose of this study is to understand how the making of fan films presents new possibilities for gender, sexuality, and race expression in popular culture fan fiction. By looking at several *Harry Potter* fan films on *TikTok* and *YouTube* and analyzing the adaptation process in source texts to fan fiction, this chapter investigates how fan films can be used as literary texts to analyze how gender and race are reconstructed in these adaptations.

Before discussing the chosen fan films, it is important to discuss the definition of fan fiction as it pertains academically and relevant platforms on which they are composed today. In the past, some authors, for instance, Anne Rice, vehemently abhorred fan fiction about their works.[5] Other authors, J. K. Rowling included, accept it as long as the writers are not making any money from it.[6] The definition of fan fiction, according to Sheenagh Pugh, is "writing, whether official or unofficial, paid or unpaid, which makes use of an accepted canon of characters, settings, and plots generated by another writer or writers."[7] Canon is the source material created by the original creator of said characters, settings, and plots and serves as the basic form of guidelines from which all fan fiction writers base their adaptations. How much or how little fan fiction writers use is what keeps the art of fan fiction active since it allows writers to stick as close to or as far from the source material as they please. As Pugh states, "Canon is a framework to write against," and fan fiction writers

---

[5] "Important Message From Anne On Fan Fiction," *Anne Rice: The Official Site*, Accessed September 10, 2023, http://annerice.com/ReaderInteraction-MessagesToFans.html.
[6] "Approve or Disapprove: What 8 Famous Authors Think of Fan Fiction," *Fansided*, Modified November 9, 2021, https://winteriscoming.net/2021/07/04/8-famous-authors-think-fanfiction-george-rr-martin-anne-rice-jrr-tolkien/5.
[7] Sheenagh Pugh, *The Democratic Genre: Fan Fiction In A Literary* Context (Seren 2005), 40.

take this to varying extremes, writing everything from canon-reliant stories to those labeled "Epilogue What Epilogue (EWE)" on fan fiction sites (these stories tend to ignore anything that happened in the *Harry Potter* series after the end of the Battle of Hogwarts) to completely new storylines that pull canon characters into scenarios otherwise never imagined in their original existence.[8]

Many storylines in fan fiction are reused so often or seem as plausible as any canon event that they become "fanon." Bronwen Thomas defines fanon as "the process whereby material is created as an addition or supplement to the canon becomes accepted and used by other fanfiction writers."[9] The fan consensus that Draco Malfoy is a misunderstood child rather than a true blood-supremacist villain is one example of these fanon moments. Thomas also mentions "Janet Maybin and Neil Mercer's concept of 'dialogic' canon," or the intersections between canon and fanon that run linearly to each other, meaning storylines that intersect either with or occur in the background of the main plot without making changes to the plot itself.[10] Some examples of this include prequel stories such as those about the Mauraders (James Potter, Sirius Black, Remus Lupin, and Peter Pettigrew, who together created the Maurader's Map in the *Harry Potter* series), stories about background characters that fans have decided are underdeveloped and deserve more focus through parallel storytelling, and sequel stories that are set up to take place after the canon story has ended, focusing on further developing already existing storylines to determine how characters may have acted once the creator of the said characters has decided to end their story. Regardless of how much or how little canon is adhered to, all fan fiction relies on the author's ability to suspend disbelief for their readers. Their world-building creates a blueprint for understanding that the things that occur within this world are the standard; everything that happens within it must then make sense, no matter who writes it.

Fanlore (fanlore.org) has a comprehensive list of every website where one can find written *Harry Potter* fan fiction. There are 105 active archival sites (not including those labeled 'defunct') for all sorts of character pairings, themes, sexual preferences, and multi-universe stories. *Archive of Our own*[11] and

---

[8] Pugh, *The Democratic Genre*, 40.
[9] Bronwen Thomas, "Canons and Fanons: Literary Fanfiction Online," *Dichtung Digital Journal Fur Kunst Und Kultur Digitaler Medien*, vol. 37, no. 9 (2007): 2. https://doi.org/10.25969/mediarep/17701.
[10] Thomas "Canons and Fanons," 2.
[11] *Harry Potter*, on *Archive of Our Own*, https://archiveofourown.org/works/search?work_search%5Bquery%5D=Harry+Potter.

FanFiction.net[12] are two of the most used sites in the United States, with approximately 483,327 and 845,000 stories (as of September 2023), respectively, making *Harry Potter* one of the most popular worlds to fan fictionalize on both websites when filtered in descending order. Authors on these websites can sub-label all their works, choosing from several worlds within *Harry Potter* about which to write, including books, movies, Hogwarts-Era, Pre- and Post-Hogwarts, Marauders, Founders, and Next Generation. Those who choose any of the first seven tend to have one major thing in common: the desire to fill in any gaps that they feel exist in the original canon, making them fix-it fics by default. As Thomas states, "Fanfiction precisely aims to extend the fictional world of the source text and to even go beyond it to create alternate universes (AUs)."[13] Indeed, fan fiction readers tend to find themselves seeking out fan fiction because they have exhausted – or are exhausted with – the limitations of the canon and are asking for more.

The *Harry Potter* world is extensive, and it seems as though each year, Rowling is adding something new to keep up with demand. However, fan readers and fic writers alike still find themselves looking for alternatives to Rowling's work while still maintaining the same worlds. A certain level of presumption can be made regarding how familiar fan fiction readers are with the source material; however, it is unfair to assume that everyone has read the books. Many have only seen the films, and while that is valid, there is always more information in the books than the movies will ever provide. As such, the *Harry Potter* Wiki contains a wealth of information that many fans use to find information about the *Harry Potter* series that was not included in the films or was provided later by the author after the novels were published.[14] As the name suggests, the *Harry Potter* Wiki is a Wikipedia-style archive centered entirely on characters, events, settings, creatures, spells, and other points from every corner of the franchise, including books and films. This website is a treasure trove of source information for fic writers, particularly for those looking to keep material in their fics as close to canon as possible. For example, it matters to some to get Hermione Granger's birthday correct, and the *Harry Potter* Wiki provides that information and more. What writers do with that information is up to them, and the endless possibilities available keep the process alive.

---

[12] Harry Potter, on *FanFiction.net*, https://www.fanfiction.net/search/?keywords=Harry+Potter&ready=1&type=story.
[13] Thomas "Canons and Fanons," 3.
[14] For example, J.K. Rowling mentioned Dumbledore's sexuality after the books had been published.

From one site to another: TikTok and YouTube

Fan film is a much newer development in fan fiction writing, as writers move from one-shots and multi-chapter fics to complex screenplays in a way that mirrors the path of the original canon stories. While there will always be fans who prefer the original aspects of reading a book (or a written online story), there are fans who enjoy and even prefer watching a live-action version because of a different personability and relatability in watching real people bring their favorite characters to life. In her article, Anna Wilson discusses "affective hermeneutics" or "knowing through feeling."[15] This process involves readers and viewers understanding the stories through an empathizing process and implies a deeper personal connection with the stories that result in better critical engagement with the material. Wilson explains the importance of affective hermeneutics when she states:

> Affective hermeneutics direct focus toward moments of high emotion in a text that stimulate equally strong feelings in the reader; these heighten a sense of empathy, connection, or intimacy between the reader and the characters in the text. Affective hermeneutics also seek to fill the gaps in canon through attention to the emotional lives of the texts themselves.[16]

Many fan fiction writers employ affective hermeneutics in their stories to build the connections between their fix-it fics and the audience brought in through the original texts, and both affective hermeneutics and fix-it fics are designed to fill similar gaps in the overarching storylines. Still, fan film creators arguably achieve this better than traditional fan fiction writers because they physically embody those roles and visually engage their fans beyond words on a page.

On a smaller visual scale, there are many *TikTok* content creators that do an immersive character development in three minutes or less. Some of the most popular included Chanel Williams (@chanwills0), who does an often humorous, but sometimes more critical, presentation of Professor Minerva McGonagall;[17] Ash Valmont (@ashvalmont), who presents a version of young Sirius Black (Harry Potter's godfather);[18] and Lou (@cultsweaters),[19] who

---

[15] Anna Wilson, "The Role of Affect in Fan Fiction," *Transformative Works and Cultures*, vol. 21 (2016): paragraph 2.4. https://doi.org/10.3983/twc.2016.0684/
[16] Wilson, "The Role of Affect," paragraph 2.4.
[17] Chanel Williams, (@chanwills0), *TikTok*, https://www.tiktok.com/@chanwills0
[18] Ash Valmont (@ashvalmont), *TikTok*, https://www.tiktok.com/@ashvalmont.
[19] Lou (@cultsweaters), *TikTok*, https://www.tiktok.com/@cultsweaters.

portrays multiple characters from the canon, both male and female. They have an equal distribution of videos that are both comical presentations of the characters and deeply emotional ones, often set to equally emotional music/scores, meant to provide viewers with snippets of otherwise unseen or hard-to-understand moments their chosen character(s) has gone through. The affective hermeneutics involved in even these short clips provide deeper connections for the creators playing them and for the viewers upon who's algorithmically designed "For You Page" (FYP) they appear. Additionally, like many fan fiction writers who deal with writing genders that are different from their own, *TikTok* cosplayers like Lou (@cultsweaters), who plays multiple genders in their videos, can provide evidence for the performative aspects of gender along with their character presentations, and how those performative aspects translate from paper to screen. In their article, Maria Karlsson and Christina Olin-Scheller discuss Lindgren Leavenworth and M. Isaksson's 2011 study, in which the latter:

> claim[s] that the fan fic writers are in dialogue not only with the source text, but also with cultural structures in general when renegotiating genre and gender conventions. In this perspective the dichotomy between male and female sexual identities can be blurred in the fan fics, and as a consequence the fans can explore queer alternatives to the heteronormativity of popular culture.[20]

While cosplay does provide a wonderful outlet for gender exploration, for content creators (particularly those identifying as non-binary and gender non-conforming) who actively and consciously explore gender in their daily lives, the ability to do so with their favorite characters also provides an ability for their viewers to do the same vicariously.

Alternatively, some content creators find that sticking to same-gender casting for their fan films is their prerogative. They make sure to cast their projects with actors and actresses who resemble the canon characters as much as possible (either based on the film actors or the book descriptions). The theatre production of *Harry Potter and the Cursed Child* began their debut shows with black actors cast as Hermione Granger and Rose Granger-Weasley, which has carried on being used in every production worldwide thus far. This is a canon break from the source material by another canon production, but content creators who make larger-scale fan films rather than smaller cosplay videos

---

[20] Marie Karlsson and Christina Olin-Scheller, "'Let's Party!' *Harry Potter* Fan Fiction Sites as Social Settings for Narrative Gender Constructs," *Gender and Language*, vol. 9.2 (2015): 170. http://doi.org/ 10.1558/genl.v9i2.17330.

have been able to make their own choices for what their characters will look like while remaining partial to canonicity. Sasha Sloan, for instance, has made sure to cast her fan series, "The Noble House of Black," according to canon portrayal from the original films. Sloan's series, in which she also is cast as Draco Malfoy's pure-blood mother Narcissa Malfoy née Black, is centered on the adolescent and young adult lives of the three Black sisters, Bellatrix LeStrange, Narcissa, and Andromeda Tonks, as well as their extended family (including Sirius Black), their spouses, and their relationship to Voldemort. The entire series is posted one three-minute video at a time to *TikTok*[21] and cross-posted to her *YouTube* channel as well.[22] This still developing prequel series is canon-reliant, or dialogical canon, since it presumably will end where the *Harry Potter* book series begins. Details of their fates can be found in everything from the books to the films, to the Harry Potter Wiki. The point of the series is to provide pre-Hogwarts information about how the Black family and their relatives found themselves involved with Voldemort that is not specifically discussed in any of Rowling's works, giving fans background information for many of their favorite morally gray and outright dark characters to try to empathize with – or justify their hatred for – these characters to a greater extent, thus both working with pre-established and underdeveloped canon and creating new canon in its own right. One of the most interesting parts of this fan film series is that it appears like a classic silent film, meaning it is entirely set to music, lacking verbal dialogue besides captions, making the process of affective hermeneutics entirely reliant on blocking (that is, the physical movements of an acted scene), music, and, to a certain extent, recognizability of the characters in the scenes. There is an interesting effect in watching Bellatrix LeStrange devolve into madness while her sisters struggle to protect her and the families they are growing, or in seeing how close Sirius Black is with his brother Regulus, who is already dead before Rowling's books begin their tale. Since the original series introduces these characters once they have already reached their maddened states, these types of fix-it fics provide context for their devolvement by explaining why they appear as they do in the original texts, thus providing the audience with another source for affective hermeneutics because of the deeper analysis into the origin of those character choices. Essentially, audiences are provided with more understanding of *why* Bellatrix or Sirius are the way they are rather than being expected to accept that Bellatrix is just crazy, or Sirius is just alone.

Along with Sloan's series, *YouTube* features an entire tag group dedicated to "fan films," including, but not limited to, *Harry Potter* films. These films, like

---

[21] Sasha Sloan (@shashaesloan), *TikTok*, https://www.tiktok.com/@sashaesloan?lang=en.
[22] Sloan, "The Noble House of Black."

written fan fiction, range in topic and length and prove the extent to which fan film creators are willing to go to produce quality performed fan fictions. For example, Conrad Studios on *YouTube* has produced a three-part fan film titled "Mudblood," which combines live-action acting and incredible special effects to produce a spectacular, borderline-cinematic quality experience of a *Harry Potter* fan film that, like Sloan's work and many others, is free to watch. The series runs parallel to events occurring during *Harry Potter and the Half-Blood Prince* and possibly into *Harry Potter and the Deathly Hallows*. The episodes follow a sixth year from Hogwarts who finds herself in possession of one of the many horcruxes (an object imbued with a piece of one's soul) created by Voldemort, entrusted to her dark mentor by Bellatrix LeStrange née Black, which the young witch stole and ran away with to America. The events do not interfere with actual canon. Instead, they diverge on a side-quest involving two canon characters who otherwise have no major effect on canon lore and answering several plot-hole questions, including whether the Magical Congress of the United States of America (MACUSA) was aware of the magical war occurring in England (in short, yes), and how one obtains a dark mark (a symbol of Voldemort's followers).[23] While they are theoretical questions, the short series proposes one possible answer, establishing fanon that is used in other similar stories.

Another full-length prequel-style fan film, "Voldemort: Origins of the Heir," by Tyrangle Films, centers on the origins of Voldemort, including his connection to Salazar Slytherin (one of the Hogwarts founders), his turn to the dark side, and the events that led to his first disappearance just before the First Wizarding War.[24] This hour-and-a-half film provides the theoretical existence of other heirs to the Hogwarts founders while explaining in detail canon information regarding how Tom Riddle (Voldemort's pre-Dark Lord persona) created the first four of his seven horcruxes, thus filling in several plot gaps and offering extra information that can be used as fanon later. The special effects quality of these fan films, including Sloan's "Noble House of Black" series,[25] is high quality considering the limited resources for many fan film creators. It is evident how much work the creative teams have put into creating "realistic" (to the fantasy world) productions that help uphold the suspension of disbelief for their audiences while maintaining affective hermeneutics with their characterization. Bronwen Thomas makes a particular note on canon theory, recalling Astrid Ensslin's work when she states that Ensslin "demonstrates that the concept of the canon has never fully been stable, but is always evolutionary, and very often

---

[23] Conrad, "Mudblood."
[24] Pezzato, "Voldermort: Origins of the Heir."
[25] Sloan, "The Noble House of Black."

highly contested."[26] As these fan films and *TikTok* content creators show, canon can be manipulated in various ways to include side stories and prequels (and sequels, which is an entirely unique branch) that do not disrupt canon material but rather add to it in ways that are buildable and adaptable while still maintaining the integrity of the provided world.

Away from the strictly dark magic side of prequel series exists the short film "Dumbledore and Grindelwald – The Greater Good," which is marked as a prequel to *Fantastic Beasts and Where to Find Them: The Secrets of Dumbledore*. Created by Broad Strokes media in 2013, this seventeen-minute film depicts a fight between Albus Dumbledore and Gellert Grindelwald, the two main focuses of the third *Fantastic Beasts* movie. The summary on the video states that this film is "set almost a hundred years before *Harry Potter and the Sorcerer's Stone*; it is the end of a friendship, the beginnings of the dark wizard Grindelwald, and the tragedy that left the Dumbledore family in ruins." The short film introduces fans to Ariana Dumbledore, Albus's sister, who is only mentioned briefly in the canon series when his brother Aberforth Dumbledore points out a portrait of Ariana to Harry, Hermione, and Ron as they attempt to escape Death Eaters who are hunting them through Hogsmead Village. All that is mentioned of her in the main series is that she died, and Aberforth blames Albus for her death. In the fan film, we see a fight between Albus and Grindelwald, with Aberforth in attendance, that results in Ariana's death.[27] This fan film employs a quick but detailed example of affective hermeneutics to show a deeply saddening background story that was only briefly mentioned in the main canon. It aims to help fans of the stories understand more about Albus and Grindelwald's sordid past, why Aberforth blames Albus for their sister's death, and explore why Albus is known continuously for being too reckless. While the *Fantastic Beasts* prequel films provide more historical context for the *Harry Potter* series, they still lack explanations for choices that certain characters made during the canon presentations, and these fan films act as further fix-its by providing context into character development and plot points glazed over in the original productions. The authors are free to create their own storylines with the canon characters while bringing fans a visual experience beyond a literary one.

A voice for the people, by the people

Many fan films on *TikTok* and *YouTube* involve some masking of the creator's voices so as not to disrupt the suspension of disbelief. This is either done by lip-syncing to pre-made sounds (audio clips from shows or movies, music lyrics,

---

[26] Thomas "Canons and Fanons," 4.
[27] Zagri, "Dumbledore and Grindelwald."

sounds from other creators, among others) or cutting the voices and background audio altogether in favor of setting the video to music reminiscent of the Silent Film Era (Sasha Sloan uses this technique for her fan films). Recently, however, a new trend that developed on *TikTok* is changing the format of audio creation for creators. Late February to early March 2023 saw the emergence of artificial intelligence (AI) audio files emerging in place of pre-made audio files. This process involves creators attempting to replicate an actor or character's voice through programs such as ElevenLabs and using the voice files to overlay their creations. Thus far, there has been little use of these audio files for the traditional lip-sync videos that cosplay creators prefer, but these files are being used for fan films that are the product of 'Frankenclips.' These videos comprise non-related film clips that are cut together to make a longer, cohesive clip. This process comes from a creator's preference for specific actors who portray certain characters that otherwise do not interact but are given the illusion of interacting through the splicing together of such clips. This is a popular form of video creation for *Harry Potter* characters with limited or no interactions that fans believe would be a better fit than the canon provides. Recently, creators have been using AI voice generators to add audio clips over or within existing audio clips to make the transitions between smaller clips flow better or fill in gaps where dialogue does not exist.

One example of this process has been gaining popularity for creators who make Mauraders Era fan films. There is a vaguely agreed-upon fan-casting for the four Mauraders as teenagers or young adults, and creators who prefer to lean into the internet's decision have used clips from these specific actors' repertoires to create these Frankenclips of possible interactions. The fan cast includes Ben Barnes as Sirius Black, Andrew Garfield as Remus Lupin, Aaron Taylor-Johnson as James Potter, and Dane Dehaan as Peter Pettigrew. As such, creators have taken clips from films that these actors have been in—typically ones that match the age range or costume choices—that best fit the creator's vision for fanon interactions. The most popular Mauraders pairing to do these Frankenclips with a pairing labeled 'WolfStar,' which is the fanon romantic pairing of Remus Lupin (the Wolf half, for his werewolf curse) and Sirius Black (the Star for his namesake). This 'ship' (a romantic pairing decided on by fans) results in Frankenclips, comprised of films that star Barnes and Garfield spliced together to create seemingly cohesive interactions. These Frankenclips use as many of the original audio files as possible, but since they are not related films, some inconsistencies may arise. Therefore, some creators will expunge audio from certain clips until it makes sense. Thanks to AI voice creations, creators can replicate – nearly accurately – the intended actor's voice and insert their own bridging dialogue between clips.[28] The result is a fan film that is more believable and gives both audio and visual qualities that are consistent throughout.

The possibilities associated with AI voice generators run parallel to the possibilities associated with deepfake media.[29] Now, creators can mimic not only the visual aspects of a certain character's likeness but also their voice, opening new avenues of filmmaking that – if the image or sound is public domain – can include recognizable characters and persons within their fan creations. Because the technology is new, the legality of this form of creation has yet to be validated, making the process dubious at best. However, since fan fiction and fan films exist outside the copyright sphere if the creator is not doing this work for profit, it is hard to say if AI audio-visual developments will come under fire for now.

Conclusion

Fan films are continuously being developed on both platforms, with *TikTok* featuring the benefit of short, spotlighted content, while *YouTube* allows for more feature-film-length productions. In both instances, fan fiction writers can take a popular fan pastime to a more expressive and inclusive level than before, providing the fix-it fics that fans are after while adding the benefit of visual performance. While fan fiction is written in multiple languages, so too are these fan films expanding globally, with "Voldemort: Origins of the Heir" being one of the many examples of a foreign-made fan film since the creators and many of the actors are Italian. In fact, the film is partially performed in Italian and then dubbed – or the process of removing the language audio from a video and replacing it with a different language audio for different audiences – in English. Additionally, as Jennifer Duggan points out in her article, "the digitization of fan fiction has diversified and democratized fan fiction-centered communities, making them more accessible to all fans despite their ages, financial means, ethnicities, nationalities, linguistical knowledge, sexualities and genders."[30] The inclusivity of fan fiction and, as they arise, fan films allow for an increase in accessibility through diverse production mediums and introduce greater avenues for fan involvement in their favorite literary worlds. As can be seen

---

[28] Teddy (@searchingforplanes), *TikTok*, https://www.tiktok.com/@searchingforplanes, has created several Frankenclips using AI voice generation.

[29] Deepfakes are AI-generated media in which a person in an image or video is replaced with someone else's likeness through CGI-like programming.

[30] Jennifer Duggan, "Who writes Harry Potter fan fiction? Passionate detachment, 'zooming out,' and fan fiction paratexts on *AO3*," *Transformative Works and Cultures*, vol. 34 (2020), https://doi.org/10.3983/twc.2020.1863.

through many of these fan films, creators can make decisions on gender, race, and sexuality with as little or as much context as they want, and much like written fan fiction, creators can play with the source material to make it fit into their vision for where the canon should go. Once film theory elements are used in the analyses of fan films, the genre opens further investigative opportunities for a deeper understanding of the individual films and the whole genre. It will be interesting to see the lengths future fan fiction and fan film creators go through to continue this literary and now cinematic artistry to keep the fandom alive and canon ever-expanding.

Bibliography

"Approve or Disapprove: What 8 Famous Authors Think of Fan Fiction." *Fansided.* Modified November 9, 2021. https://winteriscoming.net/2021/07/04/8-famous-authors-think-fanfiction-george-rr-martin-anne-rice-jrr-tolkien/5.

Duggan, Jennifer. "Who writes Harry Potter fan fiction? Passionate detachment, 'zooming out,' and fan fiction paratexts on *AO3*." *Transformative Works and Cultures*, vol. 34 (2020). https://doi.org/10.3983/twc.2020.1863.

Faraj, Conrad, director. *Mudblood: Part 1.* YouTube, 2021. https://www.youtube.com/watch?v=9hGwd7d857E&list=WL&index=3. Accessed January 14, 2023.

———. *Mudblood: Part 2.* YouTube, 9 Jul. 2021. https://www.youtube.com/watch?v=o7RDcRX0tV0&list=WL&index=1. Accessed January 14, 2023.

———. *Mudblood: Part 3.* YouTube, 17 Dec. 2021. https://www.youtube.com/watch?v=hC6N3_iCVZ4. Accessed January 14, 2023.

"Harry Potter." *Archive of Our own.* Accessed March 1, 2023. https://archiveofourown.org/tags/Harry%20Potter%20%20J*d*%20K*d*%20Rowling/works.

"Harry Potter FanFiction Archive." *Fanfiction.* Accessed January 10, 2023. https://www.fanfiction.net/book/Harry-Potter/.

"Harry Potter Wiki." *Fandom.* Accessed January 10, 2023. https://harrypotter.fandom.com/wiki/Main_Page.

"Important Message From Anne On Fan Fiction." *Anne Rice: The Official Site.* Accessed September 10, 2023, http://annerice.com/ReaderInteraction-MessagesToFans.html.

Karlsson, Marie and Christina Olin-Scheller. "'Let's Party!' Harry Potter fan fiction sites as social settings for narrative gender constructs." *Gender and Language*, vol. 9.2 (2015). http://doi.org/ 10.1558/genl.v9i2.17330.

"List of Harry Potter Archives." *Fanlore*, Accessed January 10, 2023. https://fanlore.org/wiki/List_of_Harry_Potter_Archives.

Pezzato, Gianmaria, director. *Voldemort: Origins of the Heir.* January 13, 2018. *YouTube*, https://www.youtube.com/watch?v=C6SZa5U8sIg&list=WL&index=2&t=1277s. Accessed January 10, 2023.

Pugh, Sheenagh. *The Democratic Genre: Fan Fiction In A Literary* Context. Seren, 2015.

Sloan, Sasha, creator. "Noble House of Black." 2021. *YouTube*, https://www.youtube.com/playlist?list=PLXRzEyWb-mn-Vvypoed6G7L8Bi_uMzGT9. Accessed January 14, 2023.

Thomas, Bronwen. "Canons and Fanons: Literary Fanfiction Online." *Dichtung Digital Journal Fur Kunst Und Kultur Digitaler Medien*, vol. 37, no. 9 (2007). https://doi.org/10.25969/mediarep/17701.

Wilson, Anna. "The Role of Affect in Fan Fiction." *Transformative Works and Cultures*, vol. 21 (2016). https://doi.org/10.3983/twc.2016.0684.

Zagri, Justin. *Dumbledore and Grindelwald - The Greater Good - Secrets of Dumbledore Prequel*. December 3, 2013. *YouTube*, https://www.youtube.com/watch?v=OGHBwk0quxs. Accessed 10 Jan 2023

Chapter 11

"It ruins the gritty realism of a man who fights crime dressed as a bat": Satire, Parody, and Multimodal Intertextuality in *Holy Musical B@man!*

Meghan N. Cronin
Indiana University of Pennsylvania

Abstract: In this article, Cronin considers multi-modal forms of the fix-it fic as a means of satirizing past versions of the original content. She examines a satirical musical, *Holy Musical B@man*, to explore the evolution of the superhero characters, specifically those belonging to the Batman franchise. Cronin points to intertextuality as the primary mode of satire, investigating how hypertext and hypotext play roles in connecting original content with the fix-it fic. Her analysis ultimately demonstrates that satirical fix-it fics in any genre is useful in probing our understanding of humanity and identity. **Keywords:** multi-modal, musicals, hypertext, hypotext satire, intertextuality, humanity, Batman, superheroes, fix-it fics.

***

Look! Up in the sky! Even without finishing this iconic phrase, one knows it is from the *Superman* comics. One may not have followed the comics from the beginning, but still know it is Superman because they have heard this phrase told, echoed, and parodied through allusions in countless movies, television shows, and various other media forms. By realizing that superheroes are recognizable through allusions to other media forms, one can better examine cultural values and desires. These links between superheroes, comic books, and outside culture demonstrate what is referred to as intertextuality. Simon Dentith defines this in his book, *Parody*, by using phraseology adapted from a Russian theorist:

One designation, for written discourse, of what Vološinov describes for speech as 'the chain of utterances,' is intertextuality. This can be characterized initially as the interrelatedness of writing, the fact that all written utterances—texts—situate themselves in relation to texts that precede them and are in turn alluded to or repudiated by texts that follow.[1]

Popular culture builds upon its predecessors, laying new knowledge and new references atop the old. Nevertheless, how can we understand this concept? I posit that it is beneficial to build a framework to examine intertextuality through satire and parody. Satire is often a rather nebulously defined term, subject to many different views over many different times. Robert Phiddian's approach to satire best describes this concept, "[satire] is a rhetorical strategy (in any medium) that seeks wittily to provoke an emotional and intellectual reaction in an audience on a matter of public (or at least inter-subjective) significance."[2] Though often employed to be comedic, satire has another equally important requirement: to make an audience stop and contemplate what something is implying through less overt means. Specifically, I propose building this framework through an internet, fan-made satirical musical called *Holy Musical B@man! Holy Musical B@man!* was created by StarKid Productions and premiered on *YouTube* on April 13, 2012.[3] In this show, the creators are not moralizing about proverbial good and bad; instead, they are pointing out the ridiculousness that permeates the genre of superheroes and villains through a visual and auditory fan fiction. They are also forcing the evaluation of the opinions, ideals, and values established within the genre of superheroes. This fan musical is multimodal; it evaluates comic books, Hollywood films, and silver screen programs through the mode of a satirical musical. In today's popular culture, there is an increasing necessity for multimodal intertextuality due to the rise of the superhero genre in literature, television, and movies. By examining the types of satire found in *Holy Musical B@man!*, which offers a self-reflective, self-critical view of the multimodal genre, I establish a framework for analyzing and understanding the evolving desires and values of humanity concerning ideas of power. Satiric fan fiction is an excellent way to explore these ideas, and such fan fiction falls under the umbrella of fix-it fics. Fix-it fics address problems and concerns found within original texts, bringing these concerns to light for wider audiences. This

---

[1] Simon Dentith, *Parody* (London: Routledge, 2000), 5.
[2] Robert Phiddian, "Satire and the Limits of Literary Theories," *Critical Quarterly* 55, no. 3 (October 2013): 44. https://doi.org/10.1111/criq.12057.
[3] StarKid Productions, *Holy Musical B@man!*, directed by Matt and Nick Lang, 2012, *YouTube* video.

acknowledgment of the issues found within a topic or genre is exactly what *HMB* accomplishes through its creation.

Fan fiction, especially in visual modes, shares many similarities with cult cinema, which has been an academically accepted genre longer than other forms of fandom studies. Cult cinema relies on fans rather than critics to carry on its popularity. It operates outside of the mainstream or dominant culture, which can be seen using the term 'cult.' A film gets elevated to 'cult status' through its fans, who build its popularity by sharing and discussing it. Fan fiction, and thus *HMB*, are created through this manner of sharing and discussing. Though superheroes have reached mainstream culture, fan fiction has not necessarily followed, at least to some scholars and critics. These similarities in creation, content, and fandom between cult cinema and fan fiction offer a new pathway to understanding the particulars of *HMB*.

Like cult cinema, *HMB* and superhero movies and shows rely heavily on parody, satire, and intertextuality. In the chapter "Intertextuality and Iron" of Jamie Sexton and Ernest Mathijs's book, *Cult Cinema: An Introduction*, they write that parody and satire often go hand-in-hand, "The terms need not be mutually exclusive, as parodic discourse can also be satiric: for example, an artwork may parody and mock a former text (or set of texts) and also critique social attitudes related to such texts."[4] Fix-it fics seek to critique the original text or visual media. Thus, *HMB* uses parody to mock the genre and its fans by satirizing the ideas and values established in the different modes of the superhero genre. This method of mockery is not always harsh critique; it can be lovingly done without outright vitriol toward the texts it is parodying or satirizing.

Sexton and Mathijs also examine parody and satire specifically concerning intertextuality. They write, "Among the most prominent terms that play a role within cult cinema are parody, pastiche, irony, and related terms such as satire. These modes, to varying degrees, can be understood as forms of intertextuality: where one text refers to another text or, more frequently, to several other texts."[5] Fascinatingly, these complicated moments of interconnectedness between satiric and parodic forms reflect the vast interdependence of the influential texts and forms used within *HMB*. To differentiate between the intertextual texts, Simon Dentith uses the terms hypotext and hypertext, which he defines as "the former denoting the preceding or original text upon which the latter, the hypertext, performs its parodic transformation."[6] In my examination, *HMB* is

---

[4] Jamie Sexton and Ernest Mathijs, "Intertextuality and Irony," in *Cult Cinema: An Introduction* (Newark: John Wiley & Sons, Ltd., 2011), 224.
[5] Sexton and Mathjis, "Intertextuality and Irony," 224.
[6] Dentith, *Parody*, 13.

the hypertext, and it relies on a great swath of hypotext, particularly the original DC comics, all major *Batman* and *Superman* movies until *The Dark Knight* and the 1960s Adam West television show. The hypertext, *HMB*, sets out to critique the various hypotexts and reinforces that *HMB* is operating as a fix-it fic, whereas it is 'fixing' these hypotexts.

Before diving into the production and analysis of *HMB*, it is imperative to discuss the historical context of the superhero genre and establish its relevance to academic study. This genre, though it dates back over eighty years, has only been legitimized in academia within the last thirty years. This is perhaps because of the original target audience, boys, and young men, who were not the same audience as those seeking more established scholarly pursuits. In 1938, the genre evolved from the very first superhero comic book, *Action Comics #1*.[7] It introduced the world to Clark Kent, a newspaper reporter by day and his by-night alter ego, Superman. Within a year, Bruce Wayne/Batman was also introduced. Superman and Batman were created to make heroic storytelling more accessible to people and to provide a distraction from the Great Depression and the initial stirrings of the Second World War. Heavily influenced by pulp fiction novels, these comics told stories of strong, good men fighting bad guys and saving beautiful women. Pulp fiction novels can trace their ancestry through adventure novels, romance, and even the epic. Glorious deeds done for the good of humanity by the best men humanity can offer are quite timeless tropes and characters. Alex S. Romagnoli and Gian S. Pagnucci describe what superheroes inform us about humanity and cultural ideals in his book *Enter the Superheroes*:

> Superheroes embody the ideals that culture holds dear: that good will triumph over evil, that with great power comes great responsibility, and that the hero will always save the day in the nick of time. They are a metaphysical representation of our desire for a world that is better than the one in which we live…Superhero stories offer us a meta-textuality: if we can create a good place in the world of superheroes, then there is hope that we can also someday make our own world a better place than it is now.[8]

If one were to remove 'superheroes' from that quote and replace it with 'Arthurian knights' or 'ancient Greek heroes,' it would automatically be considered a scholarly observation. Like other forms of literature, the superhero genre

---

[7] Alex S. Romagnoli and Gian S. Pagnucci, *Enter the Superheroes: American Values, Culture, and the Canon of Superhero Literature* (Lanham: The Scarecrow Press, Inc., 2013), 6.
[8] Romagnoli and Pagnucci, *Enter the Superheroes*, 97.

contains character archetypes so well established by now that they could be considered mythological figures. Captain America is a good-natured, all-American hero who sticks up for the little guy and hates bullies of any kind, be it the bullies of back alleys in Brooklyn or the Nazis he fights in Europe. The Joker is a chaotic villainous entity who 'just wants to watch the world burn' and finds violence to be quite the laugh. Similar character archetypes can be found in drama and satire as well. Therefore, it is not quite a leap to link superheroes and villains with these previously academically established character archetypes, especially when examining a satiric superhero musical.

One reason comic books have not been taken seriously in the past is that they rely on heavy amounts of illustration through cartoons. Pulp fiction novels were not illustrated, so comic books borrowed structure ideas from the novels and added brightly colored cartoons to aid the audience's imaginations. Though there can be a childish tilt to the concept of cartoons, cartoons and caricatures were initially found in magazines and newspapers read by adults. In fact, cartoons, and thus comic books, can find their roots in overtly satirical magazines covering both social and political satires.[9] With this in mind, comic books can be seen as what Glenn Wilmott calls a tradition of 'cross-writing':

> In addition to viewing comics as a diverse social and economic institution, we consider comics as a mercurial creative tradition that crosses institutional boundaries, both as an artistic practice and as a symbolic network over time. This is a cross-writing tradition in two ways: formally, in its roots in what has been called caricature, understood as an iconography or kind of style, and thematically, in what I will call its animalization, understood as an iconology or vehicle for ideas.[10]

By this definition, Wilmott attempts to bridge the gap between popular culture and scholarship. The defining aspects of comic books are that they have stories outlining battles between forces of good and evil or broader societal issues and that they contain artistic illustrations. By combining these, the art becomes symbolic or iconographic as time passes, and the art also operates as a vehicle to present the ideas within the text portion of the comic book. When examining satire created about the superhero genre, this tradition of multiple layers of meaning through text and art makes the intentions of the satire clearer as one has both the text and the art from which to draw.

---

[9] Glenn Wilmott, "Comics as a Cross-Writing Tradition," *Jeunesse, Young People, Texts, Cultures* 6, no. 2 (February 2014): 98. https:// doi.org/10.1353/jeu.2014.0012.
[10] Wilmott, "Comics as a Cross-Writing Tradition," 98.

Now that I have covered the historical context and justification of the superhero genre, I will examine the particulars surrounding the creation of the multimodal text *Holy Musical B@man* (*HMB*), created by StarKid Productions, a theatre company that found its start at the University of Michigan.[11] StarKid initially rose to fame with its first online musical, *A Very Potter Musical*, in 2009, which both parodies and satirizes the *Harry Potter* series. Its next foray into lovingly mocking pop culture was *Starship* in 2011, which drew inspiration from the *Alien* franchise, *Transformers*, and even *Star Wars*. At the time of *HMB*'s premiere in 2012, the superhero genre was experiencing a major boom in Hollywood. Batman had received his first television series in the 1960s, starring Adam West as the caped crusader. The 1970s, 1980s, and 1990s saw the increasing popularity of superhero movies, such as the *Superman* movies starring Christopher Reeves and the numerous *Batman* movies starring Michael Keaton, Val Kilmer, and George Clooney. However, the turn of the twenty-first century saw things ramping up even further. By the premier of *HMB*, there had been two Christopher Nolan *Batman* movies starring Christian Bale, three *Spider-Man* movies, two *Fantastic Four* movies, a *Superman* live-action television show, numerous animated television series, and the start of perhaps the most ambitious multi-movie franchise, the Marvel Cinematic Universe (MCU), which had six different movies released as *HMB* began its run. All these shows and movies influenced the theatre production, but none more than the Nolan movies or the West television series. These influences are seen in the choices the company and actors made about the characterizations. Alfred, Batman's trusty butler, is modeled after Michael Caine's version of Alfred found in the Nolan movies. Out of respect for the late Heath Ledger, the company created a different main villain, Sweet Tooth, though he is heavily influenced by Ledger's Academy-Award-winning Joker. The Batman of the musical spans both the Nolan movies and the West show, voiced like Bale but dressed like West. Finally, Dick Grayson, a.k.a. Robin, is the classic TV Robin of the West show both in character and costume. More influence of Nolan and West is seen in certain song titles; "Dynamic Duet" is in reference to the classic West nickname of "Dynamic Duo," and "Dark, Sad, Lonely, Knight" is in reference to the Nolan movie, *The Dark Knight*.

The production of *HMB* satirizes all forms of Batman media: the comics, the original 1960s television show, and all movies from Keaton to Bale, as well as other DC comic entities from comics to movies. Within the musical itself, *HMB* also satirizes die-hard fans and the relationships those fans have with Batman. The specific intertextuality of *HMB*, how parody is used in it, and the

---

[11] "About," StarKid Productions (StarKid Productions, LLC.), accessed March 13, 2023, https://www.teamstarkid.com/about.

relationship with fans can be seen as a parallel to cult films in a quote from Sexton and Mathijs:

> Parody's importance as a cultic form of filmic expression is that it relies upon broader cultural knowledge to function effectively. In this sense, it can sometimes appeal to a prominent sector of cult cinephiles: viewers with an extensive knowledge about cinema as a whole, gained through heavy viewing and associated information seeking. Extensive use of parody will more likely be fully understood by such viewers, who will have an increased likelihood of spotting the allusions at work in a parodic text.[12]

With increased knowledge of Batman media, fans can find deeper connections and allusions to other forms of Batman media snuck into the musical by the creators. That is not to say that this extensive knowledge is necessary to understand or enjoy the musical or the topics it satirizes. Because of the great permeation and saturation of superheroes in today's popular culture, there is hardly a person who has not heard of Batman or Superman. They have become mythic figures whose characters and stories are as familiar as would King Arthur have been to Elizabethan England. According to Sexton and Mathijs, cult films, and therefore the musical *HMB*, "will tend to function in a manner that minimizes the exclusivity of their operations: this is achieved through scattering references so that a film does not necessarily depend on the recognition of one referent text, and also by creating scenes that can function effectively even if the parodic referent is not spotted."[13] To make something like this musical inaccessible to casual fans would cause further nichification to an already niche topic. Therefore, spreading allusions throughout the musical allows for a scavenger hunt for those highly familiar with the different hypertexts.

The production of *HMB* puts all forms of Batman media and the audiences that eagerly consume them under a microscope. It forces its own audience to stop and think about the ridiculousness of the genre while critiquing problematic aspects that have been found through closer examination over the many years of Batman's existence. It does this by asking the audience to reject the willing suspension of disbelief, drawing back the curtain on the genre as practice. There are various elements of the musical that parody or satirize different modes of content. However, the most important is split into three categories: things that parody or satirize the comic books, moments that

---

[12] Sexton and Mathijs, "Intertextuality and Irony," 226.
[13] Sexton and Mathijs, "Intertextuality and Irony," 226.

parody or satirize Nolan's movies, and elements that parody or satirize the West television show. Each of these categories critiques the different desires and values of humanity concerning ideas of power. Given the differences in time between the creation of these various hypotexts, the mainstream culture, and values will have changed greatly. What may have been popular or what values were had were no longer necessarily what they are today. Audiences and fans are aware of this, and much of the time, this is how fix-it fics are created. The hypertext of *HMB* is created in this fashion.

The idea of being someone else, of having a secret identity, is one of the major targets of satire in *HMB*. There is an instance of Batman ordering pizza to the Batcave, and the address given is his other identity's house, Wayne Manor. The pizza delivery people ask each other, "I wonder if Bruce Wayne knows Batman lives under his house?"[14] and do not make the connection that Bruce Wayne is Batman. Batman himself has trouble when it comes to distinguishing between his identities; he attempts to introduce himself as "I'm Bruce Man, I mean, Bat Wayne, fuck. I'm Batman. Fuck. I'm Bruce... Wayne," or as 'Bruce Wayne' but then crosses that out and writes 'Batman' and somehow, thanks to comedy, the citizens of Gotham are none the wiser.[15] Yet, he knows that Superman is Clark Kent and places the item that defines the difference between Kent and Superman, his glasses, on Superman's face. Green Lantern comments on this by asking Superman, "[your identity,] it's a secret?."[16] One other notoriously questionable aspect of the comics is the fact that Batman seems to randomly acquire orphan boys, which is vastly concerning to modern audiences. Alfred alludes to this by checking the newspaper for 'orphans for sale.' Then he brings Dick Grayson to meet Batman.[17] Dick refers to this weirdness too, "It's the same old song and dance, take in the young acrobat and watch him flip around a bit," which, to today's audiences, sounds particularly pedophilic.[18] Fix-it fics often have an aspect of pointing out inconsistencies in the texts about which they write, whether it is unresolved homoerotic tension or obvious plot holes. To the audience, Batman and Superman's dual identities are evident plot holes, yet to the other characters in the musical, they are not. The willing suspension of disbelief can only go so far, and the fic, *HMB*, highlights this while trying to resolve the issue.

When discussing supervillains, Superman and the Green Lantern realize that all the villains are formulaic: "guy in a suit, thing on his head, making puns."

---

[14] *Holy Musical B@man!*, Act 1 Part 1, *YouTube* video, 8:09.
[15] Act 1, Part 6, *YouTube* video, 2:37.
[16] Act 1, Part 4, *YouTube* video, 3:37.
[17] Act 1, Part 3, *YouTube* video, 13:08.
[18] Act 1, Part 6, *YouTube* video, 4:11.

Some examples they use are "The Riddler? Guy in a suit, thing on his head," and "Mad Hatter? Guy in a suit, thing on his head."[19] This formula is visibly emphasized in the following scene, "Rogues Are We," which features all the classic major villains in Batman. The villains all make puns that correspond to their theme, such as "enough pussy-footing around" by Catwoman, and "Batman has put my operations on ice, my assets are frozen," by Mr. Freeze.[20] By satirizing the villain trope in this way, one can see that because of the seventy-odd years of superheroes and villains up to the point of the show's creation, many aspects of comic books have become so common they are very nearly cliche. Also, the only separation between villains within the Batman canon is their theme. An ironic twist is that the villains also understand this, but not about themselves. The villains comment on Two-Face and his plots, which are 'two-themed.' He attempts to enlist their help, but they guess his plans to "rob the Second National Bank of Gotham of their two-dollar bills on a Tuesday," which they immediately turn down because of how stupid they believe his gimmick to be.[21] One can see that we as a society still value good triumphing over evil, as we are led to root against the seemingly incompetent villains, particularly Two-Face. However, by emphasizing the ridiculousness of the villains, it is clear that audiences are tired of the same cliches that oversaturate the genre of comic books. Through this revelation and emphasis, the musical attempts to fix the tiring cliches on which the genre was previously reliant, once again reinforcing *HMB*'s designation of fix-it fic.

Before examining the satirizing of Nolan-era Batman within the musical, it must be noted that there is hypertext specifically for Nolan's Batman media: Frank Miller's *Batman: The Dark Knight Returns* series. This series is pivotal for the decisions Nolan makes as a director for his *Batman* movies, and therefore, it is necessary to understand when looking at the satirization of Nolan-era Batman found in *HMB*. According to Jenna Cortiel and Laura Oehme, "[Miller] thus uses the superhero figure to tackle fundamental pressures put on key American cultural narratives, addressing their entanglement with risk, technology, and biblical notions about the end of the world."[22] This series, which premiered in the 1980s, reflected the changing social and global society during the Cold War. It was grittier than the original arcs of Batman comics. The

---

[19] Act 1, Part 4, *YouTube* video, 3:59.
[20] Act 1, Part 5, *YouTube* video, 2:31.
[21] Act 1, Part 5, *YouTube* video, 3:54.
[22] Jenna Cortiel and Laura Oehme, "*The Dark Knight*'s Dystopian Vision: Batman, Risk, and American National Identity," *European Journal of American Studies* 10, no. 2 (August 2015): 2. https://doi.org/10.4000/ejas.10916.

move from comics to West-era and then from West-era to Miller's *Dark Knight* reflects the changing world views in America at the time. At the turn of the twenty-first century, Miller premiers his sequel series to the *Dark Knight* series, *Batman: The Dark Knight Strikes Again*. Where the first series dealt with the Cold War, this series deals with post-9/11 America and the shifting ideas of American identity. Cortiel and Oehme describe Batman and his influence in both series as thus:

> [I]t would take Frank Miller's darker, more complex Batman character in *Batman: Dark Knight...* and *Batman: The Dark Knight Strikes Again* (2001-02) and his more distinctly noir vision of Gotham City to fully express the dystopian in its critique of contemporary American culture. There is also a particular pattern to the darkness in Miller's *Dark Knight* that points beyond both the comics medium and superhero fiction towards fundamental questions concerning the crisis of American national identity at the turn of the millennium.[23]

The 1980s and 1990s required a shift from the distractive, overtly hopeful Batman comics. Frank Miller's *Dark Knight* series sought to update Batman to fit the time and world events, fixing what he saw as a Batman that was incongruent with the world in which he lived.

With the advent of the Batman movies of the 1980s and 1990s, which premiered after Miller's *Dark Knight* comic run began, costumes and content were dialed down and made more realistic. Also, at this time, Batman had taken a grittier, noir-like feel, a major departure from earlier comics and the Adam West television show. This change is reflected in the Nolan-era as well. These changes between the West and Nolan-era are played out in *HMB* from the beginning of the musical. Prior to Robin's introduction in Act 1, Part 6, Batman mainly fights in a realistic manner reminiscent of the hyperviolence of the Nolan-era Batman movies. Fights are more graphic, and Batman is a tougher, more dangerous fighter. He no longer traps his foes in nets. He breaks noses and tibias and fires guns from his Bat-Plane that take out his enemies' kneecaps. Our Nolan-influenced, pre-Robin Batman treats all perpetrators of crime in the same category no matter what they did. This dark version of Batman is seen in the opening number of the show. A shopkeeper realizes that he accidentally took a dollar with him instead of putting it in the till. Batman shoots at him, just as he had shot at the gangsters who were racketeering mere moments before. It sounds harsh on paper, and it is, once the viewer rejects willing suspension of disbelief. However, Batman plays it off as a joke, laughing

---

[23] Cortiel and Oehme, "The *Dark Knight*'s Dystopian Vision," 2.

while he comments to Alfred that he is "Crippling misguided youngsters I've never met."[24] There is an ironic moment critiquing the violence of Gotham as a whole. Commissioner Gordon states that Gotham has recently reduced the crime rate in the city. In celebration, the ensemble pulls out their weapons and shoots their guns in the air. Commissioner Gordon then comments, "It's still the highest in the world, but we're getting there."[25] It is treated as a humorous moment, but the audience can see it is critiquing the necessity of such violence in the story. Since Gotham is an American city, it is also critiquing that such violence is nearly commonplace in real life as well. Americans still value power but are beginning to question whether it comes at such a high cost, and *HMB* brings this forth to be fixed.

Moving on to examine the critiques within the parodying and satirization of the West-era influences, it is helpful to define the term that best suits this concept: camp. In his book, *The Cambridge Introduction to Satire*, Jonathan Greenberg describes camp as a style involving humor, parody, irony, and detachment. He continues to define this and expands on their meaning to his definition:

> [I]rony gives camp a double vision: on the one hand it offers an appreciation or celebration of that which is melodramatic, operatic, and sentimental, but on the other it requires a detachment from the perceived intentions of the artwork that allows a critical recognition of the artwork's aesthetic failure.[26]

Camp works exceedingly well with the West era and musical theater for both entail over-exaggeration and its inherent theatricality or melodrama. Greensburg's idea of detachment within camp is particularly important to *HMB* as the musical seeks to make the audience stop and critically interact with the genre. It does not want the audience just to accept everything as written; that is not the goal of fix-it fics.

Dentith, in his book *Parody*, describes parody in a way that also fits well with camp. He writes, "One of the typical ways in which parody works is to seize on particular aspects of a manner or a style and exaggerate it to ludicrous effect."[27] The musical takes the ridiculousness of the West-era and further exaggerates it to an insanely ludicrous effect. The West-era is silliness personified, filled with goofy puns, unmanly giggling, and elements of pure slapstick. In *HMB*, the

---

[24] *Holy Musical B@man!*, Act 1, Part 3, *YouTube* video, 1:36.
[25] Act 1, Part 2, *YouTube* video, 0:22.
[26] Jonathan Greenberg, *The Cambridge Introduction to Satire* (Cambridge: Cambridge University Press, 2019), 50.
[27] Dentith, *Parody*, 33.

West-era camp is brought on through the addition of Batman's new sidekick, Dick Grayson's Robin. When Robin joins him, Batman's fights take on a more slapstick feel. He still is hyperviolent, for he often manages to harm the people he is supposed to be 'helping,' but now he is slap-fighting and kicking villains in the shins. This shift is in reference to the childish qualities brought on by Robin, a child based on the 60s version of Robin. The childish version of camp allows for another moment of visual humor, in this case, visual irony. The man tasked with playing Robin is in his thirties. His costume comprises brightly colored briefs, but unlike Batman, he is not wearing tights underneath, and his incredibly pale and hairy legs can be seen. The citizens of Gotham constantly refer to this, and they can be heard asking about the location of Robin's pants at least four separate times throughout the show. This silly relationship is further explored in the most camp musical number of the show, "Dynamic Duet," which sees Batman and Robin fighting crime while pausing to sing a high-pitched, upbeat song about their friendship. It is filled with dance moves and lyrics reminiscent of love songs, which plays up the camp aspect. This new version of Batman seems even sillier when one thinks about how he was recently a very gritty, dangerous character who punched first and asked questions later.

By combining the Adam West and comic-esque costumes with the feel of the Nolan-era (and its predeceasing movies in the eighties), StarKid is critiquing the true ridiculousness of the genre across all forms. This critique is amplified by the slapstick-style fighting Batman takes part in after he is joined by Robin. In the awkward meshing of two very incongruent takes on Batman media, the musical draws even more attention to what current audiences think are the values and desires of Americans as a society and comic book fans. The musical seeks to draw attention to this and fix it to truly fit this day and age.

Later in the musical, we hit the beginning of the major climactic action. Sweet Tooth's minions have taken 3,000 people hostage in Gotham Square. Sweet Tooth sets up a Facebook poll and makes Gotham vote on who to save: Robin from Sweet Tooth's clutches or the people in the Square from a lethal sour Warhead in the water supply. Batman sees this poll and is conflicted about who to save. He finally decides that since Gotham hates Robin, they will vote to sacrifice him. He runs off to save Robin himself at the expense of the people of Gotham. President Barack Obama calls Superman to intervene and stop Batman. These events lead to one of the most satirical musical numbers of the show, "The American Way." This song is in three verses: one sung by Batman, one by Superman, and one by Sweet Tooth. Through these verses, the song presents three conflicting views of what America is, what it stands for, and what it wants. Superman sings the first verse:

SUPERMAN:
Truth and liberty and justice all are in jeopardy tonight
All we cherish here, and all the values that we hold dear
Are in the balance tonight
'Cause we're American
And it's America
And in America
We do what's right
The firetruck's here for the kitty in the tree

SUPERMAN & CITIZENS:
Oh, the American way!
SUPERMAN:
And if the cops can't come, you can always call on me

Superman represents the classic, idealistic America, which concentrates on the arbitrary ideals of 'truth' and 'justice' and what is 'right.' He is for the police and other emergency workers but recognizes that they are in demand and thus states that he can fill in for them if someone is needed. This belief in Superman is seen as stemming from his initial time of character creation, the Great Depression. However, America has changed over the nearly one hundred years since Superman's creation. This view may no longer be sustainable or what we want or value.

The next view of America comes through the eyes of Batman. He has returned to his Nolan-era violent persona as Robin is facing death. Batman sings the following verse:

BATMAN:
Tonight it's personal
I'm unleashing my arsenal
To rain blood tonight
Tonight I'm gonna save my bro
And if all the city has got to go
Then so be it
'Cause it's America
And I'm American
And in America
I do what I like

> If money can't fix it then I haven't found it yet…
> Be a born billionaire and have your butler build a jet
> CITIZENS:
> That's the American way!

With the rise of capitalism, especially after the war boom revamped the economy, America has become individualistic and concerned only about wealth. Batman does not need to do what is considered good because he experiences freedom in America. He is extravagantly wealthy and will throw money at problems rather than work for a solution. He forgoes the common good to do what he deems 'right' himself, saving Robin and dooming the citizens of Gotham. The musical points out the absurdity of this capitalistic and individualistic view of Batman, especially when it clashes with Superman's view.

To further complicate this, the final verse is sung by the villain, Sweet Tooth, who has an even more incongruent view of America in relation to Superman's and Batman's views. The music slows down and has a darker feel than the previous verses. Sweet Tooth is joined by the other villains and sings:

> SWEET TOOTH:
> Tonight we're taking back the town
> We've got the bat trap set we're gonna catch the clown
> In America tonight!
> We've got a warhead ready in the water supply
> Tonight The Bat and his bull won't fly
> So, Robin, goodnight!
> 'Cause it's America
> And we're American
> And in America
> We fight!
> Never gonna win til your enemies are dead

Sweet Tooth represents the darkest view of American identity and values: the over-militaristic, over-violent, and over-reacting America found after the wars in the Middle East. He is the embodiment of the America that sees winning as no longer having any enemy left to fight because the enemy is dead. His view is very clearly the most villainous, but Batman's is also uncomfortable.

By situating all three of these views together, the song forces the audience to re-evaluate what it means to be American. It forces the audience to examine what leads to these views and whether we should continue to support them.

Superman portrays the supposed good values of America: truth and justice, as well as trust in policing institutions. However, it is that truly what people want, especially now after the Black Lives Matter movement and the increasing need for police reform? Batman represents the mindset of 'pull-yourself-up-by-the-bootstraps,' though everything was handed to him, and do people want that after the wealth gap has expanded to unthinkable dimensions? Sweet Tooth is the harsh reality of much of American global politics, and do audiences want that when thousands of innocents have been killed by the American military for no discernable reason other than supposed 'peace'? In the end, the situation is 'fixed' by deus ex machina time travel, and, in a way, both Superman and Batman's views stand. Batman saves Robin and kills Sweet Tooth. Just as the Warhead is going to be dropped and the hostages killed, Superman flies around the world backward and forces time to go back. Superman stops the Warhead and saves the people of Gotham. The final fix of this fix-it fic is time travel, an often-chosen plot device that seeks to fill in plot holes. Time travel was the only option that would allow both Robin and the people of Gotham to survive. However, as time travel is not currently possible in the real world, what is this trying to tell us? The creators are drawing further attention to these views of America and its values, seeking even further fixes. Even though the musical is a fix-it fic, it does have its own limitations to what it can fix.

Satire and parody are often used in quite humorous manners. They make us laugh, but more importantly, they make us think. Fan fiction seeks to do the same. Fix-it fics come from this critical engagement with the text or texts. The intertextuality that links satiric and parodic fan fiction to the content they question is building up to require awareness of more and more hypertexts. Today, we can see this in the layering of the MCU, as to fully appreciate and understand the newest shows or movies, one is required to be familiar with over thirty-two movies and two dozen multi-season television shows. For multi-dimensional understanding and critique of *Holy Musical B@man!*, over seventy years of multimedia content must be covered and reconciled. However, by examining satires of the superhero genre, such as *HMB*, we can formulate a framework that allows us to understand and analyze multimodal intertextuality. This framework aids our evaluation of the ever-changing views, ideals, and desires inherent to today's culture in America. As a fix-it fic, *Holy Musical B@man!* draws back the curtain on the ever-changing status quo of American culture as represented in comics media.

Bibliography

"About." StarKid Productions. StarKid Productions, LLC. Accessed March 13, 2023. https://www.teamstarkid.com/about.

Cortiel, Jenna, and Laura Oehme. "The Dark Knight's Dystopian Vision: Batman, Risk, and American National Identity." *European Journal of American Studies* 10, no. 2 (August 2015): 1-25. https://doi.org/10.4000/ejas.10916.

Dentith, Simon. *Parody*. London: Routledge, 2000.

Greenberg, Jonathan. *The Cambridge Introduction to Satire*. Cambridge: Cambridge University Press, 2019.

Griffin, Dustin. *Satire: A Critical Reintroduction*. Lexington: The University Press of Kentucky, 1994.

Phiddian, Robert. 2013. "Satire and the Limits of Literary Theories." *Critical Quarterly* 55, no. 3 (October): 44-58. https://doi.org/10.1111/criq.12057.

Romagnoli, Alex S., and Gian S. Pagnucci. *Enter the Superheroes: American Values, Culture, and the Canon of Superhero Literature*. Lanham: The Scarecrow Press, Inc., 2013.

Sexton, Jamie, and Ernest Mathijs. *Cult Cinema: An Introduction*. Newark: John Wiley & Sons, Ltd., 2011.

StarKid Productions. *Holy Musical B@man!* Written and directed by Matt and Nick Lang. Uploaded April 13, 2012, *YouTube*. Video. https://www.youtube.com/playlist?list=PL96B8289ADF77A8C4.

———. *Holy Musical B@man! Soundtrack*. Genius, April 13, 2012. https://genius.com/albums/Team-starkid/Holy-musical-b-man.

Wilmott, Glenn. 2014. "Comics as a Cross-Writing Tradition." *Jeunesse, Young People, Texts Cultures* 6, no. 2 (February): 97-103. https://doi.org/10.1353/jeu.2014.0012.

Index

A

"A Hole in the World," 55, 56, 57, 60, 65, 68
A Very Potter Musical, 176
A/B/O, 24, 26, 29, 31, 32, 54, 56
Abby Gardner, 7
Aberforth Dumbledore, 166
Abigail De Kosnik, 37, 140
ableism, 96
abortion, 60
abuse, 56, 59, 96, 98, 154
ACT UP, 14
Action Comics #1, 174
activism, ix, x, xii, xiv, 10, 53, 58, 59, 60, 63, 64, 65, 68, 77, 99, 100, 108, 113, 114, 118, 119
Adam West, 174, 176, 180, 182
adaptation, 19, 47, 91, 110, 111, 147, 149, 153, 157, 159
Adrienne Rich, 129
advocacy, ix, x, 113
affective hermeneutics, 162, 163, 164, 165, 166
Aidaran, 48, 49, 50
AIDS, 13, 14, 101, 102, 105, 107, 110
Alaa Alghamdi, 78
Alex E. Jung, 111
Alex S. Romagnoli, 174
Andrew Robinson, xi, xii
Alexander Siddig, x, xi, xii, xv
Alexandra Alter, 66
Alexis Lothian, 114
Alfred, 176, 178, 181
Alien, 176
alienation, 4, 86

"All the Young Dudes," 84, 85, 86, 87, 89
Alpha Beta Omega, 24, *See* A/B/O
Alphas, 24, 26, 28, 54, 55, 69
Altered Carbon, 58
Alternate Universe. *See* AU
alternative storylines, 158
Alwaysanoriginal, 100, 102
Amelia Glaser, 40
America, 13, 40, 59, 67, 75, 89, 94, 95, 96, 104, 165, 175, 180, 182, 183, 184, 185
Amit Assis, 140
Andrew Garfield, 167
Andromeda Tonks, 164
Angela Nagle, 22
Anissa M. Graham, 99
Anna Breslaw, 142
Anna Wilson, 162
AnnalieseMichel, 55, 56, 57, 68
Anne Rice, 159
Annika Gonnerman, 96
Anthony Gierzynsky, 75
anti-fandom, 4
anti-fannish, 4
AO3, viii, ix, x, xi, 5, 8, 11, 12, 21, 24, 25, 26, 36, 37, 40, 41, 43, 45, 47, 48, 50, 63, 67, 74, 77, 88, 93, 98, 99, 108, 109, 115, 116, 123, 129, 130, 132, 134, 144, 155, 157, 168, 169
Archive of Our Own. *See* AO3
archives, 36, 37, 47, 49, 93
Argyle, 11
Ariana Dumbledore, 166
artificial intelligence, 167
Ash Valmont, 162

Ashkenazi, 40, 41, 45, 48
AU, 6, 45, 58, 63, 67
Audrey Fox, 7
Author God, 92, 99
authorial intent, 9, 10, 91, 94, 96
authority, viii, 10, 21, 22, 23, 29, 32, 140, 150, 154

B

Batman, xiv, 174, 176, 177, 178, 179, 180, 182, 183, 184, 185, 186
Battle of Hogwarts, 80, 160
Battlestar Galactica, 58
BBC, 141, 155
"Be Alive With Me Tonight," 28, 30, 33
Bea Smith, 123, 126, 130
Becky Rosen, 92, 99
"becoming", 37, 42, 45, 50
Bellatrix LeStrange, 80, 164, 165,
Ben Barnes, 167
Bex Taylor-Klaus, 20
bigotry, 14, 86
binaries, 125
binary identities, 4
Black family, 85, 164
bloodscout, 35, 36, 37, 39, 48, 49, 50
bonding marks, 26
bookinit, 11, 12
Braime, 144, 147, 149
"Breath Mints/Battle Scars," 79, 80, 81, 82, 83, 87, 89
"Breathe me in, Breathe me out," 30, 33
Brenda Murphy, 122, 129, 130, 131, 132, 133, 134
Brianna Dym, 78
Britta Lundin, 103, 143, 144
Broad Strokes, 166
Bronwen Thomas, ix, 160, 165
Bruce Wayne, 174, 178

Bryan Fuller, 108, 109, 110, 111, 114, 115, 119, 120
Buck v. Bell, 67
bullying, 84
Bundibird, 95, 103
bury your gays, 5, 15, 16

C

Caeseria, 28, 30
Cait Coker, 92
Candance Benefiel, 92
canon, 4, 6, 7, 8, 10, 12, 15, 19, 26, 29, 39, 44, 49, 53, 61, 62, 83, 91, 93, 98, 99, 101, 112, 116, 118, 122, 124, 129, 131, 133, 134, 141, 143, 145, 151, 157, 158, 159, 160, 161, 162, 163, 165, 166, 167, 169, 179
canonical, 9, 23, 24, 35, 37, 46, 49, 79, 82, 83, 94, 98, 121, 124, 127, 128, 130, 132
canonicity, 164
cartoons, 175
Cassidy Sheehan, 141
Castiel, 55, 56, 57, 58, 92, 93, 94, 97, 98, 99, 100, 101, 105, 144, 146
Castiellesbian, 97, 103
Castielspussy, 95
Catwoman, 179
Chanel Williams, 162
change, xiii, xiv, 21, 22, 53, 65, 68, 76, 77, 82, 85, 102, 113, 115, 143, 155, 180
Chaosinfurgency, 67, 69
characters, viii, x, xi, xii, xiii, xiv, 6, 7, 8, 10, 13, 15, 16, 19, 22, 23, 24, 25, 28, 30, 32, 44, 53, 54, 56, 57, 58, 59, 60, 61, 63, 64, 68, 69, 78, 79, 82, 84, 88, 92, 93, 94, 97, 98, 100, 101, 109, 110, 113, 118, 119, 121, 128, 129, 132, 134, 141, 142,

144, 145, 146, 148, 150, 152, 153, 154, 157, 158, 159, 160, 161, 162, 163, 165, 166, 167, 168, 174, 177, 178
Charles Xavier, 64, 65
Charowak, 67, 69
Chernobyl, 45
1967 Chevrolet Impala, 95
Christina Olin-Scheller, 163, 169
Christopher Reeves, 176
Chuck Shurley, 91
CIA, 64
cisheteronormative, 99
cisheteronormativity, 31
cisheteropatriarchial, 32
civil trial, 56
Clark Kent, 174, 178
Cold War, 179
comedic, 172
comic books, 171, 172, 174, 175, 177, 179, 182
commercial authors, 140, 143, 149, 152, 153
Commissioner Gordon, 181
community, x, xiv, 4, 8, 10, 14, 20, 21, 22, 23, 24, 29, 31, 32, 37, 38, 39, 40, 41, 42, 43, 44, 47, 48, 50, 54, 55, 68, 76, 77, 78, 79, 81, 84, 86, 88, 100, 109, 125, 148
ComradeTortoise, 42
content creators, 157, 159, 163, 166
convergence culture, 98
Corinne E Hinton, 126
Cornel Sandvoss, 4, 99, 114, 120, 133, 135
Cosmopolitan, 118
Covid-19, x, xiii, xiv, 76, 115
cruising, 113
cult following, 108
cultural *frustration*, xiii, 4, 12

D

dandelionbunny, 45, 50
Daredevil, 61, 62, 67
Dark Angel, 58
Dark Knight, 180
DC comics, 174
Dean Leetal, x
Dean Winchester, 55, 91, 92, 93, 94, 95, 97, 99, 100, 101, 144, 146
Deancritblog, 95
Deanwasalwaysbi, 98, 104
death drive, 110, 111, 112
Death Eater, 81
Declan McCullagh, 21
Deep Space Nine, ix, x, xi, xii, xv
deepfake media, 168
DefyingNormalcy, 122, 131, 132, 135
Deirdre T, 93
Demon Heart, 144, 145, 146, 147, 151, 152, 154
Derek Johnson, 133
Dertziyung, 41
Destiel, 55, 58, 91, 92, 93, 94, 97, 98, 99, 100, 101, 104, 146
"Détente," 64, 65, 68, 69
Diana Floegel, 3, 21, 99, 100
Dick Grayson, 176, 178, 182
Digital Millennium Copyright Act, 65
Dion Kagan, 101
discourse community, 37, 40
diversity, 74, 75, 76, 79, 83, 98, 144
dominant discourse, 37
Draco Malfoy, 77, 79, 81, 160, 164,
Dramione, 79
"Dumbledore and Grindelwald - The Greater Good - Secrets of Dumbledore Prequel," 158, 170
Duncan Lindsey, 124
dysphoria, 29, 30

dystopias, 55, 68

E

Eddie Munson, 8, 10, 12, 15, 35
Eddie Munson's Black Handkerchief, 12
El, 11
ElevenLabs, 167
Eli Batalion, 46
Eliel Cruz, 93
Elim Garak, xi, xii
Elisabeth Schneider, 10
Eliza Quinn, 94
Elizabeth Bridges, 97
Elmie K-E, v, ix, x, xi, xii, xiii, xv
Emma Nordin, 141
"Enslaved," 28, 30, 33
Epilogue? What Epilogue?. *See* EWE
Eric Kripke, 98, 105, 143, 145
Erik Lehnsherr (Magneto), 48, 64, 65
Erin B. Waggoner, 15
Erin M. Giannini, 92
Ernest Mathijs, 173, 186
Ernst Bloch, 113
erotica, 24, 66, 68
escapist, 97
Eve Bennett, 96
Eve Kosofsky Sedgwick, 123, 125
Eve Ng, 94
Ever Given, 41, 43, 44, 49, 50
EWE, 5, 6, 7, 17, 160

F

fan behavior, 20, 22, 27, 139
fan communities, 9, 16, 20, 24, 39, 77
fan fiction, v, vii, viii, ix, x, xi, xii, xiii, xiv, 3, 4, 5, 7, 8, 10, 11, 13, 19, 23, 24, 26, 30, 50, 53, 54, 55, 57, 58, 61, 62, 65, 66, 67, 68, 75, 76, 77, 78, 79, 82, 83, 84, 87, 88, 92, 93, 94, 97, 99, 100, 102, 108, 109, 112, 114, 115, 118, 123, 124, 125, 126, 129, 130, 139, 140, 141, 142, 143, 144, 145, 146, 148, 152, 154, 157, 158, 159, 160, 161, 162, 163, 165, 168, 169, 172, 173, 185
fan film, 157, 162, 164, 165, 166, 168
fandom, vii, xii, 4, 5, 6, 7, 8, 15, 16, 19, 20, 21, 22, 23, 24, 25, 26, 27, 29, 32, 33, 39, 40, 44, 45, 48, 49, 50, 54, 59, 68, 74, 76, 78, 79, 84, 87, 88, 92, 93, 94, 95, 96, 98, 101, 103, 104, 109, 114, 115, 116, 118, 123, 124, 129, 132, 134, 140, 141, 142, 143, 144, 145, 146, 147, 148, 149, 150, 155, 169, 173
fandom spaces, 21, 23, 32, 39, 132, 145
FanFiction.net, 21, 25, 161
Fangirl, 142, 143, 155
Fanlore, 94, 104, 117, 119, 141, 142, 145, 155, 160, 169
fannish, 4, 38, 39, 41, 43, 44, 48, 49, 50, 124, 128
fanon, 122, 130, 133, 160, 165, 167
Fantastic Beasts and Where to Find Them, 158, 166
Faraj Conrad, 158
fat shaming, 148
FDA, 14
"Feels Like Home," 122, 130, 131, 132, 135
female gaze, 122, 125
femaleness, 125
feminine-coded, 27
femininity, x, 125, 126, 134
feminist studies, 158

fix-it fic, v, viii, ix, x, xi, xiii, xiv, 4, 5, 11, 15, 36, 53, 55, 59, 60, 62, 63, 64, 66, 68, 94, 101, 108, 110, 114, 116, 122, 127, 131, 132, 134, 140, 143, 150, 153, 157
fix-it novel, 141, 143, 144, 150, 153, 154
For You Page, 163
found family, 31, 84
Frank Miller, 179, 180
Frankenclips, 167, 168
Freakytits, 124, 125, 129, 132, 133, 134
futurity, 31, 32, 38, 39, 107, 108, 110, 111, 112, 113, 115, 118, 119

G

Game of Thrones, 143, 144, 147, 148, 152, 155
Garashir, xi
gaslighting, 98, 104
gay, 11, 20, 84, 86, 100, 111, 113, 145, 146, 151
Gellert Grindelwald, 166
gender, ix, 3, 14, 16, 20, 22, 24, 25, 26, 30, 31, 54, 79, 145, 157, 159, 163, 169
genre, viii, 21, 24, 25, 26, 28, 30, 31, 32, 37, 54, 58, 96, 101, 103, 124, 125, 141, 144, 159, 163, 169, 172, 173, 174, 175, 176, 177, 179, 181, 182, 185
George Clooney, 176
Gian S. Pagnucci, 174, 186
Gianmaria Pezzato, 158
Gil Z. Hochberg, 37, 38
"glaze defects," 67, 69
Glenn Wilmott, 175
GLSEN, 14, 18
God, 10, 16, 67, 92, 97, 104
"God Bless America," 68

Gods of the Gates, 147, 148, 149, 152, 153
Good Omens, ix
Gotham, 178, 179, 180, 181, 182, 184, 185
Governor Meg Jackson, 126
Great Depression, 174, 183
Green Lantern, 178
green paladin Pidge, 20
Griboslav_Muhomorovich, 41, 42, 43, 50, 51
Gryffindor, 80, 85, 86

H

"half a heart (without you)," 11, 16
"Halflings," 58, 59, 60, 61, 65, 68, 69,
Hamlet, 157
Hannibal (Hannibal), xiv, 24, 34, 107, 108, 109, 110, 111, 112, 113, 114, 115, 116, 118, 119, 120
Hannigram, 109, 116
happily ever after, 79, 94, 99
Harry M. Benshoff, 101, 122
Harry Potter, vii, xiv, 6, 7, 8, 17, 42, 73, 74, 75, 76, 77, 78, 79, 80, 83, 84, 87, 88, 89, 101, 105, 157, 158, 159, 160, 161, 162, 163, 164, 166, 167, 168, 169, 176
Harry Potter and the Cursed Child, 83, 158, 163
Harry Potter and the Deathly Hallows, 6, 17, 89, 165
Harry Potter and the Half-Blood Prince, 82, 165
"Harry Potter and the Muggleborn Prolet," 42
Harry Potter and the Sorcerer's Stone, 166
Harry Potter Wiki, 164, 169
Hasnaa, 97, 104

"Have Your Steak (And Eat It Too)," 59, 60, 69
Hayes Code, 5
headcanons, 20, 21, 22, 23, 63
Heartstopper, 96, 103
heat, 26, 29, 30, 54, 55
Heath Ledger, 176
HedonistInk and Heikijin, 29, 33
hegemonic, 36, 47, 95, 141, 142, 143
Hell's Kitchen, 62
Henrik Linden, 99
Henry Jenkins, viii, 3, 16, 77, 100, 122, 140, 142
Hermione Granger, 79, 80, 87, 161, 163
heteronormativity, 7, 8, 9, 110, 111, 163
heterosexual, 3, 5, 6, 9, 10, 95, 99, 100, 107, 109, 129
Hogsmead Village, 166
Hogwarts, 79, 80, 81, 82, 84, 85, 87, 161, 164, 165
Holy Musical B@man!, 172, 173, 174, 176, 178, 179, 180, 181, 185, 186, 201
homoaffection, 125, 129, 134
homophobia, 86, 93, 98, 105, 146, 155
homosexuality, 101
Hugh Dancy, 108, 109, 119
Humans, 58
hybrids, 58, 59, 60
hypermasculine, 95
hypertext, 173, 178, 179
hypotext, 173

I

identity, ix, xiii, 14, 16, 17, 21, 22, 23, 25, 27, 29, 31, 32, 37, 61, 78, 82, 84, 85, 86, 87, 100, 111, 123, 141, 149, 150, 151, 178, 180, 184
ideology, 82
"If Only You Knew," 122, 127, 128, 135
inclusive, 74, 76, 77, 141, 150, 152, 154, 159, 168
Instagram, 20, 33
intersectionality, 22, 23
intertextuality, 171, 172, 173, 185
irony, 74, 173, 181, 182
"It's not a problem until it's a problem...," 29, 33
Ivan Askwith, 92
Izupie, 98, 104

J

J. K. Rowling, xiv, 6, 7, 8, 17, 73, 74, 75, 76, 77, 78, 79, 80, 82, 83, 87, 88, 89, 158, 159, 161, 164
J. Raúl Cornier, 12
J.T. Weisser, 24
jack_dearly, 9, 17
James Kirk, xi
James Potter, 84, 85, 160, 167
Jamie Elman, 46
Jamie Sexton, 173
Jane Eyre, 157
Jared Padalecki, 91, 92, 106
"Jealousy Thy Name is Keith," 27
Jeff Casey, 110, 111
Jeffrey Shandler, 36
Jenna Cortiel, 179
Jennifer Duggan, 77, 168
Jensen Ackles, 91, 92, 94, 101, 106, 146
Jewish, xiii, 35, 36, 37, 38, 40, 41, 44, 45, 48
Jewishness, 35, 37, 38, 42, 48, 49, 50

Joan Ferguson, xiv, 121, 123, 124, 125, 126, 127, 128, 129, 130, 131, 132, 133, 134,
Joaquim Dos Santos, 19, 20
John Winchester, 95
"Johnny Robert's Hypocwisy," 67, 69
Jonathan Byers, 11
Jonathan Gray, 4, 17, 114, 133, 135
Jonathan Greenberg, 181
José Esteban Muñoz, 107
Joseph Brennan, 9, 10, 17, 24
Journal of Transformative Works and Culture, 21
Judith Herman, 76, 78
Judith May Fathallah, 92, 139, 140
Julian Bashir, x, xi
Julie Levin Russo, 133
Julie Wilkinson, 93
justice system, 56
Justin Zagri, 158
JustSomeGirl92, 31, 32, 33

K

Kali Wallace, 31
Katherine Larsen, 97, 106
Kathryn Eddy, 75, 89
Kayla McCarthy, 14
Keith, 23, 26, 27, 29, 30, 31, 34, 122, 135
Kelli Wilhelm, 95
King Arthur, 177
Klance, 26, 28, 30
knot, 28
Kristina Busse, viii, ix, xv, 27, 28, 33, 54, 66, 99, 122, 135
kudos, 108, 116, 119, 132
Kyle X-Y, 58

L

Ladinokomunita, 38
Lance, 23, 26, 27, 29, 30, 31
Laura E. Felschow, 91
Laura Mulvey, 132
Laura Oehme, 179, 186
Laura Prudom, 110
Lavender Brown, 80
lawsuit, 65, 66
Lee Edelman, 107, 110
Legacy Russell, 39
legal arguments, 54, 60, 65, 68
legal issues, 57, 67
legal personhood, 58
legal systems, 55
Legendary Defender, 19
Les Amis, 63
Les Misérables, 63
lesbian, 121, 123, 124, 129, 132, 133, 134
Lesley Goodman, viii, 122
LGBTQ+, 20, 21, 23, 26, 32, 44, 76, 84, 93, 97, 100, 121
Lily Winterwood, 22
Lily's Boy, 7, 17
Linnie Blake, 96
litigation, 58, 65, 66, 67
"Little Achievements", v, x, xi, xii, xiii, xv
LiveJournal, 21, 22, 33
Lord of the Rings, 116
Lou, 162
Louisa Stein, 4
Lyman Tower Sargent, 55
Lynn Zubernis, 97
Lynn1998, 29, 33

M

macro fix, 55, 68

Mads Mikkelsen, 108, 109, 112, 119,
Magical Congress of the United States of America, 165
"make me aware of being alive," 35, 37, 39, 42, 48, 50
male gaze, 132
marginalized, ix, 16, 31, 37, 39, 53, 75, 84, 134, 139, 141, 143, 145, 150
Marianne Gunderson, 54
Marianne MacDonald, 101
Marie Karlsson, 163
Mark Duffett, 100, 141
Marlboro Man, 95
Martijn Veltkamp, 59, 68
Marvel, 61, 62, 176
Mary Sue, 61, 69, 93, 105
MaryKate Messimer, 110
masculine roles, 26
masculinity, 9, 24, 95, 96, 98, 126
mating, 26, 28, 30, 31
"Mating Bond," 27, 34
Maurader's Map, 160
Mauraders, 160, 167
May10baby, 27, 33
mental illness, 22, 133, 134
Mer_kitty, 28
metatextual narratives, 91, 99
metatextuality, 92
Michael Caine, 176
Michael Keaton, 176
Michael McDermott, 23, 94
Mike Wheeler, 11
Milena Popova, 25
Misha Collins, 92, 94, 97, 101, 105, 106
misogyny, 101, 149
MissDisoriental, 108, 116, 117, 118, 120
Monique Franklin, 9
monster, 96, 132, 133, 135

Motion to Dismiss, 66
Mr. Freeze, 179
MsKingBean89, 84, 85, 86, 87, 89
MsYukari, 122, 127, 128, 129, 135
"Mudblood," 158, 165, 169
Muggle, 75, 82, 83, 85, 89
multimodal, 172, 176, 185
Murder Husbands, 109, 116

N

N. Micarelli, 93
nakba, 38
Nancy Wheeler, 8
Naomi Seidman, 45
Narcissa Malfoy, 164
narrative, vii, 8, 11, 20, 23, 24, 26, 29, 31, 32, 45, 53, 61, 62, 64, 68, 81, 84, 87, 93, 95, 96, 97, 99, 100, 101, 115, 140, 142, 143, 149, 150, 152, 153, 169
NBC, 108, 110, 119, 120
Negative affective, 4
negative futurity, 110, 112
Neha Hazra, 122
nesting, 26
Netflix, vii, xv, 8, 11, 18, 19, 35, 112, 115, 119
Never Have I Ever, vii, xv
Noble House of Black, 158, 164, 165, 170
non-binary, 163
non-Jewish, 36, 40, 48
non-normative, 31
non-Yiddish, 36, 46
NSkellington, 28, 29, 33
Nymphadora Tonks, 79

O

O. J. Simpson, 56
Obergefell v. Hodges, 67, 69

Index

ohfreckle, 109, 120
Olivia Dade, 143, 147
Omega, 25, 26, 28, 29, 30, 31, 33, 54, 55, 57, 69
Omegaphobe, 98, 105
Omegaverse, xiii, 21, 24, 25, 26, 28, 29, 31, 32, 33, 34, 54, 55, 57, 65, 66, 67, 68, 69
Onyx_and_Elm, 80, 82, 89
oppressed populations, 68
"Origins of the Heir," 158, 165, 168, 169
Orphicdean, 101, 105

P

P. Matthijs Bal, 59
pack, 26, 28, 31, 32
palmviolet, 13, 15
pansexual, 109, 119
paratexts, 5, 36, 37, 42, 77, 88, 145, 152, 168, 169
parody, 172, 173, 176, 177, 181, 185
participatory, 4, 77, 78
Pavarti Patil, 80
Perlukafarin, 94, 105
Peter Pettigrew, 84, 160, 167
Piertotumshore, 61, 62, 69
POC, 39
police, 61, 62, 63, 132, 183, 185
political activism, 54
popular culture, vii, 3, 16, 38, 40, 101, 158, 159, 163, 172, 175, 177
positive fannish, 4
post-9/11, 95, 180
postcardmystery, 109, 120
postvernacular, 39, 46, 48, 50
pregnancy, 24, 26, 28, 31, 123
2016 presidential election, 75
prequel, 158, 159, 160, 164, 165, 166
President Barack Obama, 182

Prisoner Cell Block H, 126
problematic, 32, 58, 82, 83, 92, 94, 96, 99, 102, 141, 143, 150, 154, 177
Professor Minerva McGonagall, 162
Profoundbondfanfic, 101, 105
protagonist, 66, 95, 142, 145
PTSD, 80
Pulp fiction, 174, 175

Q

queer, xiii, 3, 5, 7, 8, 9, 10, 11, 12, 13, 15, 16, 21, 24, 29, 30, 31, 32, 36, 38, 39, 40, 41, 43, 44, 45, 47, 49, 50, 76, 83, 93, 94, 95, 96, 97, 98, 100, 101, 102, 103, 107, 108, 110, 111, 112, 113, 114, 117, 118, 121, 130, 134, 141, 142, 144, 145, 146, 150, 151, 154, 158, 163
queer bodies, 39
queer erasure, 3
queer futurity, 108, 112, 118
queer theory, 107
queerbaiting, xiii, xiv, 9, 19, 20, 21, 24, 25, 26, 28, 32, 93, 94, 101, 104, 111, 141, 143, 145, 147, 151
queercoding, 5, 9, 10, 16, 92
queering, 17, 20, 99, 100, 104
Queerklancing, 30
queerness, 4, 5, 8, 9, 10, 11, 12, 13, 15, 16, 24, 25, 27, 30, 31, 32, 93, 94, 99, 110, 111, 112, 113, 118, 141, 145, 146
Quill Ink Books, Ltd. V. Soto a.k.a. Cain, 65

R

Rabbit Lightning, ix
race, 22, 79, 83, 113, 157, 159, 169

Rachel Aroesti, 96
racism, 39, 59, 60, 63, 101
Rainbow Rowell, 142
Rainbowtyrant, 101, 105
rape culture, 55, 58
real person fiction, 59, 67, 142, 155
realfakedoors, 29, 33
Rebecca Borah, 77
Rebecca Margolis, 40
reclaim, 87, 88, 94, 140
recovery, 21, 76, 78, 79, 81, 83, 87, 88
Red Dragon, 109, 111, 119
Reg Watson, 121
Regulus Black, 86
rehabilitation, 82
reimagine, 75, 94, 121
rejection, 20, 86, 93, 111, 112, 123, 124, 127
Remus Lupin, 79, 85, 160, 167
reparative, 123, 129
representation, 3, 10, 30, 32, 37, 38, 83, 91, 94, 95, 97, 100, 101, 104, 150, 151, 152, 157, 174
repression, 75, 123
reproduction, 24, 107
retroactive continuity, 74, 83
Rhonda Nicol, 95
Ria Narai, 125
Riverdale, vii
"Rivkele Un Gitele", 42
Robbie Thompson, 92, 101, 106
Robert Phiddian, 172
Robin, xii, 176, 180, 182, 183, 184, 185
Robin Buckley, 8
Roe v. Wade, 67
rogue, 36, 38, 43, 45, 47, 49, 50
Roland Barthes, 10, 118
Ross Scarano, 110
Roz Kaveney,, 99
Rukmini Pande, 39

rut, 26, 54
Ruth Bader Ginsberg, 67
Ryan Lattanzio, 109

S

Sadie Gennis, 93
Sam Winchester, 56
sapphic, 122, 125, 129, 133, 134
Sara Linden, 99, 105
Sarah Swan, 55, 69
Sasha Sloan, 158, 164, 167
Satire, xiv, 171, 172, 181, 182, 185, 186
Scarlett Epstein Hates It Here, 142
science fiction, 45, 57, 58
Screak, 130, 132, 133, 134
Second World War, 174
sequel, 159, 160, 180
sex, 24, 25, 27, 29, 54, 57, 59, 67, 74, 89, 93, 96, 97, 103, 113, 128, 145
sexual orientation, xiii, 98
sexuality, 12, 20, 26, 30, 31, 79, 109, 114, 124, 145, 157, 159, 161, 169
Sheenagh Pugh, 130, 159
Sherlock, vii, 141, 155
Sherlock Holmes, viii, 141
Shinelikethunder, 92, 105
ship, 15, 39, 44, 49, 79, 92, 93, 109, 122, 124, 129, 130, 133, 145, 149, 151, 167
Ship It, 143, 144, 145, 148, 149, 151, 152, 153, 155
shippers, 93, 124, 125, 129, 130, 133, 134
shipping, 19, 20, 23, 91, 109, 124, 144, 146, 148
ships, 8, 23, 39, 41, 79, 83, 98, 109, 123, 133, 134
Shiro, 20, 31
Shmueskrayz, 47

ShortAngryTwinks, 12, 13, 17
Sid City Social Club, x
SiderumInCaelo, 65, 66, 69
Silent Film Era, 167
Simon Dentith,, 172
Siouxsie, 114, 120
Sirius Black, 79, 84, 85, 160, 162, 164, 167
slash, x, 3, 4, 8, 10, 19, 35, 41, 48, 92, 94, 96, 98, 99, 103, 110, 120, 145
slow burn fic, 132
Slytherin, 81, 82, 85, 165
social change, 53, 56, 65, 101, 142
social criticism, 96
social injustice, 53, 68
socio-cultural, 100
"Someone's Bound to Get It", 12, 13, 17
"SomewheresSword," 7, 17
Spicy Little Kitten, 27, 33
Spiderman, 151
Spider-Man, 61, 62, 176
Spock, xi
Spoiler Alert, 143, 147, 148, 152, 153, 155
Star Wars, 39, 67, 176
StarKid, 172, 176, 182, 185, 186
Starship, 176
StarTravel, 48, 49, 50
status quo, xiii, 83, 92, 94, 95, 97, 98, 99, 102, 185
Steve Harrington, 8, 15, 35
stickmarionette, 64, 65, 69
straight, 95, 97, 118, 129
subculture, 139, 140
"sub-culture," 13, 15, 17
subgenres, viii, 158
subtext, 5, 9, 11, 12, 13, 93, 97, 98, 109, 111
Suez Canal, 41, 43, 44, 49, 50
Suncaptor, 96, 106

superhero, xiv, 58, 64, 65, 67, 142, 171, 172, 173, 174, 175, 176, 177, 179, 180, 185
Superman, 171, 174, 176, 177, 178, 182, 183, 184, 185
Supernatural, xiv, 54, 55, 91, 92, 93, 94, 95, 96, 97, 98, 99, 100, 101, 103, 104, 105, 106, 143, 144, 145, 146, 147, 155
supervillain, 64, 65, 178
Supreme Court Justice Samuel Alitoo (with two o's to avoid legal problems) gets matpat mpregged," 69
Susan Faludi, 96
Sweet Tooth, 176, 182, 184, 185

T

tag, xi, 3, 5, 6, 7, 8, 12, 13, 19, 25, 26, 27, 35, 44, 45, 53, 63, 67, 73, 75, 91, 99, 107, 108, 115, 116, 117, 119, 121, 123, 130, 139, 157, 164,
Taylor Boulware, 96
Teddy, 79, 168
testimony, xiv, 56, 66
"The American Way," 182
"The Collars," 61, 62, 63, 69
The Dark Knight, 174, 176, 179, 180, 186
"The darkness in his eyes," 28, 29, 33
The Extraordinaries, 142, 155
The Fixer, xiv, 121, 124, 126
The Freak, 121, 124
The Good Fight, 65, 66
The Iliad, viii
The Lion King, 157
The Man From U.N.C.L.E., 41
The New York Times, 66, 68
The Odyssey, viii

"The One about Wolf Porn," 65, 66, 69
The Principle of Hope, 113
"The Secrets of Dumbledore," 166
"The Shape of Me Will Always be You," 108, 116, 120
"The Ship and the Canal," 41, 45, 50,
The Silence of the Lambs, 109
"The Things I Say," 63, 68, 69
"The Very Secret Diary of Will Graham," 108, 117, 120
"The Wrath of the Lamb," 108, 111, 113, 114, 116, 118, 119, 120
The_Broken_Dreamer, 29, 33
theodcyning, 41, 51
thepolysyndetonaddictsupportgroup, 67, 69
"there's beauty in your venom," 109, 120
"They Call Me The Taylor," 27, 34
Thomas Harris, 109,
Thomas Knowles, 95
TikTok, 9, 17, 74, 157, 158, 162, 164, 166, 168
TilDeathDoWeLove, 25, 27, 34
time travel, 185
Timemidae, 41, 51
TJ Klune, 142
Tom Riddle, 165
trans, 7, 8, 24, 74
transformative, ix, 4, 6, 92, 140
Transformers, 176
transphobic, xiv, 8, 74, 76, 110
transvernacular, 40, 46, 47, 48, 50, 51
trauma, 20, 21, 22, 24, 25, 26, 30, 31, 32, 38, 75, 78, 79, 80, 81, 83, 84, 85, 86, 87, 88, 93, 95, 96, 101, 106, 123, 124
trauma-informed reading, 83

tropes, 25, 26, 32, 45, 54, 55, 66, 68, 102, 174
Trump, 22, 33, 75
Tumblr, viii, 22, 24, 25, 32, 33, 74, 92, 93, 94, 95, 96, 97, 98, 100, 101, 102, 103, 104, 105, 106
Twitter, 20, 22, 33, 34, 74, 89, 110, 148, 151
Two-Face, 179
Tyler Labine, 20
Tyrangle Films, 165

U

U.S. Capitol Riot January 6, 2021, 67
U.S. Constitution, 58
U.S. Supreme Court, 57
Unforth, 58, 69
University of Michigan, 176
Urban Dictionary, viii, xv
utopia, 108, 113, 114, 117, 118
utopist, 97

V

Val Kilmer, 176
Vaybertaytsh, 47
Vera Bennett, 122, 123, 124, 125, 126, 127, 128, 129, 130, 132, 133, 134, 135
Victoria M. Gonzalez, 139
Vinegartits, 124
Vito Russo, 5
Vivid_IGuess, 67, 69
Voldemort, 76, 85, 86, 87, 158, 164, 165, 168, 169
Voltron Legendary Defender, xiii, 19, 20, 21, 22, 23, 34

W

"Want", 31, 32
War and Peace, 75
Wattpad, 25
Wentworth, xiv, 121, 123, 124, 125, 126, 129, 130, 132, 133, 134, 135
Westworld, 58
"What Else Could a Virgin Omega Do," 29, 33
White supremacy, 96
whitehorsetiger, 27
whiteness, 39
Wide Sargasso Sea, 157
Wikipedia, 161
Will Byers, 10, 11
Will Graham, 107, 108, 109, 115, 116, 117
WolfStar, 79, 83, 85, 167
womanhood, 125

X

XiuChen4Ever, 59, 60, 69
X-Men, 48, 58, 64, 65

Y

Y. Gotlib, 40
YA novel, 142, 143, 144
yellow paladin Hunk, 20
"Yentl with Zombies," 41, 42, 45, 51
"Yentl the Yeshiva Boy", 41
Yiddish, 36, 40, 43, 44, 46, 50
Yiddishkeit, 36, 38, 45
Yiddishland, 36, 38, 39, 40, 41, 43, 44, 45, 46, 47, 48, 49, 51
Yiddishness, 36, 47
Yidishe Kinder, 41
YidLife Crisis, 46, 48
"You'll only see my reflection," 109, 120,

"Your Sex I Can Smell," 29, 33
YouTube, xi, xiv, 46, 94, 97, 104, 105, 157, 158, 162, 164, 166, 168, 169, 170, 172, 178, 179, 181, 186

Z

zade, 63, 69
zeerogue, 27
zines, viii
Zishe Landau, 41, 44

ד

"װאָרט" "די אונגעהײַערע צװײשנספֿער פֿונעם", 41, 51
"דערציונג," 41, 51

www.ingramcontent.com/pod-product-compliance
Lightning Source LLC
Chambersburg PA
CBHW072235290426
44111CB00012B/2108